D1271781

TYPE and
TYPEFACES

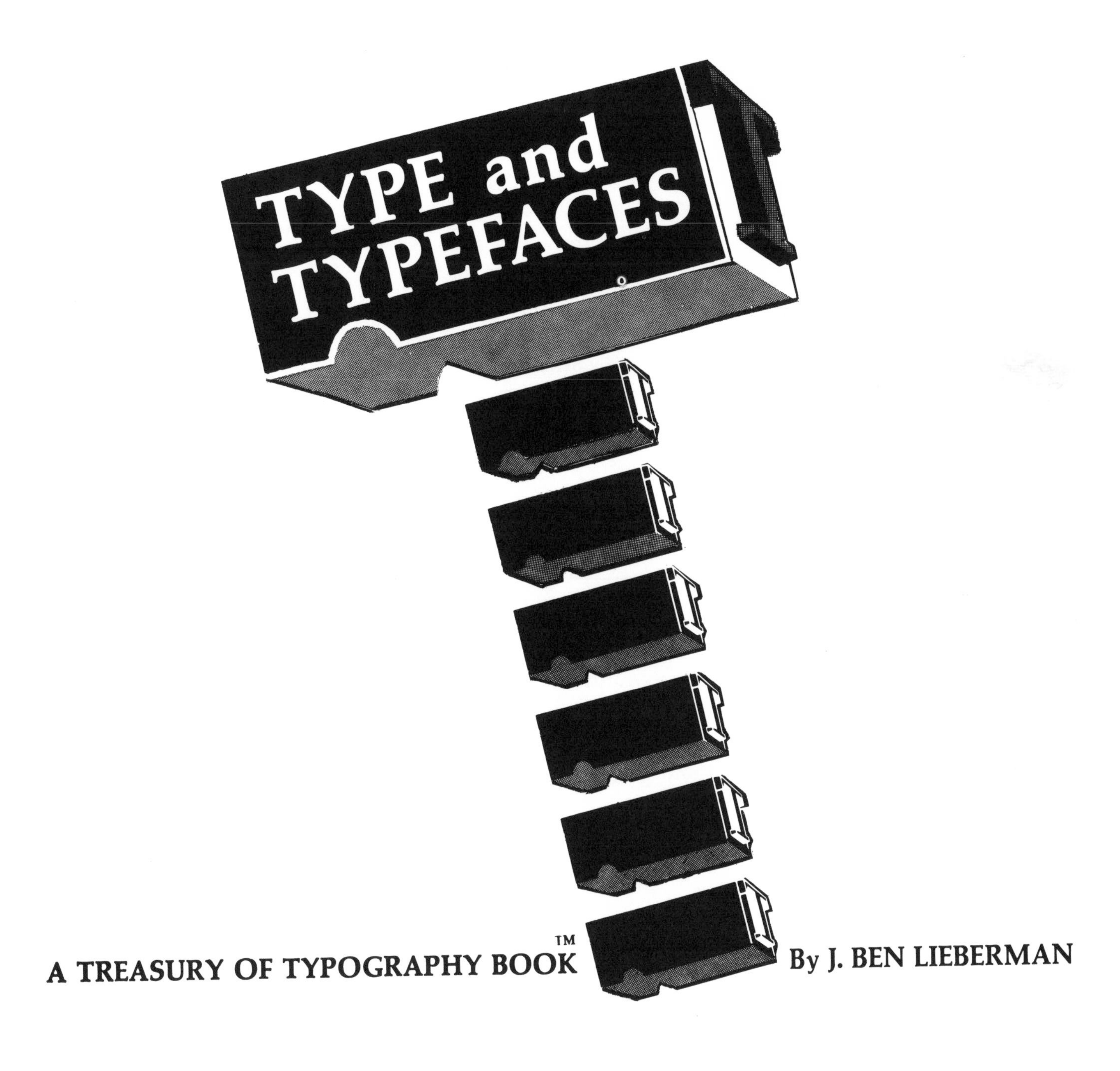

A TREASURY OF TYPOGRAPHY BOOK™

By J. BEN LIEBERMAN

M THE MYRIADE PRESS: New Rochelle, New York

DEDICATED TO THE MEMORIES OF
BEATRICE WARDE and PAUL A. BENNETT
(*see Page 85*)

Book I, The Treasuries of Typography Series™

A Treasury of Typography Book, A Treasure of Typography Book,
The Treasuries of Typography Series and The Treasures of Typography Series
are trademarks of The Myriade Press.

SECOND EDITION

Published by The Myriade Press, 7 Stony Run, New Rochelle, N.Y.10804
Manufactured in the United States of America.

First edition (published as Types of Typefaces)

Second printing, 1967; third printing, 1968

LIBRARY OF CONGRESS
Cataloging in Publication Data

Lieberman, J Ben.
Type and typefaces.
(A Treasury of typography book)
First published in 1967 under title: Types of
typefaces and how to recognize them.
Includes index.
1. Type and type-founding— History. 2. Printing—Specimens.
I. Title.
Z250.L6 1977 686.2'24 77-24401
ISBN 0-918142-01-6
ISBN 0-918142-02-4 pbk.

Library of Congress Catalog Card No. 77-24401

ISBN: Trade Edition, 0-918142-01-6
Paper, 0-918142-02-4

26 (?) Letters

Aa Aa Aa A a Aa Bb Bb Bb B b B

C C C c C C Dd Dd Dd D d Dd Ee

Ee Ee E e Ee Ff Ff Ff F f f Ff G

g Gg Gg G g g Gg Hh Hh Hh H h

h Hh Ii Ii Ii I i Ii Jj Jj Jj J j J J

j Kk Kk Kk K k k Kk Ll Ll Ll L

l l Ll Mm Mm M m m Mm Mm N

n Nn Nn N n n Nn O O Oo O o O P

Pp Pp P p p Pp Qq Qq Qq Q q q

Qq Rr Rr Rr R r R Rr S S Ss S

s S s s s Tt Tt Tt T t t Tt Uu Uu U

u U u u U V V v V V v V v V W W w

W w W w W W X X x X x X x X x

Y y Y y Y y Y y y Y y Z Z z Z z Z z Z z

RAU

Everybody looks at typefaces all the time —just as you are now. Rather, you are looking *through* the printed letters, not *at* them.

The next statement may surprise you, under the circumstances: you are right *not* to be looking at the type designs while you are reading. A type designer is a success precisely because readers do not notice his design. A peculiar statement to start off a book devoted to typefaces? As you read on just a little way, you will find out why it is not peculiar at all.

Of course, this book encourages you to look *at* typefaces, too. In fact, the whole point of the book is to give you a way of looking at typefaces that will open up a wonderful, exciting world that most people never discover.

There are literally *thousands* of different typefaces, quite aside from different sizes of the same ones. They are of all conceivable kinds, because when someone conceives a new type of typeface, then that one is produced, too. *Why?* That's part of the story this book tells.

You will read about one of the great treasures of our civilization—our remarkable collection of typefaces—what this book calls the TYPORAMA. There is no other word to describe the incredible, fascinating range and variety of designs and letter forms that have been created to print our ideas, opinions, facts, deeds, sales messages and literature.

As you get to know this Typorama better, you will find you can enjoy and use your new knowledge in quite a variety of ways:

- You will be looking at all the printing that surrounds you, in a fresh and meaningful new way.
- You will know better how to order printing and judge its quality whenever it becomes your responsibility.
- You will discover that a career in printing or the other graphic arts can be fascinating and rewarding.
- You will find that the history of civilization is written on the faces of our printing type, and that types and printing are keys to understanding our great cultural heritage.
- You will realize how the lore of printing ties into almost any field you are interested in.
- You may even want to make a hobby of one of the many possible activities related to type, as described towards the end of the book.

. . . It is a magical moment when one first discovers the Typorama. We hope you will enjoy it to the fullest!

GETTING TO KNOW TYPEFACES

CHAPTER 

From beginner to designer of type in one easy step

YOU DO NOT have to know anything about typefaces, or even printing, to understand this book. But you probably will find that you *do* know quite a bit that is related, and this will make your understanding easy.

Most people, however, are not trained to notice the very small variations that make typefaces differ. Therefore, this first chapter is a little do-it-yourself project to get you into the middle of things quickly and painlessly. It will take only a few minutes with pencil and paper. You will very likely have fun doing it, and *maybe* you will discover that you are a great designer without knowing it.

o |

What you are going to do is design a type alphabet, from the circle and the line printed above. These are exactly the same starting "elements" that a now-world-famous type designer, Paul Renner, used in the 1920's to create the typeface called Futura. This face became an instant success, helped change typography around the world, and is still very much in use.

After you have finished your design, you can compare what you did with what Mr. Renner did, by looking on Page 8.

In making each of the letters, you will encounter many of the problems that have to be settled in type design. Don't worry about coming up with the "right" answers—or even the same answers as Mr. Renner. Just enjoy yourself while creating something you probably never thought you could do.

Take your pencil—preferably a soft black lead pencil. And take blank paper thin enough to let the solid circle and line show through it. Add an eraser and some kind of straight-edge or ruler.

Now, using those basic **O** and **|** shapes, start out to design what printers call the "lowercase" alphabet—that is, the small letters (a, b, c) as distinct from the capitals (A, B, C). You will need a few other shapes, which you can make by adapting these two shapes any way you wish. It is probably best to go through the alphabet in order and design each letter without worrying about details. Then, review what you have done and make. changes so that the letters follow the same general rules of construction (*your* rules) and thus look as though they really "belonged" together.

To see what this means, look at the different kinds of little "a" here:

You can form the letter in one way by putting the vertical line against the outside of the circle, as in (1), making the vertical line the same length as the outside diameter of the circle. Put your sheet of paper over the circle at left above and trace it; then lay the paper over the vertical line where you want it against the circle, and trace that. The vertical line can be longer, if you wish, as in (2).

Of course, as shown in (3), you can decide that instead of touching the outside of the circle, the vertical line should go right over the right side of the circle. (The dotted lines show where part of the circle is covered over.)

Or, as in (4), you can have the vertical line touch against the inside of the circle, cutting off the rest of the circle. (Again, the dotted lines show where the circle would normally have gone.)

You may even think of a different (and better) way to design the letter. For instance, you might put a line over it, as in (5).

Once you have the "a" settled, and have it drawn on your paper, you are ready to design the "b." In many typefaces, the only real difference between "a" and "b" is that the "b" is a backward "a" with a longer stem. If you like that idea, trace in your letter next to the "a," and make the stem longer. Only, how *much* longer? For the moment, at least, the right answer is: whatever looks best to you.

The letter "c" is often just a circle with part of the right side cut away. But how much? Where? And what do you do about the cutting itself—how do you "treat" the ends of the line, as designers say? As (1) shows, you can go perpendicular to the line of the circle itself, or horizontal as in (2), or maybe one of each (3), or an "overcut" (4).

(1) (2) (3) (4) (5)

Or, again, maybe you can think of something you like better.

Well, "d" is just the "b" backwards, as in (5). Or is it?

And "e" is the letter "c" with a cross line, isn't it? But, how far up do you put the cross line? High (1), medium (2), or low (3)? Now that you're thinking about that problem, will that change your thinking about the opening in the "c"? Should the "e" cross line be straight across (4), or slanted up (5) or down (6)? How do you treat the meeting point—straight (7), or curved (8), or pointed (9), or jutting out (10)? Or some other way?

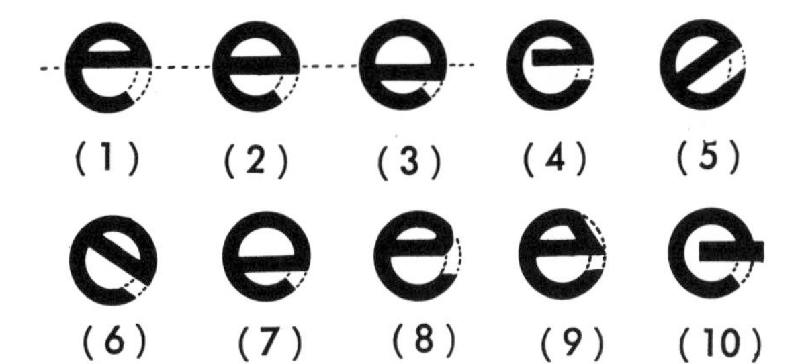

Is it possible that the cross line should not be the same thickness as the circle and the stems of "a," "b" and "d"? These are things you must decide.

The "f" perhaps poses a new kind of problem. You can take part of your standard circle and use it for the curved top of the "f" as in (1), or you can make a different kind of curve (2). How much curve is part of the problem. Where it joins the stem is another part: should it be quite high, as in (1) and (2), or lower on the stem as in (3)? How far down should it go on the other side? As far as in (1) or (2) or (3)? Or maybe even lower, as in (4)? Do you put the cross line even with the cross line of the "e" as in (5), or even with the top of the circles as in (6)? How thick should the cross line be?

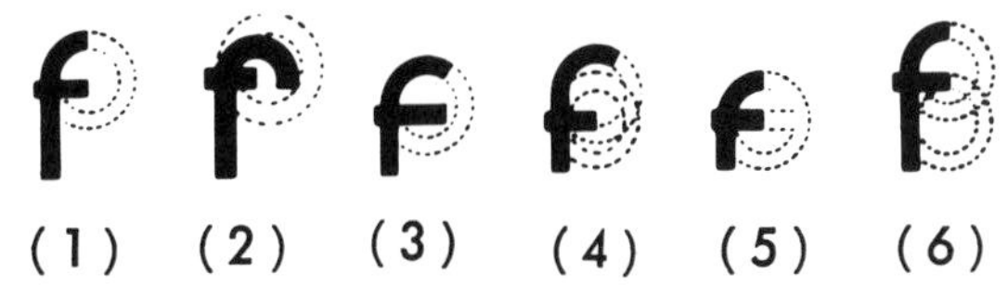

You are well on your way now. Go ahead and finish the rest of the small letters in the alphabet. But don't make a chore of it—remember, it's just for fun, and to introduce you to some of the problems that you probably would never think of otherwise.

Designing your own typeface will prove to you that there is no such thing as a *right* way to solve the different problems. There are many "right" ways and thousands of

THERE'S MANY A WAY TO MAKE AN A

The Futura small "a" is probably not the best, much less the only way, to make an "a." Here are some random samples of others:

a a a a a a a a a a

abcdefghijklmn
opqrstuvwxyz

This is the lowercase Futura alphabet as designed by Paul Renner in 1927 from the elements you used, a circle and a line. (See Column 1 below.)

different solutions—to meet different tastes and serve different purposes. That is why there are thousands of typefaces in existence and more coming out almost every week.

When you have finished your alphabet, and made the changes needed, compare it with Futura (above), reproduced here in the same size as the letters you have traced from the **O** and **|** elements. Look at each Futura letter separately, and then lay your sheet over the Futura letters to see where Renner made subtle little changes, such as thinning one side of the circle on some letters. If your designs look anything like Futura, you should feel pleased indeed.

If they do not, console yourself by turning to the Specimens of Typefaces in the Appendix starting on Page 97 and compare

RENNER'S 'LITTLE DIFFERENCES'

aaov

To make Futura *look* geometrical, Renner had to deliberately avoid *being* uniform, because of optical illusions. He thinned his curves (left a) where they meet the stem to avoid (as in right a) looking too thick. And the o has to go above and below the line, and the v below it, to appear to be *on* the line. Look again at the full alphabet above to see Renner's other "optical adjustments" and similar niceties that make the face *look* so even. (Renner got much help from his foundry in all this adapting, though; see top of P. 48.)

Futura with other standard so-called "sans serif" faces which are more or less based on the same lines—Gill Sans, Kabel, Metro and Univers, for example. You will see that the originators of these faces designed differently, too. Note what general effect you get from each one, and decide which you like best, and why.

As you go through the rest of this book, you will gain more and more information, and with this you will understand what was behind your feelings. Meanwhile, what can you make of all these "sans serif" alphabets?

The principal point is that there is no uniformity from one letter to another in a typeface even when it looks *very* geometrical. Those little differences, added together, give a typeface life and character, and convert it from just mechanical-drawing letters.

If you wish, with that same circle and line you can design capital letters. However, you may have designed enough by now to serve the purpose. Certainly you have learned the lesson well if your eye is beginning to note where some letters are wider than others, how different parts are joined, and how parts are changed to fit together.

You know now that one kind of typeface can be designed from a circle and a line. You will soon discover that this is *not* the usual starting point, and that in fact it took more than 350 years after the invention of printing before anybody began to think along those lines.

Why should that have been the case? As you come to understand, later in this book, you will know a good deal about type.

CHAPTER 

Type designs – how and why they are different

CONSERVATIVE ESTIMATES put the number of typefaces in use today at about 3,000, with at least 10,000 different designs having been used at one time or another over the past 500 years. This probably makes you wonder: Why so many? Can there even be so many differences? How can anyone hope to learn anything about typefaces if there are so many?

This chapter will answer these questions, and show you how to divide all typefaces into just two divisions, as a start towards learning a simple system for dividing typefaces into basic groupings called "styles." In due course, the book will explain these styles, with detailed illustrations, and you will then have the key to understanding the whole range of typefaces.

Types, like all of printing, are tools in communication. Printing puts information into someone's hands, influences him to feel or think a certain way, or prompts him to take or refrain from taking a certain action. The typeface is the trigger part of that tool, so to speak, because it determines the way the message looks to the reader—pleasant, pretty, messy, painful or threatening—and this in turn affects the reader's reaction to the printed message.

A great number of men, therefore, have taken great pains through 500 years of printing history to shape type designs that will meet one or more of the various needs or purposes which printing serves. The 10,000 typefaces are the result.

That doesn't mean there are 10,000 different needs. Most of the designs are attempts to meet a common need better than before, especially the need for a readable and yet space-saving typeface for books, magazines and newspapers. And as your do-it-yourself designing showed, there are innumerable differences possible in the way letters are drawn.

Actually, as the box below shows, almost all printing can be divided into three broad kinds:

To catch a person's attention, in order to sell him something. This is printing for advertising, posters, promotional materials,

The function of one kind of type: *to catch the eye.* **LOOK AT THIS!** The function of this kind of type: *to set the mood.* FESTIVAL OF BAYREUTH	The words you are now reading have a message for you—namely, that with a good reading type, the meaning comes through clearly, and you don't even pay any attention to the letters as such, much less their design. *Right?* The function of this kind of type: *to convey meaning without catching the eye.*

political campaign materials. To "catch the eye," in competition with a mass of other ads with other typefaces, many designers think they must create constant "novelty," with typefaces which have some *new* or different peculiarity—some unusual design that will call attention to itself.

To produce a printed piece for an occasion. This covers such things as programs, menus, presentations, invitations, certificates, and documents to match historic periods, etc., and also such mundane "service" items as tickets, invoice forms, etc. Here, the function of the typeface is to "catch the mood"—solemn, gay, reverent, loving, important—whatever may be needed. Through the generations, certain typefaces have come to symbolize certain moods: Old English for a holiday touch on a Christmas

Old English PLAYBILL

card, or a design like Playbill for a suggestion of entertainment. The good designer finds fresh ways to use typefaces to create a given mood, but "mood faces" as such, like the "selling faces," have their special peculiarities to convey some special feeling.

To convey information or make literature readable. In this group are the books, magazines and newspapers (that is, their non-advertising pages). Typefaces for reading at any length are best when they perform a function exactly opposite the other types: they *avoid* catching the eye with peculiarities, or unusual designs, so that nothing will hamper the eye's easy, fast and pleasant flow, to move the printed meaning off the page and into the mind.

The first two kinds of printing have led to typefaces with virtually every imaginable sort of "different" design. The third kind of printing has tended to discourage such noticeable differences. Thus, there are two basic kinds of typeface—one with special peculiarities, and one avoiding all peculiarities.

To see what this means, take a minute to look at the page of newspaper front pages, at the right. In particular, look at the big lines of type, usually called "streamers" or "banner headlines."

Some of those typefaces are very much like what you are used to—in fact, as you may have noticed, this is true of all the headlines in the first vertical column. These are what we can call STANDARD typefaces. They will do for newspaper headlines, and for almost anything else. Not the very best designs to use, perhaps, but they will never look peculiar or unusual, when used in a size appropriate to the purpose.

But the typefaces in the second column all differ from those standard typefaces in one particular way: they are SPECIAL faces that will do well in certain special circumstances for special purposes, but they do look peculiar—very unusual indeed!—used as a newspaper banner line.

The top one is a typeface called Goudy Text; it looks right on a church document, or an old-fashioned Christmas card, but here it is not being used in *its* special way. The next typeface is named Stencil, and this tells you its special purpose is to give a stencil effect. It will never do on a wedding invitation. The third face is called Park Avenue—drawn to imitate elegant handwriting. Fine for a stylish invitation, or a lady's personal stationery, perhaps, but not for a newspaper headline or grocery listing. The bottom one is a typewriter face deliberately made to look like typewriting instead of printing, and hardly useful, therefore, when you want something to look *printed.*

The first and basic division, therefore, is into STANDARD and SPECIAL typefaces.

As you look at typefaces to decide whether they are standard or special, you will find borderline cases, of course, which can go either way. In some, the attention-getting part of the design is subtle or slight. Others have been used specially so often that they have become accepted as ordinary. Do not worry about these now. If you can divide the 10,000 typefaces roughly into the two basic divisions, you are well on your way to being their master.

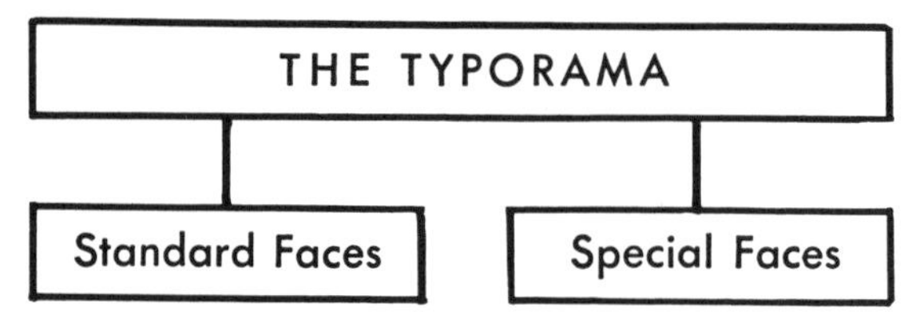

Tribunal and Times

THE WEATHER

THURSDAY, SEPTEMBER 2, 1965

UN ACTS TO PRESERVE PEACE

REMAP PLAN REBUFFED, HE RETALIATES — Johnson Asked Help, He Says

Mammoth Dallas Port Project OK'd

Taylor Given Aid Post

STEEL TALKS REACH 'HARD, TOUGH' STAGE — Tackle Issues on Pay, Pensions

15,000 in Cleveland Greet Lone Sailor

TITLE OF CONSULTANT CREATED BY JOHNSON

2 COURTS BAN INTERFERENCE WITH SCHOOLS

President Seeks Full Support for Domingo Rulers

Tribunal and Times

THE WEATHER

THURSDAY, SEPTEMBER 2, 1965

UN Acts to Preserve Peace

REMAP PLAN REBUFFED, HE RETALIATES — Johnson Asked Help, He Says

Mammoth Dallas Port Project OK'd

Taylor Given Aid Post

STEEL TALKS REACH 'HARD, TOUGH' STAGE — Tackle Issues on Pay, Pensions

15,000 in Cleveland Greet Lone Sailor

TITLE OF CONSULTANT CREATED BY JOHNSON

2 COURTS BAN INTERFERENCE WITH SCHOOLS

President Seeks Full Support for Domingo Rulers

Tribunal and Times

THE WEATHER

THURSDAY, SEPTEMBER 2, 1965

UN ACTS TO PRESERVE PEACE

REMAP PLAN REBUFFED, HE RETALIATES — Johnson Asked Help, He Says

Mammoth Dallas Port Project OK'd

Taylor Given Aid Post

STEEL TALKS REACH 'HARD, TOUGH' STAGE — Tackle Issues on Pay, Pensions

15,000 in Cleveland Greet Lone Sailor

TITLE OF CONSULTANT CREATED BY JOHNSON

2 COURTS BAN INTERFERENCE WITH SCHOOLS

President Seeks Full Support for Domingo Rulers

Tribunal and Times

THE WEATHER

THURSDAY, SEPTEMBER 2, 1965

UN ACTS TO PRESERVE PEACE

REMAP PLAN REBUFFED, HE RETALIATES — Johnson Asked Help, He Says

Mammoth Dallas Port Project OK'd

Taylor Given Aid Post

STEEL TALKS REACH 'HARD, TOUGH' STAGE — Tackle Issues on Pay, Pensions

15,000 in Cleveland Greet Lone Sailor

TITLE OF CONSULTANT CREATED BY JOHNSON

2 COURTS BAN INTERFERENCE WITH SCHOOLS

President Seeks Full Support for Domingo Rulers

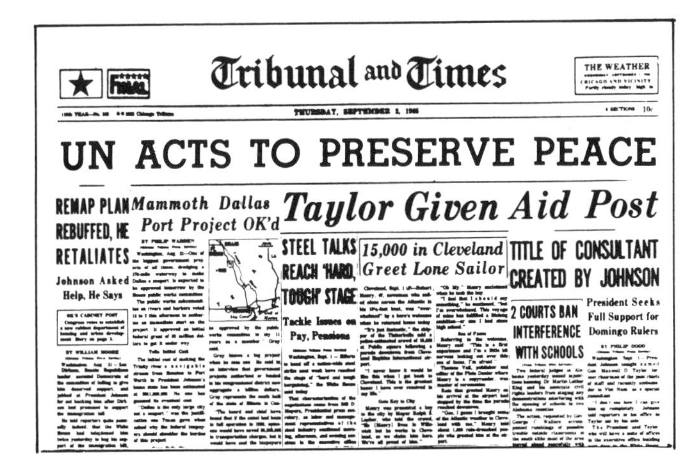

Tribunal and Times

THE WEATHER

THURSDAY, SEPTEMBER 2, 1965

UN ACTS TO PRESERVE PEACE

REMAP PLAN REBUFFED, HE RETALIATES — Johnson Asked Help, He Says

Mammoth Dallas Port Project OK'd

Taylor Given Aid Post

STEEL TALKS REACH 'HARD, TOUGH' STAGE — Tackle Issues on Pay, Pensions

15,000 in Cleveland Greet Lone Sailor

TITLE OF CONSULTANT CREATED BY JOHNSON

2 COURTS BAN INTERFERENCE WITH SCHOOLS

President Seeks Full Support for Domingo Rulers

Tribunal and Times

THE WEATHER

THURSDAY, SEPTEMBER 2, 1965

U N Acts to Preserve Peace

REMAP PLAN REBUFFED, HE RETALIATES — Johnson Asked Help, He Says

Mammoth Dallas Port Project OK'd

Taylor Given Aid Post

STEEL TALKS REACH 'HARD, TOUGH' STAGE — Tackle Issues on Pay, Pensions

15,000 in Cleveland Greet Lone Sailor

TITLE OF CONSULTANT CREATED BY JOHNSON

2 COURTS BAN INTERFERENCE WITH SCHOOLS

President Seeks Full Support for Domingo Rulers

Tribunal and Times

THE WEATHER

THURSDAY, SEPTEMBER 2, 1965

UN ACTS TO PRESERVE PEACE

REMAP PLAN REBUFFED, HE RETALIATES — Johnson Asked Help, He Says

Mammoth Dallas Port Project OK'd

Taylor Given Aid Post

STEEL TALKS REACH 'HARD, TOUGH' STAGE — Tackle Issues on Pay, Pensions

15,000 in Cleveland Greet Lone Sailor

TITLE OF CONSULTANT CREATED BY JOHNSON

2 COURTS BAN INTERFERENCE WITH SCHOOLS

President Seeks Full Support for Domingo Rulers

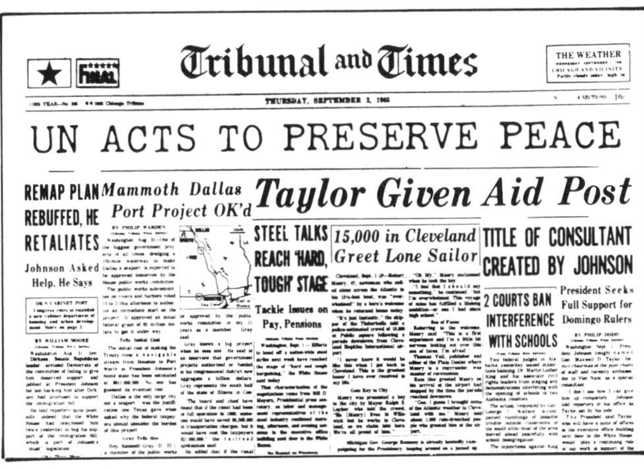

Tribunal and Times

THE WEATHER

THURSDAY, SEPTEMBER 2, 1965

UN ACTS TO PRESERVE PEACE

REMAP PLAN REBUFFED, HE RETALIATES — Johnson Asked Help, He Says

Mammoth Dallas Port Project OK'd

Taylor Given Aid Post

STEEL TALKS REACH 'HARD, TOUGH' STAGE — Tackle Issues on Pay, Pensions

15,000 in Cleveland Greet Lone Sailor

TITLE OF CONSULTANT CREATED BY JOHNSON

2 COURTS BAN INTERFERENCE WITH SCHOOLS

President Seeks Full Support for Domingo Rulers

The big headlines show standard and special faces (see opposite page)

CHAPTER 

The major differences in typefaces

DIFFERENCES IN LETTER FORMS can be small or great. However, before we get into the precise differences among the shapes of letters, it will be helpful to take a somewhat closer look at the two major groupings—standard and special typefaces—to see what really makes them differ from each other.

THE SPECIAL FACES

The basic clue here is the special *purpose* of a typeface. What is the type supposed to do? There are six main special purposes.

SIMULATES. Some typefaces simulate, or imitate, certain kinds of lettering—and writing. These are used when a graphic designer *wants* the lettering to look like something other than regular printing.

Typewriter STENCIL

CARTOON Park Avenue

You noted among the examples of newspaper headlines that there were types intended to look like typewriting, stencilling or handwriting. These are simulates.

RESIDUALS are for a special kind of imitation. Before type came into use—even before the alphabet was completely worked out, as you will soon see—there were many varieties of hand-lettering and handwriting styles in use in Europe. Some were beautiful

Cursive Italic Uncial

LOMBARDIC

and certainly different, and some (like the examples shown) are still in use in typefaces cut to imitate the lettering of ancient days.

One of these is our ordinary *italic* type, used now for the special purpose of emphasis.

ADAPTED. Some typefaces are changed greatly from the shapes of standard typefaces for various reasons. Some have been

Ringlet

UMBRA

PROFIL

adapted, or altered, for purposes of decoration—ornaments have been put on them, or patterns, or fancy flourishes, or they have been surrounded with flowers. Some faces, made into huge letters and really decorated, are used as initials. Some letters get a mixture of different adaptations.

MANNERED. These typefaces are something like the standard faces, but there is always something "wrong," or at least different. They all have some quirk, some odd style about them that is quite noticeable, such as unusual sizes or shapes, or long h's,

Black Squared Special

VERTICAL Wide

p's and q's, or special blackness. These differences, properly used, help set a special tone, style or mood. That is why, for all the similarity, they cannot be called "standard."

NEWFORMS. These are different from standard faces, too, and very deliberately so. Some are experimental—in efforts to find a more legible or simpler alphabet—and

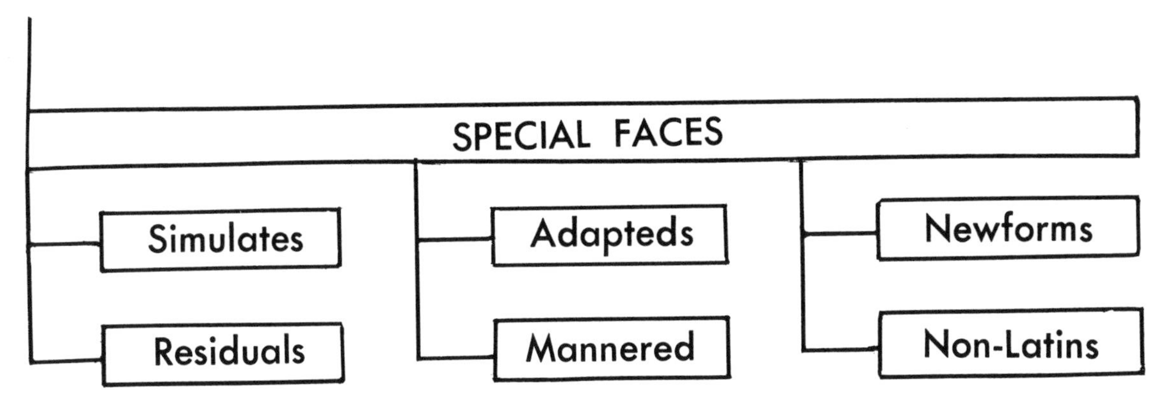

some are used for new electronic purposes, as in computer scanners, which need

æ b c d ee f g h ie j k l m n œ p r r s t
wh ch th th sh ʒ ŋ a a a au e i o u
PITMAN INITIAL TEACHING ALPHABET

0 1 2 3 4 5 6 7 8 9 MAGNETIC

precise differences so they can tell the letters apart electronically.

NON-LATIN. Our alphabet—called "Latin" for reasons which will come clear later—is by no means the only way of expressing language. At least parts of the Bible, for instance, have been printed in

מְדִינַת יִשְׂרָאֵל HEBREW ألْحَمْدُ لله رب ٱلْعَالَمين ARABIC

русский язык RUSSIAN रम्यान्तरः कमलिनीहरितैः सरोभि- SANSKRIT

more than 1,500 different languages, using scores of different alphabets (sometimes called "scripts") which have been put into type.

These, then, are the SPECIAL faces. Remember that each had a reason for being born, and that each can perform an assignment, can help messages reach the reader. Even the most outlandish are part of a wonderful human heritage.

STANDARD FACES

After the great differences among the Special faces, the Standard faces look very much alike. However, the Standard typefaces, in sheer wordage, perform the bulk of the world's printed work and very small differences can mean a lot. You will find, therefore, that most of the concern about typeface design through the centuries has focused on what might seem very subtle changes.

One simple little part of most Standard typefaces—the cross line at the end of a stroke or main line—is the key that opens the door to seeing the differences. It is called a "serif" (SEHR-if), and the art below shows it in some detail, along with some of

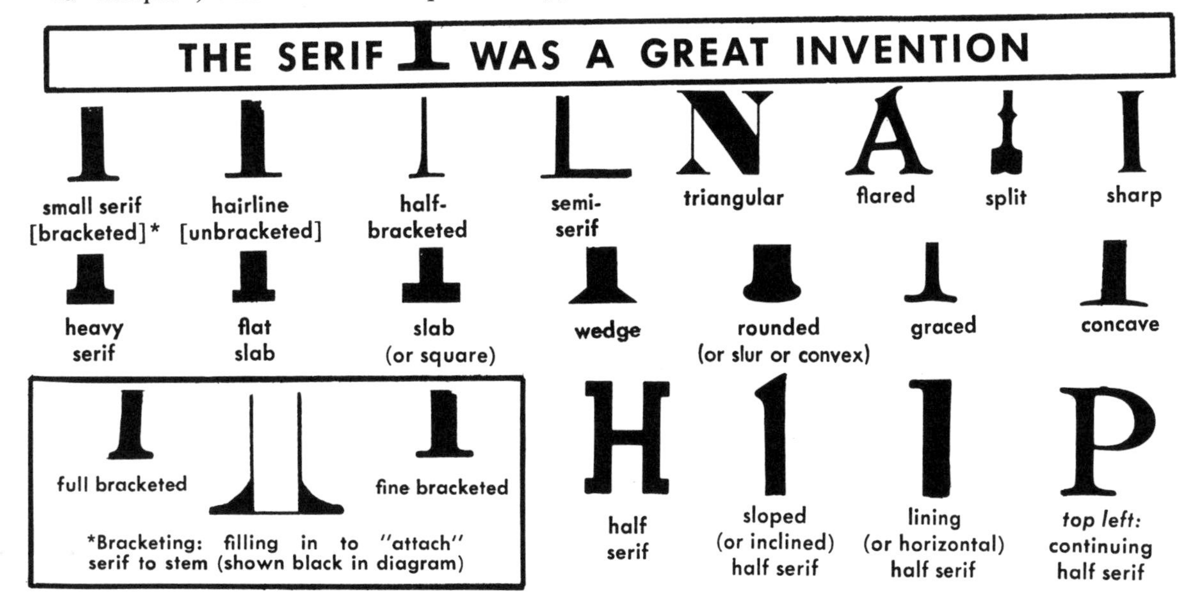

the ways it can be treated. (These differences are by no means arbitrary or accidental; there are reasons and long history behind each one, as you will see.)

What is important is that these different ways of making a serif, or leaving it off altogether, provide us with an easy way to begin recognizing different standard faces. It is by no means the only way, and the serif is often not the most important element of a type design. But because in a good type design the treatment of the serif ties in very closely with the treatment of the rest of the letter, the serif becomes a highly reliable key to the whole design.

On this basis we can divide standard typefaces into three categories—small serif faces, strong serif faces and sans serif faces. ("Sans" is French for "without.") You will see the differences clearly here:

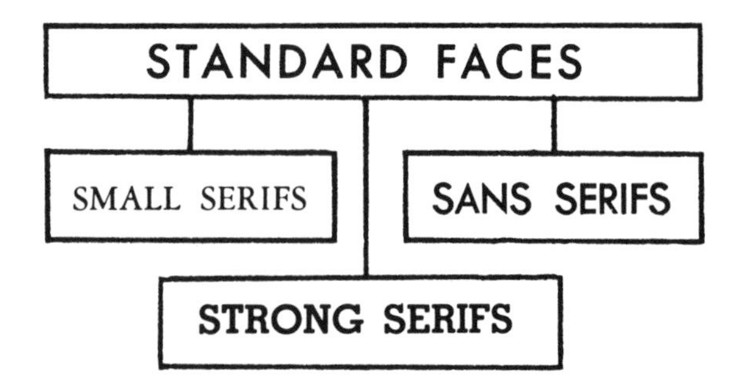

THE ELEMENTS OF LETTERS

As the chart on page 15 shows, making tangible what we discovered in designing Futura, there is almost no end to the combinations of elements of letters. So typefaces are skinny and fat, graceful and crude, tall and squat, mannered and rude, rough and slick, sunken-in and popped out, thin and thick, intended to whisper or shout.

Note that all of these differences in appearance are created by changing only tiny lines or areas of the type design. A typeface as such has no other way to express a tone or mood. If a type in print seems to say "I'm happy," most of the "gayness" is coming from the way the graphic designer used it and from what the message itself says.

One feature is not shown in the chart, because it is more than just a design element of type, being fundamental to the whole design of letters as such—that is, the width allowed each letter. Normally, letters have different widths, the l and W generally providing the greatest contrast.

The ordinary (non-proportional) typewriter is an example of what happens when flexibility in width cannot be allowed. In the typewriter, each letter has exactly the same space to fill, because the carriage moves the same distance each time. Thus, the i and l have trouble filling the space, while the M and W can barely squeeze in:

s a w m i l l

To remedy the situation, early typewriter makers usually put strong serifs in their typefaces. Here you see the difference with serifs:

sawmill

No one has a right to expect a beautiful face on a standard typewriter, since some letters are bound to be thin and some crowded, making the page look spotty. To improve on this, manufacturers began producing typewriter "proportional spacing" machines—that is, the carriage move varies for each of three or four different width letters. Thus, the letters can look like this:

sawmill

Printing type allows much greater variations in width — 12 different widths on the least flexible casting machine, and an infinite number on hand-casting devices. The different letters can be shaped to their

FGHIJKLMN

"natural" width according to the ideas of the designer, not simply forced into a standard measure.

Differences so small that one can hardly measure them make the differences between standard typefaces. Yet even when the differences are almost microscopic in separate letters, a line of type or a paragraph can reflect such a total difference that even national character can be exhibited—one

SOME OF THE CHANGEABLE ELEMENTS IN OUR LETTER FORMS

The basic shape of the letters (see Frontispiece)
Variations within a given basic shape
The proportions of the parts of a letter
The width of a given letter
The "weight" or "color" (blackness) of a letter
Contrast among parts of the same letter
The distribution of "stress" (thickening) of a line
The basic position or force of the stress (see Page 18)
The "quality of line" (see Page 18)
The kind of contour or outline
The treatment of endings (see Pages 13, 31)
The treatment of surfaces
The stance of the letter: leaning or upright
The "alignment" of the letter along a reading line (see Page 61)
Differences in kinds of strokes (see Page 31)
Differences in punctuation marks
Differences in dimension (e.g., third dimension)
Differences in size as such

can say there is a Dutch-English school or a French school of type. On such minute

French School

Dutch-English School

variations do beauty and success rest for a typeface.

You may think you will never be able to see these differences, and in a sense that may be true, since no one really observes all these characteristics in detail. And yet, after a little study, you will be able to distinguish one typeface from another, just as you can tell a carefully-dressed person from a dowdy one, without being able to say in words precisely what makes the difference.

More than that, because you will be turning now to the story of how typefaces "happened"—a quick look at the remarkable inventions that made them possible and shaped them—you will soon learn where patterns and styles came from, and why. Then, suddenly, this great welter of type pieces and parts will form into a unified whole and make sense.

THE 15 GREAT INVENTIONS
BEHIND OUR TYPEFACES

CHAPTER 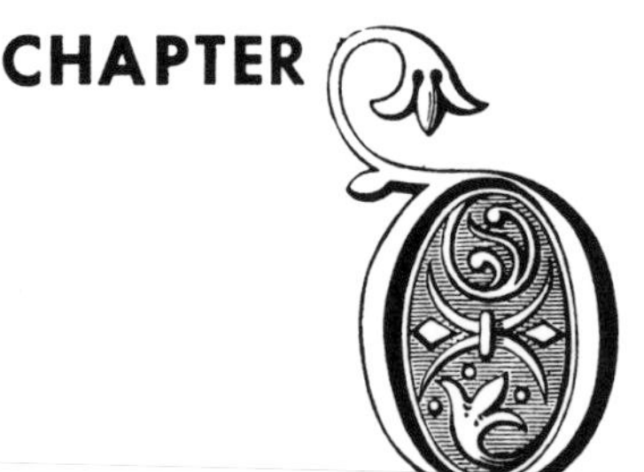

The invention of the alphabet for reading aloud

ELEPHANTS' MEMORIES are reputedly greater than men's, but mankind has won mastery of the Earth because it has remembered its past experience and put it to use. The elephant has not. One difference lies in man's *alphabet*, which made written memory possible.

How the idea of an alphabet was invented and how our Latin alphabet developed are fascinating stories in their own right. There is always a temptation to start with the first picture-writers who drew objects that could be recognized—perhaps 10,000 to 25,000 years ago—and then trace the series of steps that resulted in a set of abstract symbols that do not look like pictures of anything, but stand for sounds of the voice.

For practical purposes, however, we can begin at the end of this process—with the abstract symbols after they lost their pictorial meaning.

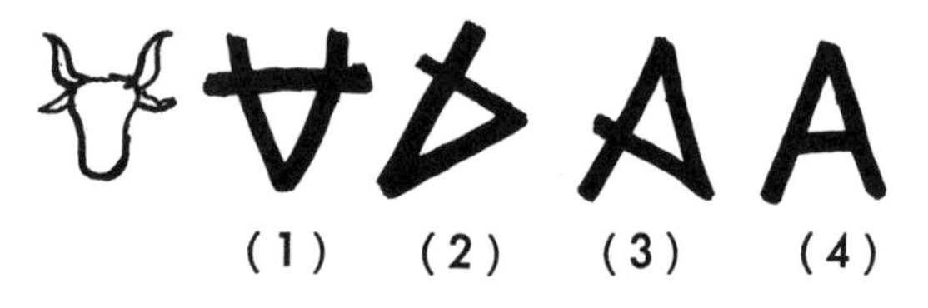

What happened is shown above. By the time of the Phoenicians, about 1500 B.C. (they generally get credit for developing the alphabet we have inherited), the first letter of the alphabet was pronounced something like our A and called "Alef" (AH-leff). This was the Phoenician word for "ox," and the symbol (1) actually looked like the head of an ox.

When the Greeks took the letter Alef from the Phoenicians, about the 9th or 10th century B.C., they did not know (or care) that it was supposed to represent an ox head. They changed the name (and sound) slightly to Alpha. (Alpha does not mean ox; the Greek word for ox was *bous.*) Over a period of time they altered the shape somewhat (2), and turned it upside down (3). Ultimately it became Alpha in Greek and then Ah in Latin (4).

Pictures had been turned into marks without pictorial meaning (called letters) which stood for particular sounds of the voice instead. This was the invention of reading aloud.

WHAT THE LETTERS MEAN

Similar scrambling, turning upside down, and a change in sound happened to many letters. Both Greek and Latin, at the start, were read from right to left (as the Semitic languages still are). At one point, the Greeks wrote *boustrophedonically*, a great word which means "the way the ox ploughs." The plough went to the edge of a field, and then turned around right there and ploughed in the opposite direction. In other words, if the first line of Greek read from right to left, the next line read from left to right, and the following line from right to left again.

To do this, the letters often were turned around for the backwards line. When the language finally settled on reading from left to right, some letters were turned around permanently.

READ TO THE RIGHT
TFEL EHT OT NEHT DNA (mirrored)
AND THEN RIGHT AGAIN
TFEL EHT OT NEHT DNA

The Latin alphabet consisted of symbols for sounds which were understood by those people who used the letters to read and write, but there was no meaning at all in the letters themselves. There was only one rule: *Letters stand for sounds, and only those sounds agreed upon by the users.*

Letters can be added or dropped, and changed in pattern or sound, whenever the users of the alphabet agree to the change—and only when they do. That is the way the J, U and W came late into the Latin alphabet.

In Africa today, most of the nations are adopting the Latin alphabet so the local language can be written, printed and read. Many of these languages have sounds not covered by the Latin alphabet, so new letters are added for the purpose.

The government of then Southern Rhodesia adopted the Latin alphabet in 1932, with six extra characters

ɓ ɗ ȿ ʋ ŋ ʐ

added for special sounds. But in 1955, those six characters were dropped, and the Latin alphabet is now used just in its standard 26-letter form, because the new letters had added more difficulties than they ended.

TWO LETTERS THAT FAILED

þ thorn

ſ long s

They were dropped because they were not needed and were confusing. The thorn was Old English for th, making "the" look like "ye," and the long s looked like an f. (See Page 85.)

Even China is moving toward replacing its ideographs with the Latin alphabet.

The history of alphabets and shapes of letters is a history of such experiments. Because no alphabet or letter form is perfect, and because languages continually change, some experiments end successfully, some letters are accepted for special purposes and some not at all.

The vast collection of typefaces we have is really a living museum of all the experiments that have been successful since the Latin alphabet was first developed.

THE GRACEFUL ROMANS

Greek art is generally considered superior to Roman art in grace and beauty (especially in the sculptures of the feminine form). But if you compare the Greek and Latin alphabets, it is the Greek letters that are cold and severe with many straight lines, angles and points, while the Romans have graceful curves that balance the lines and angles, to create interesting variety.

ANGLES AND CURVES

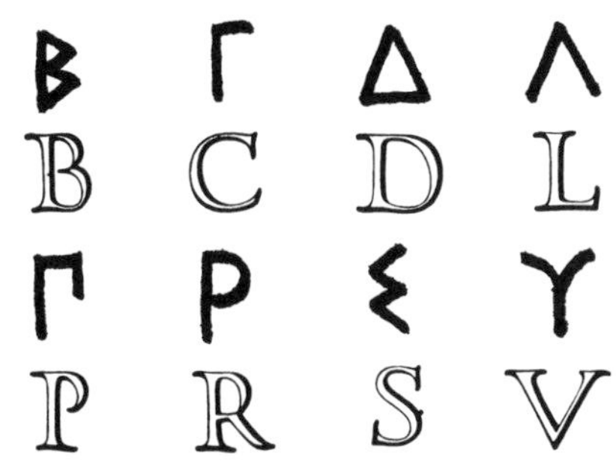

Here are the Greek (top) and Latin letters that differed, as of classical Roman times. The Greek letters were angular because they were shaped when scribes were still writing on surfaces that hindered a free-flowing hand and curves. The later Romans had smoother surfaces and better writing tools.

These letter forms have come down to us as inscriptions in monuments still standing in Rome and elsewhere. Whoever patterned these letters worked out the proportions (the variable widths of l, w, etc., referred to in Chapter C) so well and gave the letters such beauty and legibility, that their effect on letter design has lasted up to the present day. As important as the proportions of the

ABCDEFG
ILMNOP
QRSTVX

THE TRAJAN COLUMN IN ROME (114 A.D.)

These "Trajan letter" shapes, cut into the stone panel (shown by white) 10 feet above ground in pedestal of column, are considered the perfect Roman-proportioned form, and still guide type designers. They are not all the same size here because they were taken from different lines graduated in height so they would all look the same size to the viewer on the ground.

THICK and THIN CURVES

Roman writing with flat pens still affects most of our typefaces, in their thick-and-thin lines. The same pen held at the same angle but moved in different directions produces lines of different widths. Two pointed markers held together and moved as a flat pen will create the same thick-and-thins in outline, to guide stone lettering. This thickening, especially when curved, is called *stress* (or *shading* or *modeling*).

letters was the "quality of line"—a delicate and graceful thickening and thinning of

ABC **ABC**

the curves, as shown by comparing these first three capitals with the next three "monotone" or one-thickness letters.

Quality of Line: INCISED

INLINE

—Hunter College, Bruce Rogers

"Quality of line" is the subtle difference in letters made by different tools and materials. Thus, the sharp edges, precise curves and lines chiseled into stone in three dimensions give "incise" lettering a quality of grandeur, impersonality, depth and authority. This will come clearer as you compare all the kinds of line in this book and see how type (which has a quality of line of its own) has faces which capture the lines of the other processes as well—even incised as in the type example above (Augustea Inline).

These letters are sometimes called "incised" because they were cut in, and sometimes "lapidary" because they were cut in stone (*lapis*).

Experts believe the letters may have been sketched out on the stone with a double-marker that had the same effect as a broad-edged pen. (See drawing.) Or perhaps they were simply drawn with a square brush on the stone in the manner of the modern skilled sign painter. Then the chisel cut them along the pattern. Thus, the letters we credit to the chisel might have been developed originally by writing masters, whose work surfaces, less durable than stone, have long since perished. Or the stone-cutters may have created the design themselves.

In either case, these early Roman letters reflect the same principles as handwritten letters—principles still in effect for the most part today. Our typefaces are curved, thick and thin, because handwriting with flat pens shaped ancient letters that way.

Another important contribution by the ancient Romans was the serif. To finish off a letter, to make it look right (the abrupt finish of a stub stroke hardly matched the grace of those curves), the serif was needed. It also solved the technical problem of getting the chisel to cut a clean, neat end. The handwriters discovered the same thing—before or after the stone-cutters—and the serifs have been with us ever since.

Almost every reading test has shown that small serifs, properly designed, help reading by providing a horizontal guideline and by tying together the letters of a word to form a single picture for the eye to grasp.

The Romans did not know this. They did not even use a space between words and ran allthewordstogetherlikethis. Their alphabet was used for reading aloud, which was so slow that the eye could pick out the separate words.

Silent reading, which is of course much faster, would have been quite another matter, and not alone because of the lack of spacing. Although the ancient Romans invented a serviceable alphabet and gave it beautiful form, it completely lacked something of equal or even greater importance for silent reading—small letters. Their alphabet consisted of capital letters only.

CHAPTER

The invention of the book

WRITING AND LETTERING are not enough. We need a simple and repeatable way to set down words (and pictures), so that many copies can be made and circulated afar. We also need words in permanent, lasting form that can be cherished and studied.

That is why the next invention, the book, and the almost simultaneous idea of publishing—making duplicate copies and distributing—are not only worth noting, but rejoicing over.

The first "book" format was the papyrus roll invented in Egypt around 4,000 B.C. and used in ancient Greece and Rome. Papyrus was a very thin version of what we call plywood today, made from the pith of the papyrus reed into sheets and pasted into long strips that could be rolled up. "Scribes" were employed to write manuscripts on the rolls, and to make copies. But a roll is not as convenient as a book for storage, for handling in reading, or for finding particular places in the text. Moreover, it is a task to reroll to the starting position after use.

Proverbially, therefore, too bulky or long a roll was a great evil. So manuscripts were divided into a series of rolls—another nuisance in storing and finding. All this worked to limit production of copies.

Our true book format started about 300 B.C. in Greece or Rome with the "codex," a loose-leaf note-book made of two or more flat pieces of wood tablet hinged together on one side, and used for ordinary writing purposes, such as business transactions.

At first, the inside surfaces of the wood were covered with a thin layer of wax, and the writer scratched his letters in the wax, using a stylus which had a sharp point at one end and a flat edge on the other (to smooth out errors). Eventually, leaves of parchment (specially treated sheepskin) were inserted between the boards, and the codex became more like the book we know. After the codex became a true book (in the 1st century A.D.), its use for formal, important manuscripts increased steadily and ultimately more or less forced the invention of true printing from type to meet the demand.

There is no question that books were cherished from the start. There was a magic in creating a book. So books were produced with care and reverence, and with a sense of beauty. "Initial letters," such as are in the chapter heads of this book, decorated the pages, and special pains were taken with all lettering.

You will see in the next chapter what the production of books, therefore, did to the shape of letters, and how an even more remarkable invention resulted.

BEGINNINGS of the BOOK

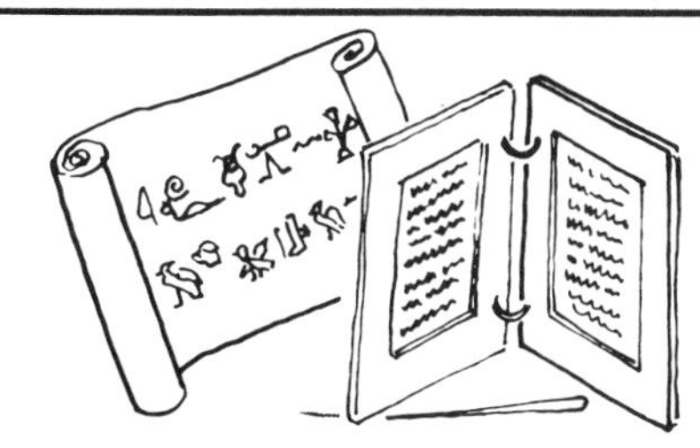

The first "book" was a roll of papyrus in Egypt. The Greco-Roman "codex"—two tied wax-coated boards written on by scratches with a pointed stylus—led to the handwritten book, still called a codex, and still the book form we use today.

CHAPTER F

The invention of small letters

THE INCISED ROMAN capital letters were majestic for inscribing a monument, but they were not ideal for use in books or for many other purposes. So in due course, letter forms were changed to serve these other purposes. Between the incised letters and these new forms, the Latin alphabet was given the shapes that still govern *our* typefaces today.

The inscriptionists—the stone-cutters along with other artists and craftsmen who carved inscriptions, initials, decorations and messages in jewels and armour—had cut with a sharp-edged tool into a hard surface, stone or metal. Their letters could not be formed as written letters are, by one stroke or a curving sweep of the hand, but had to be cut a little at a time according to a pattern. Since the process was slow, they felt they might as well cut the most beautiful letters possible.

But the Roman scribes—specialists hired to put down any and all types of communication on papyrus or other writing surface—had writing tools which gave them more freedom and flexibility. Whether they "adapted" the inscriptioned capitals, or created their own styles first, they developed three different kinds of handwriting or "hands."

Roman square capitals, called Quadrata

SQUARE CAPITALS were either an attempt to copy the inscriptional letters exactly for the production of formal books, or the basic letter which the stone-cutters copied. However, even though wealthy, the manuscript collectors who paid the scribes could hardly afford to have every letter in a book made as carefully and slowly as the inscriptional style required. Cutting a few letters in stone was one thing: the whole works of Virgil was something else. Besides, the scribes were using a different tool than a chisel—a reed brush on papyrus or, later, a reed pen on parchment and vellum (vellum being a softer, more pliable and smoother version of parchment). Their lettering, therefore, inevitably differed from the inscriptional form.

RUSTIC CAPITALS. For less important books, the scribes were not as painstaking. Also, the Square Capitals were really quite wide letters, and vellum was expensive. Expense could be saved two ways (in time and material) if the writing were done in letters that were narrower and simpler to

Quality of Line: CALLIGRAPHIC

Using a flat pen, calligraphy shows the graceful flow of the human hand, with more subtle movement than an incised line can allow and more warmth than strictly geometrical lines (see Copperplate, Page 39). Incise must stay in third dimension, but the pen swells and subsides to create a ribbon line turning from two-dimensional front views to three-dimensional edge views. Always, good calligraphy has the fresh look of a unique letter created specially for you, its one reader.

Roman rustic capitals

Roman everyday hand

make. The Rustic (or Simple) Capitals (*Rustica* in Latin) were the answer.

EVERYDAY HAND. Not all writing had to be fancy. Most of it, in fact, was for recording business transactions, bookkeeping, correspondence and similar uses. This did not have to look as elegant as formal writing, and in fact could not, because it was often done in a hurry. The hand was still based on the inscriptional letters but short-cuts which were more or less legible were tried and accepted. They saved time, space and writing materials. These letters were the beginnings of the small letters we know today. An important innovation was the tendency towards ascenders and descenders—longer vertical lines ("stems")—for the b, d, h, k, l, p, q and t, and tails for g and y. This came from the natural tendency of a flowing hand to make "flourishes" or long, sweeping lines and from the fact that it was easier to make longer stems than the precise short lengths originally used.

The important point to note is this—letter forms were being changed by the tools in use and by the needs of the users. In technical terms, form follows function. We will see this principle constantly at work as the history of typefaces goes on.

EXPORTED ROMAN HANDS

While the three original Roman hands were kept in use until about A.D. 500, two events shortly after their development led to some different styles of writing.

Almost overnight, about 85 B.C., Rome became a literary force, and there were plays and poems and philosophy to be published, for reading through the whole (Western) world. Soon, on top of this, Christianity became the Romans' religion, and they began to spread it. Bibles were needed, as well as commentaries on the Bible for scholars, and other church writings.

This great volume of writing production spurred interest in improving the forms, especially in terms of economy, and thus led to three new hands:

ROMAN CURSIVE. Once everyday handwriting began to develop differences, and these differences proved valuable, professional scribes gave special attention to improving this particular kind of writing. The resultant hand is called "cursive," a term which you will understand best if you connect it with the word "course," as in the way a river flows. The incised letters did not flow, but handwriting did flow. That is,

Later Roman cursive hand

cursive writing had the feeling of a hand moving across the page as it wrote. It was reasoned that in the same way, the eye would flow more easily across the page, and the cursive was, therefore, thought to be more legible. The fact that cursive letters were born out of a flowing motion meant that their shape had to be changed from the original capital letters. More and more they were changing into our small letters, most conspicuously by the way ascenders and descenders lengthened.

UNCIALS. These letters grew out of an effort to develop a beautiful formal letter for Bibles and other important books, recognizing the fact that Square Capitals were uneconomic and the Rustica not elegant enough. With lessons that the scribes were learning from their (still more or less everyday) cursive hand, applied directly to the formal Square Capital letters, with the pen held horizontal to the letter base, the lovely round uncial was achieved by about A.D. 300:

The uncial hand

Most writers explain the name as indicating a letter one inch high, "uncia" in Latin meaning "one-twelfth." However, since there has never been a Latin manuscript found with letters one inch high, and since "uncia" in Latin also means "little by little," perhaps that meaning should apply. In any event, the uncial was a change from the standard Square Capital, achieved "little by little" over a long period of time.

Since the uncial is a beautiful letter with great stately grace and dignity, and a round fullness (sumptuousness, it has been called) it became the dominant formal book hand for some five centuries, and is still used in special typefaces for the same reasons that made it attractive then.

Note that the uncial also was beginning to develop some small letters; the "a" is a clear case. But it was still one alphabet, and it is today still classed as a capital-letter alphabet.

THE HALF-UNCIAL. Despite its name, this hand did not arise from the uncial, but developed at the same time out of need for an easier, more condensed and more readable hand for ordinary books (not Bibles). It, too, seems to have been greatly influenced by the cursive hand, and the half-uncials reflect further steps towards our small letters as the scribes took more and more liberties with the capital letters. In fact, the half-

The half-uncial hand

uncials are often classed with the small letters, and it is really quite fair to say they represent the invention of the small-letter alphabet.

Except for the letters J, U and W, the basic Latin alphabet was now formed. But the general adoption of small letters in a uniform way was quite another matter.

Class: UNCIALS

a d e g m

p r s t y

Today's uncial still has the single alphabet with its unique "uncial a" and d and e, and the letters that later divided into capitals or lowercase. Shown: *Libra.*

NOTE: This is the first of a series of "style boxes" of present-day type designs, showing the key characteristics of a style (or class) of typeface. Each box appears on the page describing the historic development which helped shape the particular style. See Page 31 for definitions of terms used; for full alphabet specimens of these styles, see Appendix I, Page 97. The classification names at the top and bottom are explained throughout the book, as the Typorama grew, and summarized in Chapter T, Page 77.

Category: Residuals (Special Faces)

WHY IT'S "L.C."

Until recent years, all type was handset, and this involved so many pieces that separate "cases" (shallow trays with boxes for each letter) had to be made for the capital and small letters. The small letters, being used far more than capitals, were placed for convenience lower and closer to the typesetter: hence *lowercase* or l.c., with capitals *uppercase* or u.c. (but usually called "caps"). Together: clc, sometimes u.l.c.

CHAPTER 3

The invention of silent reading

THERE WAS also a deeper force than the mechanics and tools of the scribes' work behind the development of the small letter, but it is a real question whether the scribes were aware of it: the invention of silent reading. This was a really astonishing feat, even though we now take it so much for granted that reading *aloud* is the unusual form.

For a moment, do not take it for granted. Look at someone in a bus or plane who is reading to himself: see him smile, frown, sigh, as he turns the pages. A piece of paper with black marks is causing that! Or pick up a classic book and read it yourself. Homer or Plato, who lived thousands of years ago and spoke a language you do not know, is talking to you, in a way that does not even create a sound—through marks on paper that you hardly even see as you skim along soaking up a meaning that certainly does not reside in them separately or as such.

Somewhere, sometime, the scribes must have become aware of this miraculous process of the human mind. Possibly it was when the uncial and half-uncial developed in separate ways—the one for Bibles (to be read aloud in church) and the other for ordinary books (to be read silently to oneself, and studied in a library).

Because of the great speed of silent reading as compared with oral reading, letter forms now had to have two particular qualities:

First, letters all had to be much easier to recognize, with more substantial variety among them so as not to be confused with one another. It became increasingly clear that small letters had much more such variety than capital letters. Second, special little differences had to be eliminated as they caught the eye unduly and interrupted the silent reader's flow across the line of writing. This meant that the form of all the letters had to be worked out so uniformly that the eye could become accustomed to seeing whole words and phrases without being distracted by unusual shapes.

One other thing had to happen, too. The eye had to have clear signals as to where sentences (and words) start and stop. When one was reading aloud, he could work out the starts and stops as he went along; he could even work out the words despite the absence of space between them. But if the eye was to move fast without distraction, it needed special signals.

The use of capitals and small letters together to signify new sentences and other

WHY LOWER CASE?

WE THE PEOPLES OF THE UNITED NATIONS DETERMINED TO SAVE SUCCEEDING GENERATIONS FROM THE SCOURGE OF WAR, WHICH TWICE IN OUR LIFETIME HAS BROUGHT UNTOLD SORROW TO MANKIND, AND

We the peoples of the United Nations determined to save succeeding generations from the scourge of war, which twice in our lifetime has brought untold sorrow to mankind, and

To reaffirm faith in fundamental human rights, in the dignity and worth of the human person, in the equal

"L.C.," in less space, is far more readable

key words grew only very gradually. In fact, we still see traces of an alternate solution tried for a while—the use of *two* small letters to start a name, as ffinch. And the w started as vv. It was not until the 10th or 11th century that spacing between words was generally adopted, and commas and other such marks were not uniform until after the advent of printing in the 15th century.

At any rate, there was no easy or immediate solution. In fact, matters got worse before they got better, and what uniformity in lettering there was began to disappear. The big reason for this (although it might have happened more slowly in any case) was the disintegration of the Roman Empire in the 5th century A.D. The Christian religion (which had spread over most of Europe) was on its own, to be adapted to local styles and customs without the unifying force of the Romans behind it. This set up new needs—for different kinds of writing to meet local tastes and customs (and in due course local languages)—in such different lands as Ireland, England, Germany, France, Spain, and Scandinavia, even in Italy itself.

EARLY NATIONAL HANDS

As Christian missionaries spread out over Europe from Rome, they had taken with them Bibles and church writings, of course. They soon had monks at work producing new copies in the monasteries they established. The uncial and half-uncial were generally the letters used, but the monks were influenced by local tastes, customs, arts and styles of decoration. Also, there was a somewhat mystic-laden alphabet out of the North, called the Runic (or sometimes Futhark, from its first six letters). Its verticals and angles combined with the rounded uncials in different ways in different localities, and out of this mixture came what

F U ThO R C G W H N I Y

EO P A S T B E M L Ng D O

The Runic (Futhark) alphabet

we today call the various "national hands," even though there were no nations then in the modern sense.

The most beautiful of these hands was the Irish, still used to some extent today.

The Irish hand

Because Ireland was never occupied by the Romans, it showed no direct influence of the Roman hands. The Irish in turn influenced the Anglo-Saxon national hand

The Anglo-Saxon hand

when Irish missionaries came into Scotland about A.D. 650. What is considered one of the most beautiful works of art of all time, the Book of Kells (now in Dublin), was produced in the Irish hand about A.D. 800.

These national hands have affected directly some of our present-day special typefaces, even though none of them proved to be in the mainstream of typographic development.

THE CAROLINE MINUSCULE

"Caroline" simply refers to Carl the Great, or Charlemagne, as we know him in Western history, and "minuscule" merely means "small letters." Charlemagne becomes a major figure in our alphabet because of his great interest in learning. In A.D. 789 he decreed that all official, legal, religious and literary writings throughout his kingdom (which in the year 800 became the entire [Holy] Roman Empire, when he was crowned in Rome) were to be recopied in a standard hand, and that all new writing was to be in that hand.

Some writers have credited this hand as

uenit malus et rapit quod semina
in corde eius: hic est qui secus uiam
est qui autem super petrosa seminat
hic est qui uerbum audit et conti
gaudio accipit illud non habet au

The Caroline hand

the personal development of an English monk, Alcuin, who served as Charlemagne's teacher. But, it seems more likely that Alcuin's real role was to persuade the great king (who could read, but never did learn to write, even though he tried) to issue the decree.

With this Caroline hand, the present small letter of the Latin alphabet was finally invented. As you can see, the Caroline letters are very much like our small letters today. Perhaps Alcuin, the first person to be identified by name with the development of writing and printing, was also the first to realize the full scope of the problems of silent reading, and to see that it needed a simple, uniform style.

THE LATER NATIONAL HANDS

For all the beauty, simplicity and clarity of the Caroline hand, it was no longer followed after a few centuries, because Charlemagne's empire and authority were gone. Also, the Caroline alphabet was not a cursive (flowing hand). Pressures of speed were being forced increasingly on the scribes, who were now commercial writers employed by publishers, rather than monks, and this served to reduce the more formal (lettering) hands into cursives. The Caroline letters had to await the invention of something that took the place of hand-lettering: printing.

One gain could be recorded meanwhile for the Caroline legacy. The idea of a dual alphabet—of using capital and small letters together—began to come into use, in part because Charlemagne's interest in reforming the minuscules had focused new interest on the majuscules (capitals).

Many different hands developed during the trend away from the pure Caroline form, but only two letter variations are important—the Gothic or "black letter" and the Italian "Humanistica."

GOTHIC OR BLACK-LETTER. The name "Gothic" came from the Germanic tribe called Goths and was applied—centuries after the Goths disappeared—to the tall, spired churches built in mediaeval times. Those who were admirers of Roman classical art and antiquities used the name Gothic scornfully since the Goths were barbarians.

As for the letter form itself, Gothic started out from the Caroline alphabet common to all. Again, it was a functional shaping of form—created by the tool being used, and probably to economize on space. At any rate, it was fast and easy to draw vertical lines with a pen and join them with hairlines; the narrow, compressed letters allowed many more words on a given page:

sā orate pro nobís.
libera nos domíne.

The Gothic hand

The small letters, however, looked too much alike. In fact, the dot over the small i was invented when it became impossible otherwise to tell an i from a stroke of an m, n or u:

domine. domíne.

Gothic really was hard to read and so far from the original Caroline hand that

ARCHITECTURE INTO TYPE

The Gothic and Roman letters really did reflect separate cultures, as their architecture shows; this same relationship appears as well with other typeface styles

WHY LOWER CASE? (2)

BEND bend bend
BLEND blend blend
PLAYS plays plays

bd pq hч uŋ чµ

Silent readers see word shapes more than they spell out (much less sound out) the separate letters. All-capital words have pretty much the same shape, but l.c. has ascenders and descenders that give variety. Do we need more? To match the reverse patterns of b-d and p-q, would it be a good idea to put an ascender on the u and a descender on the n, or a descender on the u?

Alcuin probably could not have read it. In fact, two letters were so changed—the I and V—that three new letters ultimately were added to our alphabet, the J, U and W. (The double V, pronounced double U in English, was early used in the absence of a capital.) Here you can see how:

v v=vv=w

As time went on, the trend worsened, and the letters became even more compressed, stiffer, thinner, more and more angular. The net effect in each letter was vertical; it matched the Gothic spire architecture. However, the ascenders and descenders were shortened, too, so that the white space between lines (which counteracted the vertical effect) could be reduced and so that there could be more lines per page. The resulting effect of Gothic letters on a page was one of close-woven texture. The face was in fact at the time called Textura (Latin for texture) and to this day, some black letter faces are called "Text."

ROMAN HUMANISTICA. When the Italian Renaissance began in the early 15th century, scholars delved into ancient Roman lettering. The inscriptions on monuments were clear to see—but did the ancient Romans have no small letters, no minuscules?

The leading Renaissance writing masters may never have realized that the small letter was a later invention. However, in searching back through manuscripts, they came upon the Caroline script. This was in itself 600 years old, and there was no way to tell how far back it really did reach, bibliographical practice being rudimentary. It was so *right* as a Roman style (with its grace, roundness, simplicity and clarity) that it simply was assumed to be, and called, the *littera antiqua* —the ancient letter of Rome—especially when manuscripts were found which combined the Caroline small letters and the Roman Square and Rustic capitals. The Italians, therefore, adopted it as a mate to the inscriptional capital for formal lettering. Later, scholars called it Humanistica, reflecting the humanism of the Renaissance.

It was this alphabet that was being used in Italy when printing began, and it was this letter that ultimately became the basis for all of our book faces.

In the continual process of "corrosion" by informal everyday handwriting—it began operating on this new Roman alphabet almost at once—there also developed a subsidiary form of this letter, called the "humanistic cursive," a more flowing letter form. In due course, our basic italic letter evolved from this.

Thus our Latin alphabet was invented—invented by a combination of the tools used and the new needs of silent reading, itself an amazing invention.

ter terminauit sententiam ita dif
ut homo scilicet ad agendum & ad
dum tanquam quidam mortalis d
retur: quod si recte decenterq; fac

V os Veranniolo meo & Fabullo
V erpus praeposuit priapus ille:
V os conuiuia lauta sumptuose

The Renaissance humanistic letter (left) and the humanistic cursive

CHAPTER 

The invention of universal reading: Printing

THE NEXT INVENTION, printing, was an epochal event, for it introduced a fast, economical way of producing many exact copies of a manuscript. Once information thus became generally available and there was a way to record events, to debate policies widely and to urge public action, then the balance of political power shifted. Before, the control of channels of communication was in the hands of a few persons, who could rule by keeping the people ignorant and unable to combine their interests. Now, with the invention of universal reading, the people as a whole had a way to influence each other and join in common agreement—and thus force on their rulers a new society that could serve the general interest more than the special interests.

All this came about primarily because of little pieces of metal type, called "movable" because they were each a separate letter that could be moved into different combinations with other letters to form words, as a child's ABC blocks can be moved to spell CAB. These pieces could now be made so cheaply, precisely and durably that they could be set together to print many copies of a page, and then used again to set and print off many copies of a different page. The type was used to print so many copies, in fact, that the investment was much less than the cost of having copyists make duplicates of manuscripts.

It was not movable type alone which constituted the invention of printing, generally credited to Johan Gutenberg (*c.* 1397–1468) in Mainz, Germany, in about 1440. (It is ironic that printing, which so thoroughly preserves all knowledge, has not preserved enough details about its own creation to make absolutely clear when it was invented or who its inventor was.)

In fact, printing using wood blocks had clearly been invented in China, perhaps as

GUTENBERG AND HIS MOVABLE TYPE

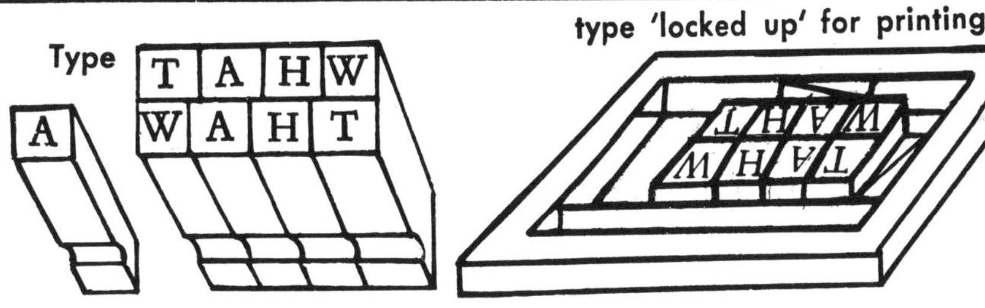

Type units as interchangeable parts form different words

Johann Gutenberg (left), or whoever it was, put together processes that are simple to understand, as this chart and those on Pages 28 and 29 show. The key is "movable type," which means that each letter is made as a separate piece of metal, so different letters can be put together or "set" to spell words, and then reused for spelling other words for other printing.

Process: LETTERPRESS

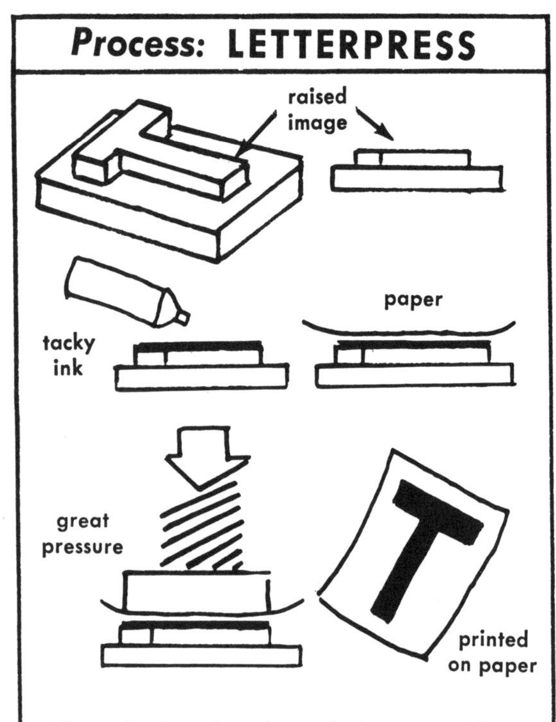

The raised surface for printing was old, as in Chinese woodblocks and rubbings (see below), but *metal* type needed stiff ink and thus much pressure, and new techniques.

early as A.D. 700. Movable type—even metal movable type—had been used much earlier than Gutenberg, both in China and Korea. But the Chinese written language requires tens of thousands of different characters, and wood-block printing of whole pages was easier than casting and setting separate characters into pages. Thus there was little incentive to develop the very different techniques required by metal type, as explained below. And Oriental printing technology, therefore, stayed with the woodblock.

What Gutenberg invented was a combination of processes and materials: he found a way to cast metal type with precision and in quantity; he found an ink that would

Text printed from woodblock

stick to the metal (as Chinese ink could not); he contrived a "chase" to hold the letters together; he adapted the wine or paper press to provide the tremendous pressure the sticky ink needed; he devised a way to deliver the printing stock (paper) without smudging, and to allow "register" or uniform placement of each sheet. All of these things had to be accomplished—and put together—before the new kind of printing could be done.

Gutenberg did all this. Furthermore, he did it at the right time in history, when there was enough demand for printing to motivate moneyed men to invest in the work and materials. To speed production, monks had been superseded by groups of literate persons working together in the cities—town clerks, teachers, notaries and commercial scribes—who wrote in a plain hand instead of the reverent hand-lettering of the past. Paper was newly available in amount and price to provide any quantity of books. But still production could not meet demand. So, printing, which could produce almost limitless quantities much faster than any combination of scribes, caught on quickly.

Gutenberg's key invention was a mould which produced a solid piece of metal type

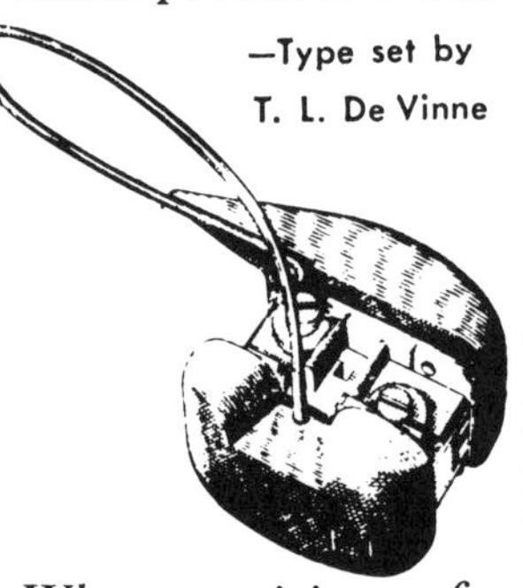

—Type set by T. L. De Vinne

The irregularity of this composition is caused by the types of the letters a and e, which are larger than the other letters, by accurate measurement, less than nine one-thousandths of an American inch. This minute difference is repeated and increased in every line, until the connection between words and lines is partially destroyed. If this use of the large a and e were continued through a dozen additional lines, the reader would be unable to understand what has been composed.

Why precision of mould (left) was important

about one inch high. The mould provided a way of making each piece of type the same height and depth. Since the letter widths were different, the sides of the mould were formed by two L-shaped walls that could close or expand the inside space. The letter was cast from a "matrix"—a pattern punched into a flat piece of brass and incorporated in the bottom of the mould.

As a first step in making the matrix, a "punch-cutter" had to cut the face of a piece

Process: CUTTING AND CASTING TYPE BY HAND

counter punch

punch

matrix

molten metal poured onto matrix held in bottom of mould

result: type

The ability to produce large quantities of letters exactly the same in appearance and size was crucial to the whole idea of "movable type." This is how Gutenberg did it.
(Note that the letter atop the type itself ends up in reverse, so it will be "right-reading" when printed.)

of type (backwards) on the end of a rod of steel. This was where the chief skill came in. Whatever way he cut the steel, that was the way the printed letter was going to look, except right-reading. (And that is why we still say a typeface was "cut.")

The steel punch was then hammered to drive a right-reading impression into a flat brass piece—with skill to a precise depth, or the letter would not be the proper height.

With the matrix now in the bottom of the mould, and the sides of the mould in place, a hot melted alloy (then, as now, lead, tin and antimony) was poured in. The type-caster gave the mould a shake with a wild motion that sometimes made uninformed onlookers think he had some weird affliction. But it was necessary to shake the liquid metal to the very bottom and force out any air pocket which would otherwise cause an airhole in the face of the type, making it worthless. When the metal cooled and hardened, it was taken from the mould by removing the expansion side. The type had a tail on it, called a "jet," from the excess metal poured in; this was broken off and the piece of type "dressed," that is, cleaned of burrs. The face of the type itself was an exact copy of the punch.

Every piece of type had to be made that way. One page of the Gutenberg Bible, for instance, contained about 4,000 or 5,000 pieces of type, but the printer had to have many times that number to print more than one page at a time and to be setting new pages while some were on the press. With extras, he probably required a stock of from 15,000 to 25,000 separate pieces of

Typecaster pouring lead into mould: from an early engraving by Jost Amman (1568)

GUTENBERG'S BIBLE TYPE

This is an exact-size reproduction of lines from the Gutenberg Bible, showing the Black Letter typeface used. There are two columns to a page.

locū unū ⁊ appareat arida. Et factū ē
ita. Et vocauit deus aridam terram:
congregacionesq; aquaꝝ appellauit
maria. Et vidit deus q esset bonū. et
ait. Germinet terra herbā virentem et
facientē semen: ⁊ lignū pomiferū faciēs
fructū iuxta genus suū. cuiꝰ semen in

type. Each one made by hand! Nor was it type alone. Spacing material—a "space" being a blank type put between words, etc.—was made the same way. (A blank type larger than a word space is called a "quad.")

Once the type was made, however, it saved many hours (if not years) of scribes' work, and produced books much faster and much more accurately. Once one copy was printed (a "proof") a printer's error ("typo") could be corrected for all copies; the scribes' errors, different in each book, remained.

PRINTER'S INK

The ink used for wood-block printing in the Orient was a thin liquid; it soaked into the wood and then soaked into the paper when the sheet was laid on the inked surface and pressure applied. Pressure was put on one spot at a time by hand rubbing. This gave a certain blur to the edges of the printing, thus making less legible the letters in a book. Furthermore, liquid ink cannot soak in or even stick to metal type.

One of Gutenberg's key inventions was an oil-based ink that was thick enough and "tacky" (sticky) enough to hold to the type and then, under pressure, to transfer to the paper stock. Chances are that Gutenberg borrowed some ideas for his ink from the oil paints which the art world had just recently developed, and from the inks used for the first copper engravings, in 1430.

A press to provide enough squeeze to transfer ink from type to paper was relatively easy once the need was recognized. The wine- and paper-makers' presses had both been developed by then. (But the pressure needed—perhaps 200 pounds to the square inch—did pose some real problems.) Techniques for locking up the type, and getting the type and paper delivered under the "platen" (the pressure plate which pushes down flat against paper and type), were not too difficult to work out. There are still presses today which use those same principles; for almost 400 years, all presses did.

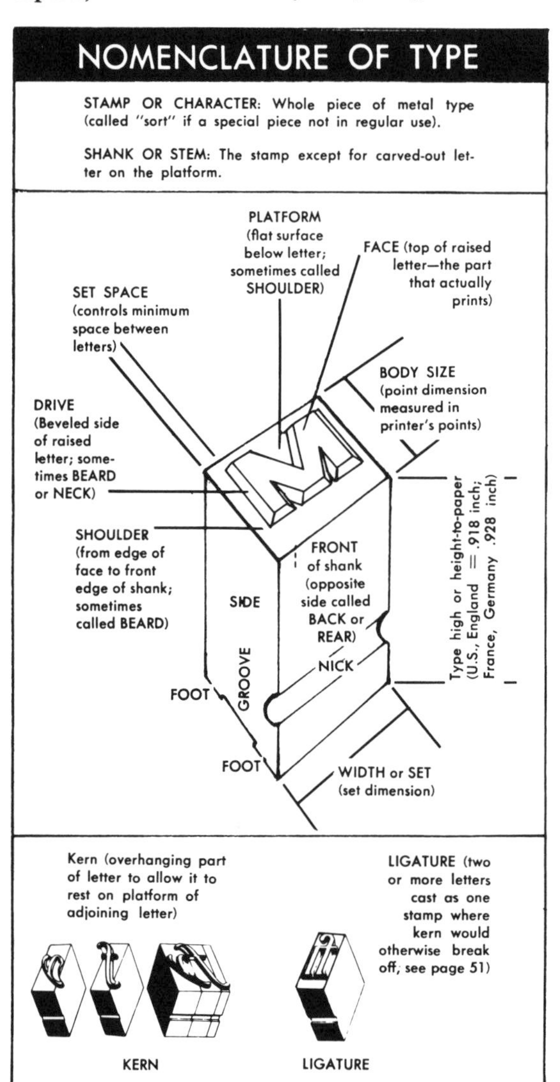

CHAPTER

The invention of typefaces

ONE PART of the invention of printing, however—the one central to this book—probably was not even given a thought at the time: the invention of the typeface as such, distinct from the hand-drawn letter.

Printing started as a cheaper substitute for hand-lettered manuscripts, and like all substitutes, it was considered very inferior. The printers, therefore, tried their best to make their work look like manuscripts, and this meant, among other things, cutting typefaces to look as much like handwriting as possible. (They probably would have done this anyhow, as a natural thing: *why* try to invent a different kind of letter?) To copy the variations of handwriting, they even cut many special combination or

APEX. Up-pointing free-ending juncture of two stems.
ARC. Curved stroke not a bowl, as C, G, bottom of j, t, u.
ARM. Horizontal or upward-sloping short stroke starting from stem, ending free.
ASCENDER. Part of lowercase letters, b, d, f, h, k, l, t extending above x-line.
BAR. Horizontal or oblique short stroke connected at both ends, as in e, H.
BOWL. The line fully enclosing a counter; complete bowl, formed by curved strokes only; modified bowl, stem forms a side of bowl.
COUNTER. Fully or semi-enclosed space within a letter.
CROSS STROKE. Stroke cutting across stem, as in f, t.
CROTCH. Pointed space where an arm or arc meets a stem; acute crotch less than 90°; obtuse crotch 90° or more.
CURVED STROKE. A curved necessary line.
DESCENDER. Part of lowercase letters gjpqy and caps JQ extending below base line.
EAR. Small stroke extending from bowl of g, stem of r.
EXTENDERS. Ascenders and descenders together.
FINIAL. Non-serif ending added to end of stroke (e.g., ball, swash, spur, hook finials).
LINK. Stroke connecting bowl and loop of g.
LOOP. Distinguished from bowl as a flourish rather than necessary part of letter, e.g., bottom of g not always enclosed.
MAIN STEM. The thicker stem, if more than one of different widths.
MONOTONE or MONOLINE. All lines same thickness.
SERIF. Line crossing free end of a stroke (see P. 13); half-serifs on horizontal arms of E, L, T sometimes called BEAKS; serifs at ends of arcs C, G, S sometimes called BARBS or cat's ears.
SET or FIT. The built-in space on either side of letters. "Set width" or amount of space can be changed by some processes.
SPINE. Main curved section of S.
STEM. Any vertical straight stroke, or principal oblique straight stroke if letter has no vertical stroke.
STRESS. Thickening in a curved stroke, such as caused by flat pen changing direction; thickest point is "maximum stress." (Stress is sometimes called "swells," "modeling" or "shading.")
STROKE. Any line necessary to basic form of letter (not serif, etc.)
TAIL. Downward-sloping short stroke or arc starting from stem (or bowl, in Q) and ending free.
TERMINAL. Free ending of a stroke with self-contained treatment instead of serif or finial, e.g., straight, sheared, acute, grave, convex, concave, flared, hook, tapered and pointed terminals.
TYPEFACE. The design or pattern of an alphabet of letters to be used together (see P. 60), to be distinguished from the face of the type stamp itself (see opposite page); called "face" for short.
VORTEX. Down-pointing free-ending juncture of two stems.

(Based on nomenclature of Joseph Thorp, courtesy Monotype Corporation Ltd.; revised to reflect current usage.)

"tied" letters, despite the economy of uniform letters:

ſt ct q; a ſſ ℞

Nevertheless, a typeface *is* different from a hand-drawn letter, and appears different on paper, for several reasons:

- Although the type might be copied from pen letters, the punch-cutter's tools force or allow slight changes that make this type look different. See how the small c "finial" is changed by the punch-cutter:

c c c c c c c c

- Since the letters are uniform (that is, all of the small "a" are the same, etc.), the typeset page will look more uniform than hand-lettering, which shows a natural variation between one "a" and another. This might be good or bad. A typeface has to be designed deliberately to have enough variation among the letters to allow interest in the page, but not so much variation as to make the page spotty and jumpy. If the hand-lettered a's are different from one another, there does not have to be any special difference from the "b," "c," etc., to allow variety. But if all the a's are alike, the "b" and "c" must be more distinctly different. And yet all the letters must have the same style to avoid unevenness. This creates a tremendous design problem.

Quality of Line: TYPE

True type quality of line—the basis of the "power of print"—is hard to define, yet even illiterates feel it. Formal and impersonal, like incised, but translated into a *rightness* of its own, as though pre-ordained, with infinite permanence. (Paper crumbles, faster than stones, but the printed message lives on.) Some typefaces copy other kinds of lines, e.g., script, but this is not the type quality meant here.

- A scribe has to draw one letter to fit after another and he almost subconsciously alters shapes to create the proper space between. Each piece of type must have its side spacing ("set") built in at the time of casting, so as to fit evenly with most letters; this means altering ideal separate shapes somewhat to work out a compromise for all the different possible combinations:

AVIATION
INVITATION

TAT in bottom line shows spacing problem that designers must try to overcome

- Mechanical considerations force letter shapes of their own (e.g., ligatures, kerns and "set"), to be detailed later in the book.

When gaps remain in typeset words, fine printers use "optical" or "visual" spacing, by putting "thin" or "hair" spaces between too-close letters and mortising (cutting away part of the type's body) so too-separated letters will fit closer.

From the very beginning, the typecutters and printers managed to do truly beautiful work. Actually, this is not so surprising. Not only had lettering been brought to a high state of art, but the punch-cutting craftsmen had a high skill, as already noted.

Furthermore, it was soon clear to a number of Renaissance men that printing was important to art and literature. It represented "the art preservative of all the arts." So the greatest men of the time were excited and helpful, and wonderful talents were brought to bear in printing.

As far as type design was concerned, there was no immediate problem. Hand-lettered models were ready for copying. All a punch-cutter or his printer-employer had to decide was which model he liked best.

But it did not stay that way long.

In time, printers learned that printed works did not have to pass as imitation manuscripts, and that typefaces designed especially for printing could be more legible and economical (because the letters were smaller, a book required fewer pages). As a result, printing developed as a separate art, creating our wondrous heritage of typefaces.

The invention of roman type

UNTIL THE 19th century, the interest in type design was concentrated on the so-called "book" faces, the small-sized types used to set the text reading matter often called "body type." The "display" sizes, even for title pages of books, were definitely considered much less important than making typefaces to serve silent reading. Except where display type is specifically referred to, therefore, the discussion in this and the next chapter is concerned with body type.

GOTHIC VERSUS ROMAN

Because printing started in Germany, where the Gothic letter was standard for the scribes, Gothic was the first typeface used in printing—including the printing of the Gutenberg Bible, which had great impact on the new craft. Furthermore, printers who learned printing in Mainz spread quickly throughout Europe, carrying their Germanic Gothic with them. Yet, within a generation, the Italian humanistic lettering emerged as a form of printing type called "roman," and won out over Gothic. Today Gothic is not a true standard typeface anywhere in the world.

How and why this happened is important to an understanding of typefaces. Yet, in a sense, it has never really been worked out.

The likeliest answer is that Gothic is easier to write, especially in the large sizes required for reading aloud, while roman is easier for silent reading, especially if the type is small. Also the costs of printing were high, and a small letter was much preferred, since it allowed the same text to be produced in fewer pages.

Gothic seemed "right" for Bibles and other church writings, and it still seems so as headings on religious documents and Christmas cards. But the bulk of reading matter is not of this kind, and roman types are obviously more practical for everyday use.

Through the centuries, Gothic has gradually been dropped everywhere. France turned to the roman faces almost immediately. In England, Gothic had been entrenched because William Caxton, the first English printer, who had enormous influence, had learned the craft from the Dutch and absorbed their use of the Gothic. Also, Caxton's helper and successor, Wynkyn de Worde, went on to print some 700 books in Caxton's black-letter types. The roman was at first considered a completely foreign invasion, and it was not until the 18th century that roman type fully took over in England. It was not until World War II that the last country to continue using Gothic as its standard letter, Germany, finally converted to roman.

Some experts insist Gothic is as legible as roman if the reader is "used to it." The test of history seems to have proved otherwise.

Class: SPIRE GOTHICS

AEGMRST

adegmpty

1 o 2 o 3 o 4 o

Also called Black Letter, or "Old English," after its long dominance in England. Caps are fanciful, varied, based on mss. illuminated initials. Basically, l.c. is "broken" roman letter, i.e., curved strokes made straight or cut up. Shown: *Goudy Text.*

Five styles: (1) Textura, no curves; (2) Schwabacher, partial curves; (3) Fraktur, half-broken, half-curved; (4) Rotunda, half and half, but rounder; (5) not shown, Freeformed, more graceful, less disciplined, often mixed adaptations of once-standard styles shown.

Category: Residuals (Special Faces)

Style: VENETIAN

AEGMRST

adegmpty

Based on Jenson, other early Venetian printers. Little contrast between thick, thin strokes; stress is diagonal; serifs are blob-like bracketed and almost "strong." Capitals tall as ascenders; proportioned to old Roman letters, some quite narrow, some quite wide. L.c. letters wide, seem rounded. Bar of e slants up. Upper serifs bracketed. A has pointed apex. Shown: *Centaur.*

Class: Book Faces (Small Serifs)

Roman type has won out because it is easier to read. Where new alphabets are being created today for verbal languages going into print for the first time, the Latin alphabet, with roman letters primarily, is the one being adopted.

The name "roman," incidentally, was not applied to type until many years later, first by the French. The word is not capitalized when applied to standard Latin alphabet typefaces. This was a nice compromise. It distinguished Latin typefaces from the Roman capitals of the classic days; it credited the Romans for the capitals and for the basic alphabet; at the same time it reminds everyone that the all-important small letters are not truly Roman but were developed by European scribes and brought to their first full form in Charlemagne's court about A.D. 800. If ever there was an international pooling of talent, it was in the development of the early typefaces—with printers of the whole civilized world participating.

Italy, and more specifically Venice, became the hub of the new printing and publishing art and industry—perhaps just because it used roman type instead of Gothic. Also, Venice, more convenient by land to the rest of Europe than Rome, was a great port through which books could easily be transported to the whole Western world. Talented people from all Europe congregated there during the Renaissance.

THE FIRST ROMAN TYPEFACES

In 1465, two German printers, Konrad Sweynheim and Arnold Pannartz, in the Subiaco monastery outside Rome, cut some type to copy the Humanistic hand letter, and cut a second, better face in 1467. Neither was a complete success, but roman type was now invented.

Quanq̃ ubi opus eſt: & in ꝑoꝛib⁹.x.quę
nr̃a ſũt aſſeramus: et in.xii.poſterioꝛib⁹
redarguamus aduerſa.Duodecim ergo
librorũ ſequentiũ primi quatuor cõtinẽt

The 1465 Subiaco typeface

Cum puraſ animaſ ſacra lauacr
Candiduſ egreditur nitidiſ exe
Atq; uetuſ uitium purgat in am
Fulgenteſ aiaſ ueſtiſ quoq; can

The second typeface, of 1467

The first great roman type was that of Jenson (who always signed his books "Nicolas Jenson the Frenchman"). Cut in 1470 in Venice, it was immediately hailed by his fellow printers and widely imitated for its beauty and legibility. It is the basic example of the so-called "Venetian" style of letter, and has, in fact, remained a major model for roman typefaces ever since. Influenced by Jenson's example, later designers used capital letters the full height of the lower case

THE TYPORAMA

ROMAN (Standard) | SPIRE GOTHIC (Special)

The division into standard and special typefaces started early in printing history

enim id ſcrutādum nobis modo eſt. Poſt H
pietate ſucceſſit: fœlice hac hæreditate a par
coniunctus quum geminos genuiſſet caſtit
dicitur abſtinuiſſe. Ab iſto natus ē Iacob q
prouētum Iſrael etiam appellatus eſt duob
uirtutis uſū. Iacob eīm athletā & exercētem
quam appellationē primū habuit: quū prać
pro pietate labores ferebat. Quum autē iam
ſpeculationis fruebať bonis: tūc Iſraelem ip

Diquead q̄ſto ſincero & ſancto Imperio, finito il ſuo facondo & beni-
gno parlare, humilmente fecime ſeruo cernuo, & cum puſilla audacia &
exiguo auſo di ſubito parendo. Sopra quelle delitioſe banche ad lato dex
tro, poſime adſedere, Cum la mia lanacea toga, ancora le prenſure, o uer la

The Jenson face (top) and Aldus face of 1495. Jenson (left) and Aldus

ascenders, although ideally smaller capitals look better.

Jenson, originally master of the mint at Tours, knew something about engraving and casting. Legend says that Charles VII sent him to Mainz to learn all he could about the new art of printing and bring it back to France. Before he could return, Charles VII was dead, and Jenson found he was not welcome. So, hearing of the great opportunities in Venice for printers, he went there, set up shop, became successful and wealthy—and made history.

Even so, Jenson's face was not as influential as one cut in 1495 by Francesco Griffo de Bologna at the instigation of Aldus Manutius (1450–1515).

Griffo was perhaps the creative genius of the team, but Aldus so far has the credit, since history calls it the Aldine roman. Next to Gutenberg, Aldus was the most famous printer of early times and the first of many great scholar-printers. A tremendously successful publisher in Venice, he edited carefully to ensure accuracy of his books' contents and continually experimented to produce books more cheaply. The Aldine roman was but one of his innovations. Another was the pocket-sized book. Before this, all books had been the much larger oral-reading size, in the tradition of the scribes and manuscripts.

Compared to the Jenson face, you will notice that the Aldine roman is more regular and still not flat; that the capital letters are smaller (not as high as the ascenders) and better proportioned to blend in with the total page effect; that the little special quirks, such as the slanted cross-bar of the e are gone; the oversized h, the jutting down d, the underslung a, the high-arching c are more in keeping with the other letters; the very faint dot of the lower-case i has been made into a real dot; the diamond-shaped colon (a Gothic style) has given way to a true comma; and the diamond-shaped period is now a rounded dot. More importantly, there is a greater difference between thick and thin lines, and in keeping with that, the serifs are not as heavy, so that the eye seems

THE "INCUNABULA"

The 60 years from the invention of printing in 1440 to the year 1500 are called the "incunabula" period, the word literally meaning "swaddling clothes," and thus loosely the period of infancy of the new tool.

By 1500, there were some 1,100 printeries set up, in all parts of Europe, and more than 35,000 different books printed, with total copies estimated at 12,000,000. (In the whole history of manuscript copying, through 20 centuries, the scribes probably had not produced anything like that total of books.) Such was the immediate effect of the printing press.

P hillyrides Chiron, Amythaoniusq; Melampus.
S æuit et in lucem ſtygis emiſſa tenebris
P allida Tiſiphone, morbos agit ante, metumq;,
I nq; dies auidum ſurgens caput altius effert,
B alatu pecorum, et crebris mugitibus amnes,
A rentesq; ſonant ripæ, collesq; ſupini.
I amq; cateruatim dat ſtragem, atq; aggeratipſis
I n ſtabulis, turpi dilapſa cadauera tabo,

The first italic typeface, cut by Griffo for Aldus to use in economy-priced books

to be able to move more easily across the page.

These may seem to be small differences, and in a way they are, but minute changes in separate letters make a substantial difference to the silent reader, whether he knows it or not, for he reads literally billions of printed letters. The question is how do they affect the eye? Jenson's is a great face, and his touches add interest and life to the page. However, the judgment through the years is that these touches slow down the silent reader. This judgment is made both by those commercial publishers who avoid Jenson (as bad for business) and those private press printers who embrace him (as good for art).

But the Aldine roman was not the ultimate type design, either. In fact, until the 20th century, its influence was not fully recognized—because the face still had a *hand*-lettered feel to it, even though it avoided the kind of personality that Jenson put into his type. The idea that the true feel of printing type is *im*personality had not yet been developed, because the days of copying manuscripts were still too recent.

Class: ITALICS

Unrelated Italic ABCDEFGH

Related Italic ABCDEF

Matching Italic ABCD

Italics have special alphabet (*a* instead of a, *f* vs. f, g or g vs. g), and k vs. k) plus hooked terminals that recall the cursive handwriting origin. Normally slanted. Shown: (1) *Arrighi*; (2) *Garamond Italic*; (3) *Bodoni Bold Italic*.

Basic kinds: (1) Unrelated—pure form based on 15c Italian hand; (2) Related—designed to blend well with a specific roman face, but still more or less "pure" italic; (3) Matched—style design same as a particular roman typeface but minimal italic qualities of slant, hooked terminals retained.

Category: Residuals (Special Faces)

THE ITALIC LETTER

Aldus in 1500 also invented the *italic* as a typeface, taking the cursive handwriting then used in the Papal Chancery and paying Griffo to cut punches in the same style. The pair did not bother with separate italic capitals, simply using the available roman capitals. (Like roman, the word italic—crediting Italy as the land of origin of the kind of letter—was a term later coined by the French and is not capitalized. At first the letter form was called "corsiva" [cursive] or "cancellarsca" [chancery]. In Germany, the name "cursiv" is still used instead of "italic.")

The idea of an italic typeface for emphasis may not seem very startling to us now, but printing had gone along for more than half a century *without* an italic (see how indispensable it is!) despite all sorts of experiments, so a slanted face could not have been a thought that occurred to every printer and punch-cutter. In fact, the first typeface for emphasis showed a different kind of thinking—a matching "semi-bold" (blacker) roman, cut in 1488 in Leipzig by Moritz Brandis.

As a matter of fact, too, Aldus did not intend italic for *emphasis*, as we have since learned to use it, but had it cut because the letter was much narrower than the roman. With it, he could get many more words on a page, and this resulted in a book he could sell cheaper. A good part of Aldus's fame rests on his efforts to make books more generally available to scholars by lowering their cost.

Immediately, other printers copied Aldus's idea, and some pirated his scholarly texts along with the new typeface. As printing production costs declined as techniques improved, books printed in roman could be sold as cheaply, and the italic book was dropped. A solid page of italic was just too hard to read, and italic never became one of our standard typefaces.

CHAPTER K

The invention of true type design

A TYPEFACE which would clearly look "printed" was yet to be invented. But it did not take long.

Just as printers had spread out from Mainz with Gutenberg's invention, printers spread out from Italy with the superior type designs that had been bred there. The French, much closer to the Italian style than the German, adopted the roman of Aldus, and then went on to create the first true *printing* letter face.

The man who generally gets the credit for this was Claude Garamont (later spelled Garamond), who became the first full-time punch-cutter and typefounder in history. (His birthdate is not known; he died in 1561.)

Type production now became the full-time occupation of professionals specially trained to think in printing terms. The result was that Garamont cut one of the greatest designs in all typographic history, a face used almost exclusively and copied (sometimes badly) for 200 years—and still today the prototype of the "old style" typefaces, with great popularity of its own. Based on the Aldus face, it added a nobility and grace, even though fully a printing face. It is a fine example of the proper combination of form and function, has the necessary feeling of impersonality but also elegance, permanence but not heaviness, interest but not sparkle, with careful blending of all parts into a pleasing, undistracting whole.

(By a quirk, Garamont's name is used today on typefaces not directly his, but cuttings done by Jean Jannon in 1615, based on Garamond. See Page 60.)

A remarkable fact about the Garamond typeface is that the small letters become more beautiful the larger the size. They were the first lower-case letters which could be used in the title of a book. (Previously, titles had always been in capitals.) With Garamond roman, lower-case type truly came of age.

THE COMPANION ITALIC—AND THE SCRIPT

Robert Granjon, a younger man who worked with Garamont, became noted in his own right, cutting many faces for printers in many countries. For Christopher Plantin of Antwerp (1520–89), the greatest printer of the era, Granjon cut approximately 10 different italic faces. One of these became the model for an italic face designed as a companion face—for emphasis and touches of grace—with old style roman typefaces, meaning Garamond in those days. This italic is considered to be a different "alphabet" from the roman because certain of its letters have a different basic shape. In addition, the

reſtituit.Fuit hic(vt Annales ferunt)Othonis nepos,
eius qui ab inſigni pietate magnitudinéque animi,ca
nente illo pernobili claſſico excitus, ad ſacrũ bellum
in Syriam contendit,communicatis ſcilicet conſiliis
atque opibus cũ Guliermo Montiſferrati regulo,qui
à proceritate corporis, Longa ſpatha vocabatur. Vo-
luntariorum enim equitum ac peditum delectæ no-

Claude Garamont and his typeface, the first true printing face

Simon Voſtre & tant d'autres, dont M. Arthur Chriſtian nous résume ici les travaux, firent merveille dans cette œuvre nouvelle.

Encouragée par plusieurs monarques, l'imprimerie n'avait, jusqu'au commencement du XVIe siècle, inſpiré en France aucune méfiance

The Granjon italic, and a "likeness" of Robert Granjon in the custom of the time

italic maintains the handwriting tradition by appearing to link letters. Such letters as the *m* and *n* have little hooks at the end of their final stroke, instead of a serif, showing their handwriting origin. But the intent and result are very clearly a *printing* face, not a hand letter, much less an imitation of handwriting.

Granjon also cut, in 1557, the first typeface designed to simulate handwriting instead of hand-lettering. Called Civilité, and based on the French handwriting of his day, it was really a cursive. But, in the centuries since, it led to the scripts, a whole class of special-division typefaces, characterized by linking letters and by a basically different pair of alphabets, based for the most part on the patterns of the French calligrapher, Pierre Moreau, in 1643.

This, then, is what Garamont and Granjon wrought: the first full flowering of true printing typefaces.

THE DUTCH-ENGLISH SCHOOL

For 200 years, Garamont's face and its recuttings were the standard of Europe, although in the mid-17th century, the Dutch, with such punch-cutters as Christoffel Van Dijck, had begun to move away from Gara-

vocabant. Laudis autem veſtræ longe pot
bulentis hiſce miſeriſque temporibus Domi
rum in fidem præſidiumque ſe conferrent p
quos non ſæva minus quam ſacrilega Anti

Van Dijck, Dutch-School old style type

mont's grace and elegance to a more solid, straightforward style. Then, in 1722, an Englishman, William Caslon, began cutting old style faces in London, based on the

Style: OLD STYLE

A E G M R S T

a d e g m p t y

Based on Aldine roman via Claude Garamont, "O.S." has more contrast between thick, thins than Venetian; stress is less diagonal; capitals are shorter than ascenders, less wide; serifs are smaller, more gracefully bracketed. Top serifs slope, bracketed. In Dutch-English school (often called Old Face) A has cupped apex, lines seem solid vs. French-school elegance, beaks of E, F, etc., more emphasized as key part of design. Shown: *Garamond.*

Class: Book Faces (Small Serifs)

THE KEY DIFFERENCES

O O O

OLD STYLE TRANSITIONAL MODERN

I I I

B E
B E
B E
K O
K O
K O

As the characteristics of roman typefaces change subtly during the period now being discussed, you will find it helpful to keep this summary of trend in mind:

From old style to modern, (1) there is more contrast in the thick-thin "stress"; (2) the stress moves to vertical; (3) the serifs become unbracketed hairlines; (4) the capitals move towards the same size, e.g., B,E wider and K,O narrower.

ENGLISH ROMAN.

Quoufque tandem abutêre, Catilina, patientia noftra? quamdiu nos etiam furor ifte tuus eludet? quem ad finem fefe effrenata jactabit audacia? nihilne te nocturnum præfidium palatii, nihil urbis vigiliæ, nihil timor populi, nihil confenfus bonorum omnium, nihil hic munitiffimus ABCDEFGHIJKLMNOPQRSTVUW

William Caslon and his so-called "old face" of 1734, controversial and great

Dutch example. The typeface which Caslon issued in 1734 was an instant success, and except for one brief period in the 19th century, it has remained popular ever since, yet it is perhaps the most controversial face in history. Some persons consider it the greatest type ever (they have popularized a motto, "When in doubt, use Caslon") and others think it overrated, a collection of mistakes, elusively out of keeping with everything. But —it works, is highly readable, alive, with warmth and open dignity that has no pretense whatsoever. Caslon is the prime example of a face in which the individual letters are nothing, but the total effect is strong and honest—the reverse of an all-star performance in which each letter has such perfection that it competes to be noticed.

The Caslon types soon eclipsed the Garamond, and it was not until the 20th century that Garamond came back into common use. In fact, until just a century ago, when a new type style was taken up, the old one was always dropped as no longer useful. Today's situation, with many different typefaces popular simultaneously, is not at all typical of most of printing history.

For Americans, Caslon has a particular importance, because it was the typeface used in the Colonial period. Both the Declaration of Independence and Constitution were first printed in Caslon, and Caslon italic and swash capitals are often used in the United States to convey a historic or American-

Caslon Antique

antique feeling. In fact, a battered-looking nondescript face has been cut to make the point more emphatic.

THE QUALITY OF "SOCK"

In looking at Caslon types in particular, and in comparing original printings with

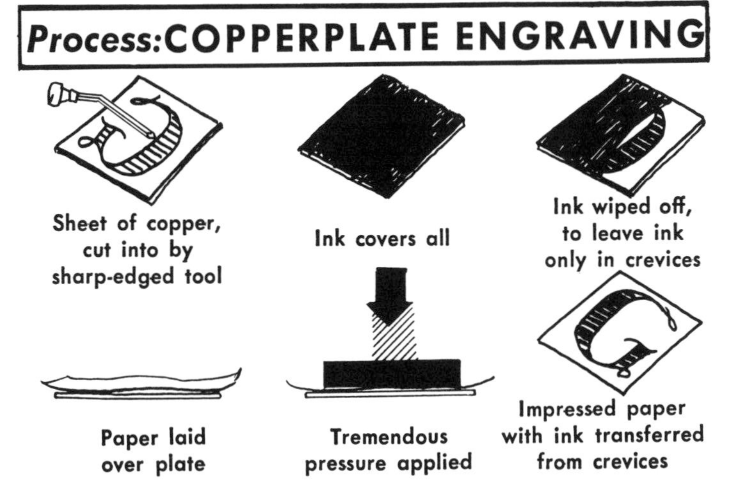

Engraving, older than printing, gradually developed its own lettering tradition not dependent on the pen or a punch-cutter's file, but on a steel point with geometric grace scratching precise lines on soft, smooth copper.

Very sharp contrast between thicks and hairline thins; clean, cool precision—in two different styles: ornate geometric curves and swelled lines, or chaste letters of straight-line geometry, with "cross-hatching" lines to create a grey half-tone.

WHAT 'SOCK' DOES

AEG AEG

Same Caslon type, with kiss and sock impression

some current uses of Caslon, you may be struck by the fact that sometimes the faces look strong and sturdy, while other times they appear thin and weak. This is your introduction to the difference in appearance caused by the way type is printed—the pressure, the kind of ink, and the paper.

Unevenness in the height of type and the thickness of paper made it necessary to force ("sock") the face of the type into the paper. The paper was usually dampened first to make this easier. From a technical point of view, in the centuries since, the objective of type-height uniformity, presswork and paper smoothness has been to get rid of sock so that no permanent indentation is left in the paper. (This is called "kiss impression.")

In a way, this is too bad, because sock provides a feeling of texture, a play of light and shadow, a special kind of life that the best manuscripts could not capture and that present-day printing has all but forgotten.

Style: TRANSITIONAL

AEGMRST
adegmpty

Faces moving from old style toward the modern style of Didot and Bodoni. Influenced by lettering of copperplate engravers on titles of their plates, thick-thin contrast is increasingly sharper; serifs are sharper in their endings and thinner, but still bracketed; finials on c, f, etc., become rounder, like balls. Diagonal shading nearly vertical; apex of A is pointed again; bowls of B nearly equal; capital letters moving more toward uniform width. Shown: *Baskerville.*

Class: Book Faces (Small Serifs)

Typefaces of Caslon's time were cut to take this into account. They were cut thinner than the finished result indicates, because sock had the effect of thickening the typeface on the paper. That is why these old type designs, when printed without sock on modern papers, seem so pale and awkward. They are being misused.

THE TRANSITIONAL FACES

It could be argued whether the "old style" period from Aldus to Caslon, some 250 years, really does represent one style of typeface, as the name indicates. In many ways, the difference between the Aldus roman and Caslon is greater than between Caslon and Baskerville, the next face of historic importance in England and America.

THE MIGHTIER PEN . . .

In the 18th century, a new pointed, flexible quill pen used in England's growing commerce led to "round" handwriting very close to copperplate thicks, hairlines (p. 39). This soon affected type design, notably John Baskerville's style.

But John Baskerville (1706–75), a wealthy manufacturer (of japanning) and amateur printer of Birmingham, England, introduced a typeface which led to a new "modern style" typeface and (ultimately) to kiss-impression printing.

Baskerville was more than 40 years old when he decided to make an effort to improve printing—the type, paper, ink and presswork. Also a master hand-letterer, he has recently been recognized as history's first type *designer*, as distinct from punch-cutter, by the evidence of printing scholar James Mosley that he was probably the earliest to work out the form first on paper. (The Romain du Roi [see Page 42] was a joint effort, not precisely followed.) His new design created a controversy that lasted 40 years and nearly broke him. He died without knowing he really was a success.

What did he do? Following a new style set by a rounder handwriting, Baskerville redesigned Caslon's type into somewhat straighter vertical and more mechanical lines, made the serifs flat and put a little more contrast into the thick and thin

have received, that I ſtill preſerve my former authority in the commonwealth: and wiſh me joy in the other of my late marriage. With reſpect to the firſt, if to mean well to the intereſt of my country and to approve that meaning to every friend of its liberties, may be conſidered as maintaining my authority; the account you have heard is certainly true. But if it conſiſts in rendering thoſe ſentiments effectual to the public welfare, or at leaſt in daring freely to ſupport

John Baskerville and the typeface that broke first him and then the Caslon foundry

strokes. This face, with more delicate and contrasting lines, required a reduction in the usual sock impression. So Baskerville created "wove," a harder, smooth, slightly shiny paper stock, and was able to print on it because he also developed much more intense and fine-grained ink.

In all past history, the handwriting tool had controlled the form of the letter. It was still true here, but for the first time *printing* technology had to be considered.

It was thus Baskerville who first made paper and ink conform to typeface design instead of vice versa, turning away from sock. His wove paper has by now made the first ("laid") paper a luxury special-effect stock. (Laid paper is textured because the fibers lie on a crude wire mesh as the sheets form; wove paper forms on a closely-woven thin-wire mesh that leaves the sheet smooth.)

Some people liked it, and some objected it was too dazzling (not restful like Caslon).

Ben Franklin, for one, was on Baskerville's side. He once tricked an American printer who was violently opposed by giving him a copy of a Caslon specimen sheet, calling it Baskerville's, and getting him to point out all he thought wrong with "Baskerville" type.

After 40 years, Baskerville's change had public taste behind it. Caslon type went out of use completely, and even the Caslon foundry had to produce its own version of Baskerville, but it had waited too long and went out of business. (However, the foundry was resumed by Stephenson Blake & Co. Ltd., the foundry which by acquisitions and mergers has ancestry in virtually every early English typefoundry, and original Caslon matrices are still available for casting.) Later, the vogue for Baskerville in turn died out. But recently it has returned to very great popularity in England and America, especially.

What Baskerville accomplished was a transition to a style of typeface that was no longer a pure pen stroke, in its serifs especially. However, he was not the first to move

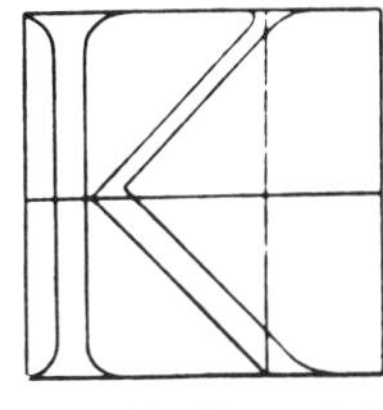
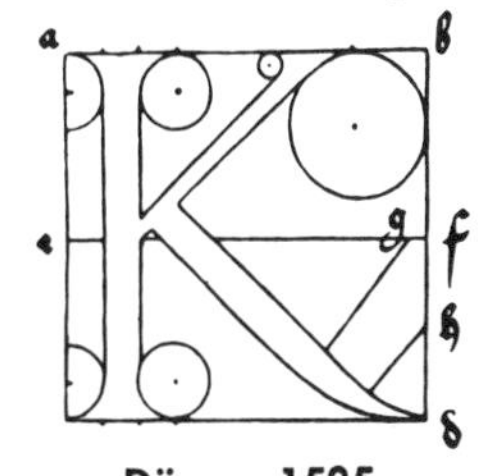
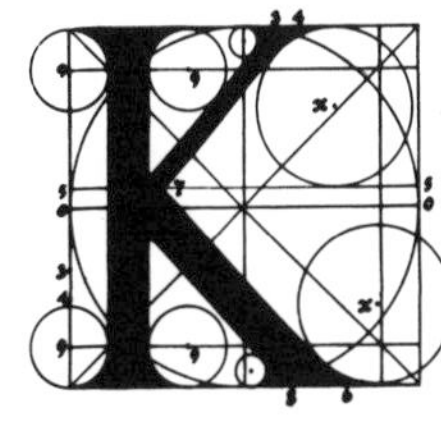

Da Moille, 1480 Pacioli, 1509 Dürer, 1525 Verini, 1526-7 Le Bé, 16c.

The most famous of the geometric designers was Geofroy Tory, 16th century. His K heads this chapter.

THE GEOMETRIC DESIGN OF LETTER FORMS

Efforts to find a geometric formula for shaping letters started in the 15th century, and have been with us since—partly for type design, and partly to teach beginning letterers. Perhaps unfortunately, no formula ever gained acceptance; but perhaps it was fortunate, too, since it left the field open to experiment in proportion and shape through the centuries. In recent times, as will be shown, two different standards have evolved—one making all capitals more or less the same proportion (a square or block) and the other using the Trajan letter proportion. In only one case has a formula geometry had any effect; for that story, turn the page.

parts. Les Hérétiques domptez, la Maiſon d'Au
orite Royale reſtablie, rendoient le Royaume
nt. Mais il manquoit au Roy un fils qui puſt
rois ans de mariage ſans enfans luy avoient pre
'en avoir jamais. Enfin, Dieu touché des vœux

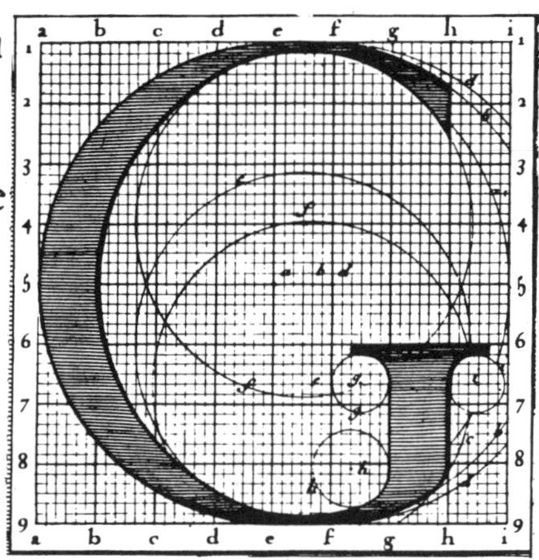

To design a new typeface in a rational manner, at the order of the King, the French Academy of Sciences developed its own geometric formula, as in the G shown. Philippe Grandjean's typeface (above) was the result. The formula, breaking with the more irregular and "natural" line of the calligraphers, enshrined the mechanical and precise copperplate engravers and led ultimately to Didot's modern style.

in that direction. In France, King Louis XIV had ordered a new style of typeface developed, and the Academy of Sciences worked out a detailed theory of design based on 2,304 little squares. Philippe Grandjean, royal punch-cutter, managed by 1702 to cut a face called the Romain du Roi, that satisfied the learned Academy without being as mechanical as the squares suggested. This face also had a more vertical stress based on the new rounder handwriting, and otherwise foreshadowed the Baskerville type—and thus it also led towards the "modern" face that France and Italy each claims as her own. It should properly be recognized as the first transitional face.

Yet, even the Grandjean face was too different for French eyes at the outset, and it suffered from lack of the better printing technology created later by Baskerville. Subtler transitional faces by Pierre Simon Fournier, called *le jeune* (1712-68), were needed to accustom the eye to the transitionals and to prepare the French for the even sharper, more dazzling "modern" typeface which was to come very soon. (Fournier came close to the modern; he even coined the term.)

THE MODERN STYLE

Firmin Didot (1764–1836), youngest grandson in a famous printing family in Paris, was highly trained as a punch-cutter from childhood. He carried the Baskerville style to its logical conclusion, and in 1783 (aged 19) created what is now called "Modern," although at the time it was called "Classical." Didot is seldom given full credit for the modern. The name more familiar is that of Giambattista Bodoni (1740–1813), an Italian. (Didot is pronounced DEE-doh.)

Bodoni was highly impressed by Baskerville, and imitated him when he became private printer to the Duke of Parma in 1768. He produced more than 100 alphabets, shown in his first *Manuale Tipografico* in 1788—and the Baskerville influence was plain. In the next year, six years after Didot, he cut his own first Modern. Actually, it was not entirely Modern as defined today; there was still a little lilt to the top serifs, and a

***Style:* FRENCH MODERN**

AEGMRST

adegmpty

Based on Didot and Bodoni, "modern" as of the 18th century and still so in terms of mechanical precision, sharp contrasts. With copperplate technique victorious, stress now completely vertical; serifs are hairlines, unbracketed; top serifs are horizontal; maximum contrast between thick and thins, the latter becoming hairlines; finials of c, f, etc., are balls. Widths of capitals much more uniform. Shown: *Firmin Didot.*

Class: Book Faces (Small Serifs)

Plus beau, plus fortuné, toujours cher à la paix,
Ton règne ami des lois doit briller d'âge en âge;
Tous nos droits affermis signalent tes bienfaits.
Le ciel t'a confié les destins de la France:
Qu'il exauce nos vœux, qu'il veille sur tes jours!
De ta carrière auguste exempte de souffrance
Que sa bonté pour nous prolonge l'heureux cours!

Quousque tandem abutêre,
Catilina, patientiâ nostrâ?
audacia? nihilne te noctur-

Firmin Didot (top) and Giambattista Bodoni, with their "modern" typefaces

little character to the outline of the face. Because the Didot face was perhaps too extreme, and Bodoni was a better printer with better connections somehow, Bodoni ended up with the major credit.

The British, closer to Baskerville, proceeded to develop Modern in a different way, into what is now called Scotch Roman.

Style: ENGLISH MODERN

AEGMRST
a d e g m p t y

Influenced by French-Italian modern, but less stark in contrast—with a touch of Caslon-like imprecision plus fine bracketing and emphasis on beaks, curled up tail on R, looped tail on Q. Capitals forced to almost equal width, cramping the M especially. L.c. a is nearly closed at top; e bar is dropped to middle. Shown: *Scotch Roman.*

Class: Book Faces (Small Serifs)

The basic modern style characteristics are there, but so are the "earmarks" of Caslon, and the result is a much more readable face than the French-Italian moderns.

With Modern, type design had now seemingly come as far as it could, from an almost hand-lettered irregular face with little contrast between thick and thin lines, with quite heavy serifs, and with slanted stresses (Jenson's) to the very mechanical, sharply defined, extremely contrasty thick and thin, extra thin and flat serifs, and vertical stress of Didot and Bodoni.

Also, in the frequent changing of typefaces from Garamond to Caslon to Baskerville to Bodoni, coupled with the increasing lack of importance of spire Gothic, a problem that was plaguing the alphabet was finally settled—the mix-up over I, J, U, V and sometimes W. Spire Gothic used the J and U instead of the I and V which had come down from Roman times, and the W had been a Gothic outgrowth of VV. The J, U and W were finally recognized as symbolizing separate sounds and given full place in the alphabet, which now became our present 26 Latin letters.

Everything, then, seemed fully settled, in the alphabet itself and its letter styles. But, in fact, within a generation, some surprising things were going to happen to typefaces!

CHAPTER

The invention of typefaces that speak for themselves

THE SCHOLARS had been the chief beneficiaries of printing through the centuries, along with religion, but in the 19th century, commerce became the printer's main customer. Printing has not been the same since.

The Industrial Revolution, which started in England in the early years of the 19th century, resulted from the broad human revolution begun by the invention of printing, among other events. With the new technique of using machinery and steam power (and later, electricity) instead of handiwork, the Industrial Revolution remade printing itself along with other industries, before the century was out. This had some direct and drastic effects on typefaces in due course—but commerce changed typefaces even more, right from the start.

More men had more money to spend, and advertising developed to create and attract customers. That in turn produced still more business and wealth. Printers got new work—"jobs," as they called them—printing the advertisements, along with commercial stationery, catalogues, time tables, trade cards, labels, and the other necessities of a manufacturing and marketing economy. With this came literacy for more and more people, and new (more earthy) tastes in reading and entertainment, also to be tempted by advertising.

One thing was obvious. The classic typefaces, designed for silent readers of books, were not suitable for shouting about a merchant's wares. So, a new kind of typeface had to be invented—one that would be *very* noticeable and "speak for itself" instead of being as inconspicuous as possible to avoid slowing down the silent reader.

The first version of this new invention was called a "fat face," a greatly thickened version of the Modern style of Bodoni and Didot. It is credited to the English typefounder, Robert Thorne, in 1803.

ABCD jkl

Thorne's first fat face. Apparently no picture of Thorne himself exists today

Within the next 25 to 30 years, typefounders did all this, as the continuing increase in commercial printing demanded more and more kinds of conspicuous faces:

● From the development of the fat face they designed "variants" for a face. Up until now, typefaces had been available in only one thickness or "weight." The new idea of varying weights led to thick (bold face), thin

Light **Condensed**

Bold **Expanded**

(light face), squeezed up (condensed) and stretched out (expanded) forms (see Page 59).

● They designed the other two of our three Standard typefaces (along with the small serifs): the strong serif faces and the sans serif faces. The strong serif category was even raised to a refined stage, with the new Clarendon and Egyptian styles fully worked out.

STRONG SERIFS

SANS SERIFS

● They took the idea of "decorated" or "ornamented" letters from the initial letters of manuscript books and spawned a really giddy variety of different letter forms for all tastes from elegant to bawdy. (Because these

Some "Victorian" type designs

styles were used prominently during Queen Victoria's reign, 1837–1901, and matched the dominant styles then in architecture, decoration, etc., these faces are often called "Victorian.")

● They designed (or copied from lithographers and engravers) three-dimensional

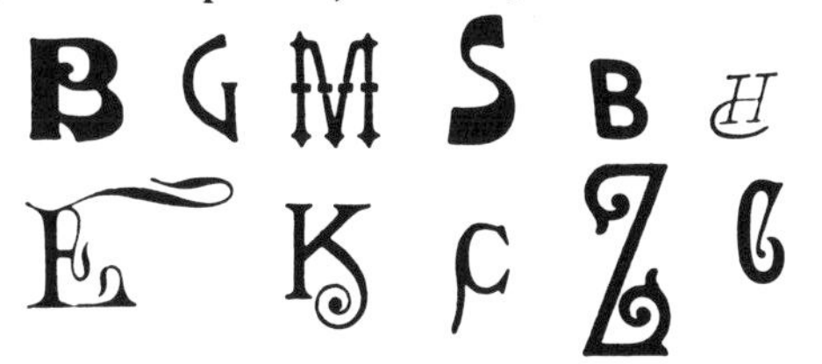

Three-dimensional letters

letter form techniques, and thus made the variety of typefaces almost endless.

● They demonstrated dramatically that letters can be pulled, twisted, turned, covered

Letters "mangled" but recognizable

over with ornaments, given embellished endings, cut into pieces, and yet still be recognized as letters—the moral being that typefaces can be created to serve any mood or need.

● They flooded the market with so *many* typefaces that the old system of identifying, by founder's name and an antiquated system of indicating type size, had to be discarded and specific proper names applied.

SPECIAL FACES VERSUS DISPLAY TYPE

Many 19th century innovations from England had roots in prior developments in other countries, especially France. Furthermore, many countries soon had comparable needs, so they joined in. The United States especially led in further development. What these typefounders did together, in just a few years, was to create the Special typeface division (as described at the beginning of this book) and broaden the range of typefaces which then became standard typefaces. It was quite an achievement of design.

Yet, to admirers of book faces (many of whom deplored the new technology), all the new "display" typefaces appeared ugly, brutish and destructive of printing standards —sinful if not downright blasphemous. The terms "jobbing" and "display" faces were soon coined to distinguish (and downgrade) them from "book faces."

Through the decades since, these terms have stuck, but the "population explosion" of typefaces has become so great and created such crossbred varieties that the terms "book" and "display" faces no longer hold as the broad divisions. The term "book

SOME OF THE NEW (19c) TYPEFACES—AND THEIR NAMES

Karnac Alpine Flirt TEMPLAR
GRECIAN ORNATE RUSTIC
MOTHER HUBBARD CABALISTIC
EXCENTRIC IDEAL Light Line Antique

Suddenly there was no limit to the styles of type —good or bad. The man who cut the most faces such as these—perhaps 135—is virtually unknown today: Herman Ihlenberg, with the Johnson Foundry in Philadelphia, *c.* 1870 to 1900.

Process: LITHOGRAPHY

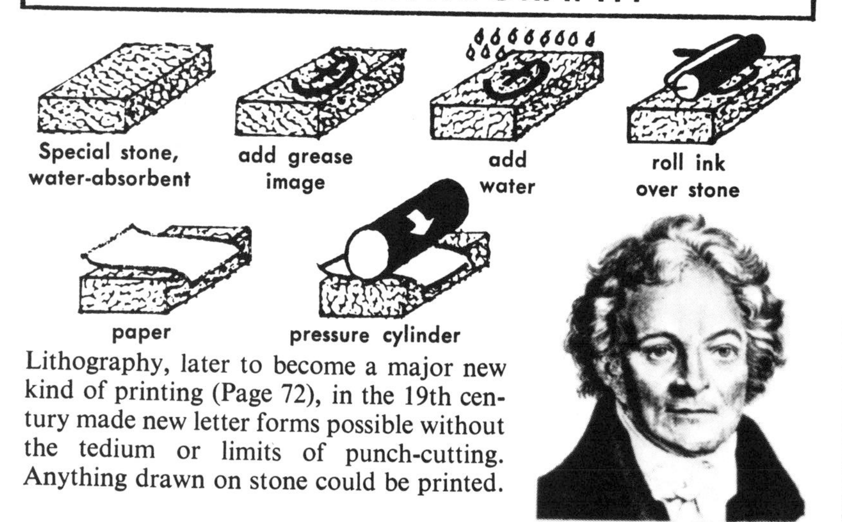

Lithography, later to become a major new kind of printing (Page 72), in the 19th century made new letter forms possible without the tedium or limits of punch-cutting. Anything drawn on stone could be printed.

Aloys Senefelder of Germany invented the basic lithographic process in 1796

The Quality of its Line

Litho imitated copperplate but was freer, more arty, softer,not as brilliant, fanciful and varied, there being no disciplining limit to the drawing on the stone.

faces," properly limited to types and sizes for sustained silent reading, applies to a still very important kind of type, but it is an increasingly smaller part of the whole "Typorama," as you will see. Many "book" faces in larger sizes become admirable *display* faces.

As the broad basis for distinctions, therefore, the terms Standard and Special will prove more useful to you.

STRONG AND SANS SERIFS

Thorne may have been the inventor of the strong serifs as well as the fat face, but another English typefounder, Vincent Figgins is usually given the credit. Figgins first showed the design, calling it "Antique," in his specimen book in 1815. This probably was because its heavy square-serifed letters were suggestive of the slab footings of the architecture and monuments of ancient

Style: CLARENDONS

AEGMRST
adegmpty

Originated in 19th century as companion bold version of English modern style, Clarendons have vertical stress but fine bracketing on otherwise rectangular serifs, as well as contrast between thicks and thins. Letters are subtly balanced, authoritatively cut. So-called French or Italian Clarendons or Antiques have exaggerated serifs, far thicker than strokes of letter. Shown: *Consort Bold.*

Class: Bracketed (Strong Serifs)

Style: EGYPTIANS

AEGMRST
adegmpty

While the term Egyptian is often used to include Clarendons (box at left), the 19th century Egyptians can be distinguished from Clarendons by their unbracketed rectangular serifs approximately the same weight as the thinner stems. Like the Clarendons, they are based on older English letter forms, rather than the geometric constructions that were to come with 20th century slab serifs. Shown: *Egyptian* (English Monotype).

Class: Unbracketed (Strong Serifs)

Egypt—which Napoleon's military campaigns at that time were bringing to the

Quousque tandem abutere, Catilina, patientia nostra? quamdiu nos

English public consciousness. In fact, the type was soon renamed Egyptian.

The first sans serif face was shown by W. Caslon IV in 1816, and he called *it*

W CASLON JUNR

"Egyptian." Not until 1832 was the serif-less idea picked up again, by both Figgins and William Thorowgood. While Figgins called it "sans serif," Thorowgood named his "Grotesque.". Both terms have stuck. Unfortunately, especially in America, the name "gothic" was also applied to this type, probably because in its early forms it was invariably a very bold [black] letter and because it lacked grace, thus "deserving" the epithet that historically stood for barbarian. This has confused matters greatly, and in this book we will distinguish between the earlier black letter as "spire Gothic" and the sans serif gothic as "grot-gothic."

These letters were originally also called "block letters" because the capitals were all about the same width and more or less square (as A, B, C blocks), not varying as the roman capitals did. And this led to a scornful jibe by critics: "Block type for blockheads."

The tradition of decorated initial letters goes back to manuscript days, but now it was adapted to the new needs. One great decorative, Tuscan, had been used throughout the Middle Ages as an initial letter in Bibles, having been invented by Pope Damasus I in the 4th century. Actually, the first full alphabet of decorated letters was cut in about 1690 by James Grover, in England, and it is still available today, under the name Union Pearl, from Stephenson Blake.

These new faces were often a matter of pandering to the desire of printers for novelties, catering to fashion rather than beauty. As a consequence, most of these faces have gone to oblivion, while the Caslons and Garamonds remain.

Not *all* faces, however, were designed for trivial reasons. At the time, England was undergoing a change to "modernism" as part of the Industrial Revolution, and people were asking questions we continue to hear today in different forms: How can art and

Class: DECORATIVES

Spurred by lithographers' freedom to embellish their letters, punch cutters learned how to match them in type, as witness above.

Decorative styles include: (A) embellished (Ideal); (B) floriated (Egmont Decorative Initials); (C) chased (Prisma); (D) materiel (Rustic); (E) foliated (Molé Foliate); (F) filigreed (Ornata); (G) inline (Neuland Inline); (H) ornamented (Sapphire), and (I) rimmed, (Comstock). Chapter T (Page 77) shows the complete range.

Category: Adapted (Special Faces)

Style: GROTESQUES

AEGMRST
adegmpty

Serif-less letters, generally monotone or monoline (same thickness throughout); capitals all more or less same width and square in basic version; l.c. letters monoline versions of roman letters vs. later geometric constructions. Early grots were generally bold or extrabold. Shown: *Franklin Gothic.*

As to name: "Grotesque" is English; U.S. calls it "gothic." Compromise "grot-gothic" is gaining acceptance. All serif-less faces are "sans serif:" sans=without. British often spell it sanserif.

Class: Grot-Gothics (Sans Serifs)

THE UNCREDITED HEROES OF TYPEFACE DESIGN

Once new typefaces went beyond designers cutting their own punches, there arose the "development" function, by which largely-anonymous draftsmen and skilled technicians in type and matrix foundries adapt original designs to meet market needs, quality standards, and technical requirements. Their contribution usually is subtle but often the difference between a face's success or failure. An extreme example is Cheltenham, the first great success of mass-produced type (see P. 59).

THE CHELTENHAM FONT

¶ It is in characters not differing in any material item from these (the designer trusts) that this new font will be cut.

THE CHELTENHAM TYPE

Quaint enough will be this type lacking exactly what chiefly gives the Italic, its qualities of dash & zip; i.e. the kerns. J.

As Bertram G. Goodhue designed it . . . .

CHELTENHAM MEDIUM

Cheltenham Medium

CHELT MEDIUM ITALIC

Cheltenham Medium Italic

. . . . and as Cheltenham emerged

the machine be reconciled? How can mass production without frills, perhaps completely automatic without human interference, get translated into a letter form? Many of the faces of the 1850's represented trial answers to that question.

By the 1850's, the answer was sans serif, a plain, stark functional design, which was seen as capturing the essence of the new age. But within a decade or two, the mood was gone, and the sans serifs were "wrong." In the 1920's, the same question was raised again, with substantially the same answer—and the answer has been debated ever since.

At any rate, as a result of the inventions in the early and mid-19th century, type was made to do much more than serve the silent reader and preserve mankind's knowledge and wisdom. Now it could also speak out to convey a message and capture moods.

THE POINT SYSTEM: HOW TYPE SIZES LOST THEIR NAMES

OLD STYLE ANT.—Long Primer

ANTIQUE CONDENSED—Pica

Old type names with approximate point size

3½	Brilliant	12	Pica (PIE-kuh)
4½	Diamond	14	English
5	Pearl	16	Columbian
5½	Ruby or Agate	18	Great Primer
6	Nonpareil (non-peh-RELL)	20	Paragon
7	Minion (MIN-yun)	24	Double Pica
8	Brevier (BRE-vee-er)	30	Five-line Nonpareil
9	Bourgeois (BURZSH-wah)	36	Double Great Primer
10	Long Primer (PRIM-er)	42	Seven-line Nonpareil
11	Small Pica	48	Canon (CAN-uhn)

3½ 4½ 5 5½ 6 7 8 9 10 11

(Lines show size of type body in printers' points)

12 14 16 18 20 24 30 36 42 48

Type sizes were first identified by name, as at left, not by a unit measure, and with slight variations. In 1737, Pierre Simon Fournier in France invented a "point system," finally stabilized by the Didot foundry in 1785. Not until 1886, when printers were buying type from many foundries and having real troubles mixing all the different sizes, did the U.S. adopt the Didot system—but with a different unit size. In 1898, England also joined, with U.S. sizes. The system is similar to inches and feet: 12 points equal one pica. It takes six picas to make *almost* an inch. (See below for details.) Besides pica, the only old term still used is *agate*, as a measure of advertising space (14 agate lines = 1 column inch). Widths of lines are in picas (this line is 18 picas wide). Body size of type is measured in points (this is 8-pt. type), except that very large "poster" type is measured in picas but called "lines" (10 line type). The "Didot point"—*corps* in French, *punkt* in German—is .0483 inch; the *cicero* (corps 12) is .1776 inch. Where the Fournier points are used, 13 of them equal one cicero. A letter cast on a wrong-sized body is called "bastard type." An *em* is a square of any body size of type; an *en* is half as wide as an em. Note that "fine print" (e.g., in contracts) is not a technical printing term.

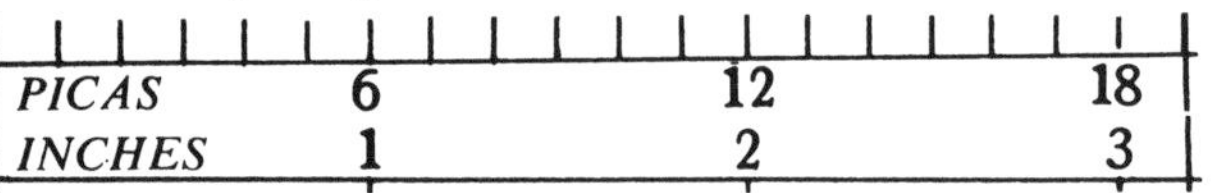

1 point = .0138 inch; 12 points = 1 pica; 72 points = .9962 inch

CHAPTER 

The invention of numbers, &, etc.

LIKE THE ALPHABET, our numbers had to be invented and shaped, and they had to be put into type. So did all the punctuation marks, the symbols we take for granted, the little printer's ornaments, the decorative borders, the pressmark and trademark "logotypes," and perhaps especially the ampersand, which has stimulated books about the many, many ways it has been drawn and cut into type, etc. For instance:

& & & & & & & &

It usually comes as a surprise to find how *late* we were in devising the present Arabic numerals we use, even though a moment's reflection reminds us that the Roman numerals were (of course!) being used in Rome at the very time the capital-letter alphabet was being given its beautiful stone-cut formulation. As a matter of fact, Roman numerals were still being used in Europe for bookkeeping as late as the 17th century (it being easier to add and subtract between two numbers with Roman numerals than *our* system). And in 1300, some European banks actually forbade the use of Arabic numerals,

I II III IV V VI VII

because, they said, it was too easy to forge a 0 into a 6 or a 9, or add a 0 or some other figure.

Originally, so scholars believe, our numbering system was invented by the Hindus, perhaps earlier than 300 B.C. About 1,200 years ago, an Indian book on arithmetic was translated into Arabic; when European merchants obtained the book and had it translated into Latin, it was credited to the Arabs, even though, as the reproductions show, the true Arabic numerals (then and

Hindu

True Arabic ١٢٣٤٥٦٧٨٩٠

now) are quite different from the "Arabic numerals" in that book.

The Spanish Moors seem to have combined the two sets of numerals, and simplified them; the earliest known European manuscript, in the Codex Vigilanus, A.D. 976, has these figures (without a zero), right to left:

After that, the changes went something like this:

1	2	3	4	5	6	7	8	9	0	
										12 c.
										13 c.
										15 c.

As in the case of the alphabet, once the numbers got printed in type, they changed their shape very little.

For the most part, the numerals in type have been cut to the same general design as the letters of the alphabet, and virtually every typeface has a matching set of "figures," as they are called in printing terms.

Two distinctions, however, can be noted.

First is the difference between what is called "old style" figures and "lining" or "ranging" figures:

RANGING FIGURES 1234567890

Old Style Figures 1234567890

As you can see, the old style figures have, in effect, ascenders and descenders like lower-case letters. Like capital letters, lining figures line up evenly at the bottom. Generally, as might be expected from the names, old style figures are more common in the more classical book faces, whereas the lining figures appear with later typefaces, and more prosaic letter forms in general. Careful printers today use both, the old style with small letters and the lining figures with capitals. Garamont is credited with the first old style figures.

The second difference is in the width of the figures. In some faces, the widths vary, as, for instance, a 1 will be much narrower than

23145678

23456178

an 8. This makes for better design. In other faces, all the figures are cut to the same width; and while this hurts the design, it does make it much more convenient for a printer to substitute one number for another in type, since they all take exactly the same space. This is very useful for tabular work.

Especially in lining figures which are cut to the same width, some of the figures are difficult to tell apart—the 3 and 8, for instance, and sometimes the 1 and 7, the 5 and 6, the 6 and 8, the 6 and 0, etc. From what you now know about how changes occur in the field of type, you will sense that the development of numerals received much less attention than the development of lower-case letters. Had there been the same kind of centuries-long experimenting with numerals as with letters, we might now have a radically different—and much more legible—set of numerals.

With the use of magnetic-ink reading devices on printed bank checks and similar computer-processed materials, we *are* finding a new kind of numeral that helps the machine's eye avoid mistaking one figure for another. Thus:

0123456789

They work for the computer's eye, but let us hope they do not take over all uses of figures. What would they do to *our* eyes!

PRINTER'S ORNAMENTS

From the earliest days of printing—the Alvises of Verona being credited with the first ones in 1478—punch-cutters and engravers began making pieces of type or stamps that were purely ornamental. These

were used to indicate the start and end of a chapter, etc. Since most of these early ornaments were based on floral themes, they were called "flowers" or "fleurons," and this name still generally applies, although since that time such motifs as cherubs' faces, crowns, harps, and stars have been introduced as useful symbolism. (The solid black ivy leaves are called "florets," dating back to fifteenth century books.) Ornaments used to "break up" a solid mass of type are called "dingbats."

In addition to the ornaments that stand alone, there are decorative type units which go together in various ways to make quite intricate borders (as for instance the one reproduced, made up of just the three pieces

shown) or other patterns. Sometimes these parts are called "arabesques" (because of the intricate Arab-style patterns they make) and sometimes simply "borders."

Granjon, who did so much else, started their popularity around 1560.

ALL SORTS OF 'SORTS'

5/8 7/8 1/3 2/3 2/3 1/6 1/3 7/8

® ℞ ♯ ♉ ♀ ©
% ℨ ♭ ♊ ⊕
± ʒ ♮ ♂ ℔
√ ♍ ☽ ※ ¢ ♃ £
□ × ÷ = ‡ § †

These are only a few of the special characters, from alchemy to music to the zodiac, that are available in type.

A FAIR SAMPLING OF PRINTER'S ORNAMENTS

Something from every style, something for every taste, in the printer's case

Some of the early type designers such as Garamont, Fournier, Didot and Bodoni cut fleurons to match their typefaces, and along with even earlier anonymous designs, these are still among the best we have. Taste in ornament use changes often; sometimes they are quite fashionable and sometimes are old-fashioned indeed.

Borders are sometimes cast in strips, and are sometimes confused with "rules," which are continuous lines. A "dash" is usually a shorter than column-width rule, but can be ornamented.

PECULIARS, TOO

As the examples at the left show, there are all sorts of "sorts," as the special characters are called by American printers. (In England, they are called "peculiars.")

Unfortunately, this difference in names extends, too, to the most common of the special characters, and this *does* cause confusion: in what the Americans call "ligatures" and the British call "logotypes." (The Americans use the word "logotype" for something very different—a piece of type with meaning on its face: a pressmark, trademark or symbol such as The). The ligature is basically a piece of type that combines two or more letters which otherwise would have a kern and would result in the kern being broken off (see Page 30).

fi fi ﬁ

Ligature (right) is one piece of type

Thus, the top part of the f would break off against another f or an i or l, or sometimes a t; therefore, we have ligatures for the fi. ff, ffi, fl and ffl (ﬁ, ﬀ, ﬃ, ﬂ, ﬄ). Diphthongs (æ, œ) are also ligatures.

Because the early printers strove to make the product look like handwriting, and because in the early italic faces especially, this involved "tied letters," as for instance, a link between a c and t or an s and t— ct. st —there are still typefaces which have this affectation. Linking adds elegance, but is usually disconcerting for rapid reading. (Technically, in the U.S., at least, tied letters are *not* ligatures.)

"Alternate characters" are special letters to eliminate too-eccentric letters (see Page 86) or to *give* particular effects, as in the case of the "quaint" characters used here in Farmer's Old Style Italic:

but mistaques will happen

Where most of our sorts or peculiars came from originally, or even all of our punctuation marks, we do not know.

WHERE DID ? AND ! COME FROM?

The Romans often abbreviated by using the first letter of a word and a period. So, *quaestio* (question) became q., gradually stylized to ?. And *io*, an expression of joy, was i., or soon !. Printers call punctuation marks "points." The ! is called a "bang."

A NEW MARK ‽ THE INTERROBANG

First new symbol since quotation marks (1671), this (in-TERR-o-bang) was created by Martin K. Speckter in 1962. It combines "interrogate" with "bang," for rhetorical statements that are both questions and exclamations (as in "What?!").

CHAPTER N

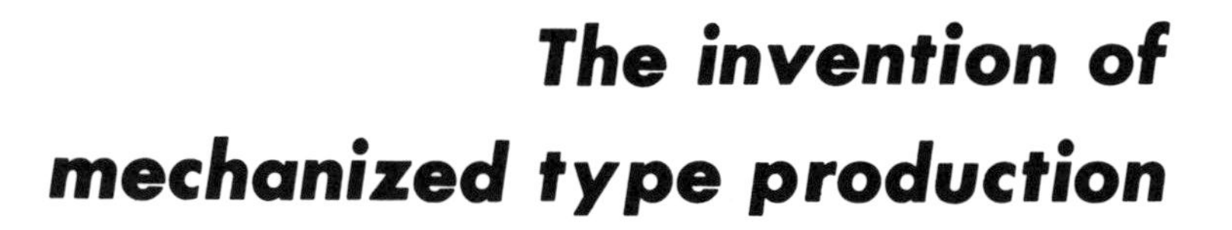

The invention of mechanized type production

PRINTING WAS ONE of the first industries to be truly mechanized. In fact, printing was so well and fully mechanized in the 19th century Industrial Revolution that it allowed itself to lag behind developments of the 20th century, and is just now moving to catch up with still higher levels of technology.

This mechanization affected type and type design, and it is worth briefly noting some of the inventions in the *printing* field.

A continuous-roll papermaking machine was finally brought to practicality in 1806, by Henry Fourdrinier in England. Previously, paper had to be made by hand out of old rags. This was not only slow and expensive, but the paper was also not uniform. It had to be printed damp and with "sock," drastically affecting the appearance of the printed type and requiring slow printing as well. By 1840, ways were found to make paper on the new machine out of wood. Now paper could be cheap and plentiful, and easily put through a press.

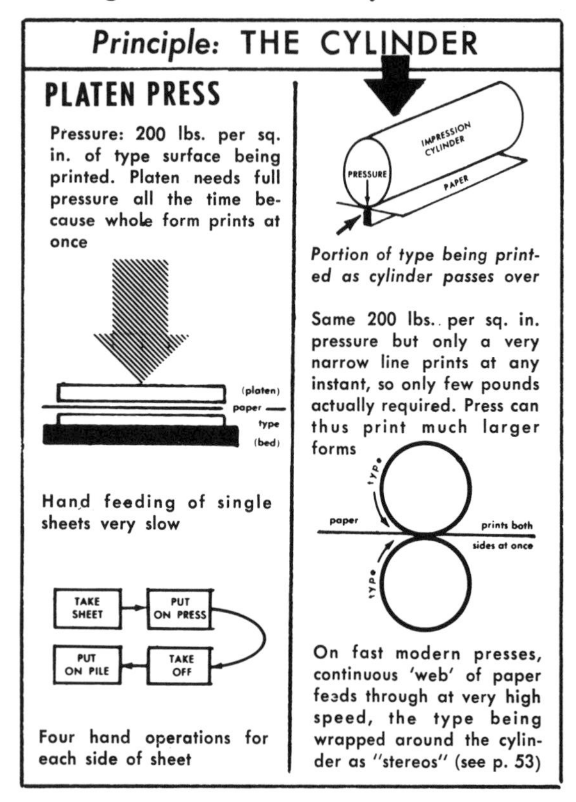

Principle: THE CYLINDER
PLATEN PRESS
Pressure: 200 lbs. per sq. in. of type surface being printed. Platen needs full pressure all the time because whole form prints at once
(platen)
paper
type
(bed)
Hand feeding of single sheets very slow
TAKE SHEET
PUT ON PRESS
PUT ON PILE
TAKE OFF
Four hand operations for each side of sheet
IMPRESSION CYLINDER
PRESSURE
PAPER
Portion of type being printed as cylinder passes over
Same 200 lbs. per sq. in. pressure but only a very narrow line prints at any instant, so only few pounds actually required. Press can thus print much larger forms
type
paper
prints both sides at once
type
On fast modern presses, continuous 'web' of paper feeds through at very high speed, the type being wrapped around the cylinder as "stereos" (see p. 53)

So simple a thing as a cylinder instead of a flat plate (platen) to deliver printing pressure made modern high-speed printing possible. The above drawings show why.

Two steam power presses that could print 1,100 sheets an hour were built in 1814 by Friedrich Koenig for The Times of London. Before that, on a hand press, 250 sheets an hour was considered fast. But Koenig's presses were just the beginning: With a way to making inking rollers and curved stereotype plates the very type form itself could be a cylinder, and presses were soon literally rolling out complete newspapers by the thousands each hour. By 1851, the Hoe Rotary press in America was producing 20,000 sheets an hour. (Today, the Hoe produces 70,000 or more complete 96-page 8-column newspapers an hour.)

These developments increased the quantity of reading matter enormously, and reduced the price at the same time. That, in turn, not only greatly reduced illiteracy, but built up a tremendous appetite for the printed word.

Printers needed some way to save the enormous expense of setting type by hand: a machine to set type cheaply. Also, hand-set type had to be "distributed" (put back in proper compartments of the type storage cases) if the type itself was to be saved for reuse, and this could be eliminated if the type could be melted down instead and new type cast again later. "Feed the hell-box" became the objective—the "hell-box" being the storage bin for old type awaiting return to the furnace for melting down.

By the end of the century, there were four different solutions to the related problems, three of them "non-distribution" systems.

STEREOTYPES AND ELECTROTYPES

The first idea was to print from a "stereotype" metal plate cast from a mould made by the type instead of printing from the original type. (This would save wear and tear on type and cut costs greatly, although it did not solve the hand-setting or redistribution problems.) Then, if duplicate plates of the pages could be printed on different presses at the same time, this would speed up production. Since it was obvious that high press speed could be obtained only by a "rotary" (wheel) motion of the plates over the paper, some way had to be found to "curve the type."

The first successful curved "stereo" came in 1805 with the printing of the New Testament at Cambridge University, England. Charles, 3rd Earl of Stanhope, is credited with the invention, although Didot, Benjamin Franklin and others had heard of or experimented with the idea earlier. Stereo is basically a way of making an inexpensive duplicate matrix from original type and then casting new type from it as shown below.

Just as whole forms of type could be cast, so could locked-up lines of large-size type be duplicated by stereo and cut apart to make separate letters. As a typecasting alternative, this never became commercially successful, but it was a method of "borrowing" an existing font of type, initial letter, ornament, etc., and it contributed to the profusion of decorative materials. Photoengraving "cuts," etched in a metal plate by photo-chemical action, also were used, like stereos.

A higher quality version of the stereotype, "electrotyping," was invented in 1839. The coated surface of the plate is copper or nickel—much harder than the lead stereo plate. Production of "electro" copies of ornaments and large letters became prevalent enough to cause economic harm to the original producers, since royalties were seldom if ever paid for the right to make duplicates. Collecting old electros has recently become a printer's hobby.

Even more importantly, the duplicate matrices could be hardened in the same way, too, and thus provide as serviceable a matrix as a "strike" from a steel punch, especially for larger sizes. Many foundries pirated typefaces in this way, but the copying process did reduce the quality of the letter, and a better way of making duplicate matrices still had to be invented.

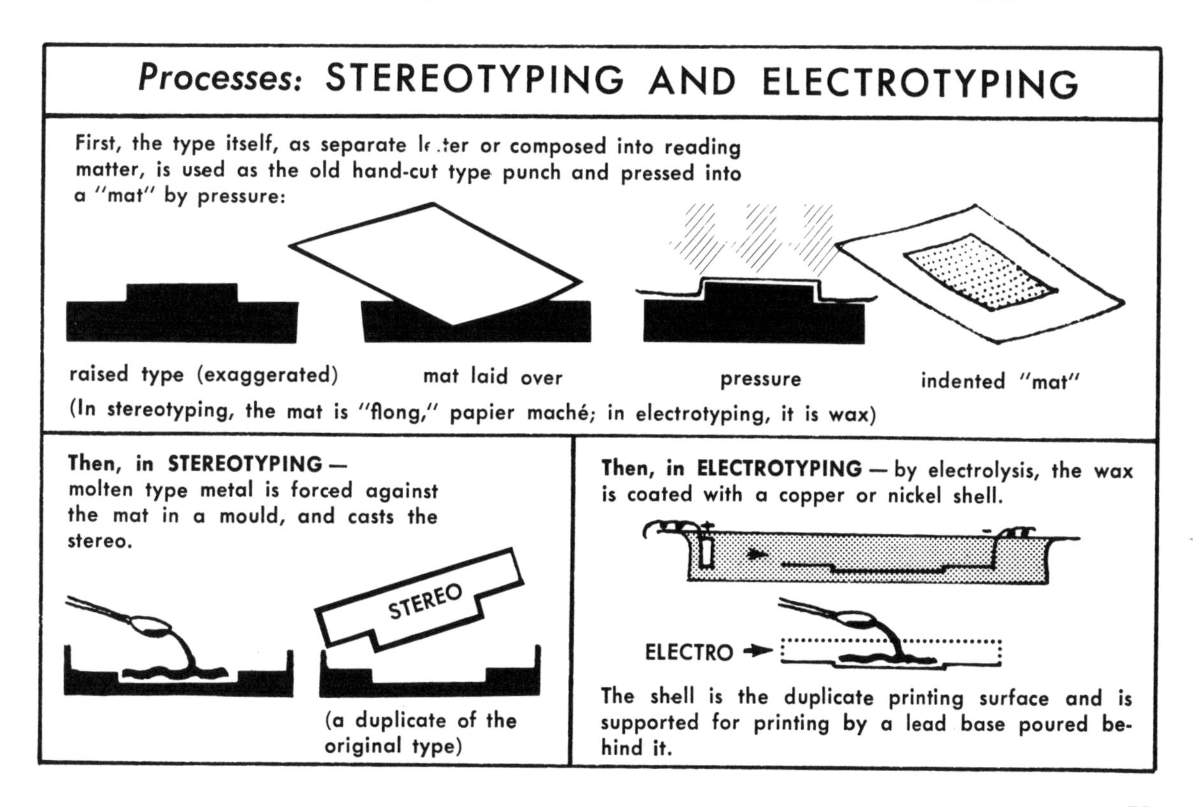

Processes: STEREOTYPING AND ELECTROTYPING
First, the type itself, as separate letter or composed into reading matter, is used as the old hand-cut type punch and pressed into a "mat" by pressure:
raised type (exaggerated)
mat laid over
pressure
indented "mat"
(In stereotyping, the mat is "flong," papier maché; in electrotyping, it is wax)
Then, in STEREOTYPING — molten type metal is forced against the mat in a mould, and casts the stereo.
STEREO
(a duplicate of the original type)
Then, in ELECTROTYPING — by electrolysis, the wax is coated with a copper or nickel shell.
ELECTRO
The shell is the duplicate printing surface and is supported for printing by a lead base poured behind it.

—*American Type Founders*

Father and son: Linn Boyd Benton (left) invented the pantographic punch-cutter, and his son Morris Fuller Benton went on to use it for a remarkable output of typefaces (see page 59)

MECHANIZED TYPECASTING

Remember how the molten metal had to be poured into the typecasting mould by hand and given an energetic shake to ensure that it would not trap air pockets which would leave a blemishing bubble on the face of the type? In 1834, this problem was overcome by David Bruce, Jr., son of a Scottish immigrant to the United States, who invented a force pump for hand casting moulds.

Four years later, Bruce also patented a true typecasting machine which not only pumped in the metal but turned out letters in a continuous row. It trimmed off their jet and made them uniform in size. Fast and precise as this machine became, it was hardly the whole solution to the problem of economical production. However, it did provide relatively inexpensive hand-set types. The basic principle is still used today for casting hand-set type, especially in display.

Type cast by the Bruce machine and its successors later became known as "foundry type" or "hand type," names which imply the use of a harder metal alloy than used by the mechanical "composition" casters which followed. The types produced by the later processes have been called by the manufacturers' names: Linotype, Monotype and Ludlow. Monotype is sometimes called "hand type," too, when it is cast in the larger sizes (by a Bruce-like caster) and put into type cases for hand-setting. We will use these terms hereafter.

The force pump later proved necessary to all the new type composition machines. But before there could be a Linotype, there also had to be a typewriter (1867) with a bar (and keyboard) which controlled the separate letters and which allowed them to be used in turn as needed. Also, since making of duplicate matrices by electrotyping resulted in poor quality, there had to be a faster, cheaper and much more uniform means than the old hand-cutting method to produce punches to make the duplicate matrices. The punches were going to be needed in great quantities, and all the punches for each letter would have to be exactly alike—impossible in hand-cutting.

THE PANTOGRAPHIC PUNCH-CUTTER

It was not until 1884 that an American, Linn Boyd Benton, found the answer. He invented a remarkably simple device, that made a uniform process out of punch-cutting by use of a pantograph. The pantographic principle allows an operator to trace a large pattern at one end and have it reproduced simultaneously as a cut-out punch in a piece of steel—in exact proportion, to the precise size desired—at the other end. The original pattern could be a wood, brass or cardboard cut-out, as big as a foot high. The pantograph could cut a punch as small as one-twelfth of an inch, precisely to the same pattern, within 1/10,000 of an inch. Perhaps more important, any desired quantity of punches could be made quickly and uniformly.

The pantographic cutter produced millions of punches and started an argument which still persists: whether the infinitely small and subtle differences caused in a typeface by hand punch-cutting are inevitably removed by the pantographic cutter, leaving only a cold, mechanically precise letter that has dehumanized printing.

A SAMPLE OF PRECISION

Our Father which art in heaven, Hallowed be thy name. Thy kingdom come. Thy will be done in earth, as it is in heaven. Give us this day our daily bread. And forgive us our debts, as we forgive our debtors. And lead us not into temptation, but deliver us from evil: For thine is the kingdom, and the power, and the glory, for ever—Amen.

Proof at left is printed from a 24-pt. type machine cast in a pantograph-cut matrix by ATF. Enlargement shows it contains whole Lord's Prayer—271 characters. Think that's small? ATF has also cut it on 4-pt. type, which is this size: ■

Principle: THE PANTOGRAPHIC PUNCH-CUTTER

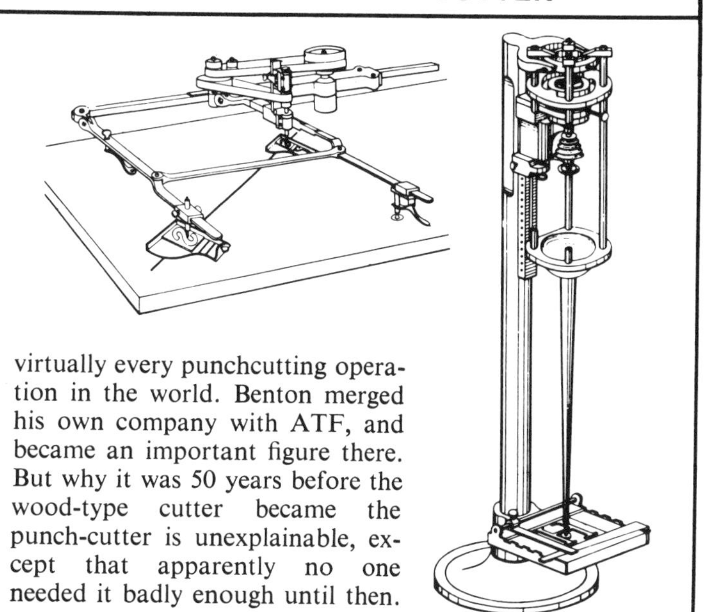

The pantograph (right, middle) was long used to make drawings larger or smaller. In 1834, William Leavenworth of upstate New York added a router (gouging bit) to it and cut duplicate wood-type letters by tracing around the original. This made wood type practical (see below). In 1884, Linn Boyd Benton, a New Yorker turned Mid-Westerner, improved the tool enough to get a patent and used it to cut metal type. Mergenthaler Linotype, in urgent need of a mechanical punch-cutter, asked him to try steel punches—and he succeeded. The machine was leased to Mergenthaler and, in due course, to Lanston Monotype as well. It is still used with refinements by virtually every punchcutting operation in the world. Benton merged his own company with ATF, and became an important figure there. But why it was 50 years before the wood-type cutter became the punch-cutter is unexplainable, except that apparently no one needed it badly enough until then.

WOOD TYPE

The pantograph was a boon, too, for the oldest way of making type—in wood. Wood for carving out initial letters and large letters of type—anything larger than one inch tall, for posters and the like—had been customary from the earliest days. Wood type made of close-grained boxwood, cut at the end of the grain, was not only durable but as precise as metal type, while being much lighter, cheaper and easier to produce.

Coming along just at the time when the Victorian-decorated faces were at their most popular, and when business, politics and the circuses needed posters with large picturesque type, the pantographs were busily put to work cutting out great quantities of wood type. Today, wooden letters of this vintage are collectors' items, and these special typefaces have been revived in a fad that may remain as a permanent style.

TYPE-COMPOSITION MACHINES

As more of the basic features of a type composition machine—the force pump, the keyboard and typebar, the pantographic punch-maker—were being developed, the pressure was on to create the whole machine, that is, one which could set a message, as a typewriter types out a word or sentence, instead of just a row of A's, B's and C's that had to be "composed" by hand into the desired words. Large prizes were offered to inventors. Finally, within a few years, two major machines became available, and then a third one primarily for display sizes.

WHAT IS TYPE?

—Woodcuts by John De Pol

To this point in our story, type was type. In 1887, Tolbert Lanston (right) even reaffirmed this with a caster that made single letters cheaply, quickly and, most importantly, already set up, ready for printing. But by then, radical changes had started. Otto Mergenthaler (left) in 1886 had made a *line* of type as one piece of metal, and this led ultimately to processes for reproducing typefaces in full pages and doing printing without using metal type at all. (See next page.)

Process: LINOTYPE COMPOSITION

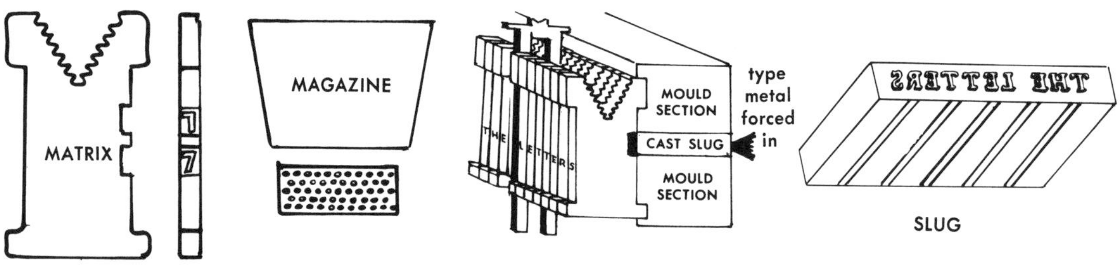

MATRIX

MAGAZINE

MOULD SECTION

CAST SLUG

MOULD SECTION

type metal forced in

SLUG

WHOLE LINE OF SPACED MESSAGE CAST IN ONE PIECE OF METAL

Brass matrix, shown exact size flat and end view, has punched-in letters on end (usually roman, matching italic). Held in "magazine" storage, mats are released by operating typewriter-like keyboard, and fall into a row, with punched ends (exaggerated black) held together against a mould. (Odd-shaped item in midst of mats is a "space-band," wedge shaped to fill out space between words.) Type metal is forced into mould and mats, and a "slug" is cast—the whole "line o' type" in one piece. Mats can be pushed up into position so italics are cast instead.

THE LINOTYPE, invented by Otto Mergenthaler, a German immigrant to the United States, was the great break-through. First put to practical use in 1886, it cast a whole spaced line of metal letters at *one time*, and in *one piece*, called a "slug." The setting of the matrices was done from a typewriter-like keyboard. After use, the matrices were automatically redistributed and the "line-o'-type" slugs remelted, to be used again later to cast other lines. The Linotype could do the work of four hand typesetters.

THE MONOTYPE was first introduced in 1887 by an American, Tolbert Lanston, and brought to full efficiency ten years later. An operator sets the type by punching holes in a paper tape from a keyboard. A second machine, controlled by the paper tape in the same way that an old player piano is controlled by a paper roll, then casts *separate letters* of type in the desired length of line, with proper spacing between words. Unlike the Linotype, the Monotype can cast letters to different "set" of space on the sides of the face. (See Page 31.)

THE LUDLOW, a device that compromised between hand-setting and expendable (remeltable) type, was invented in 1911 by Washington L. Ludlow, also an American. Matrices are set by hand in a composing stick and from this a slug is cast to the desired length, with all the letters in one piece. Then the matrices are returned to their cases for re-use. After the slug is used, it is remelted. The Ludlow is especially useful for large sizes.

Especially for body-type, what Linotype, Monotype and Ludlow did was make the printing plant itself a typefoundry again, as it had been in the earliest days—except that now it had plentiful supplies of matrices (now called "mats" for short) of great variety and machinery to cast precise type in any desired quantity, so quickly and cheaply that it could be remelted instead of having to be used over and over. And at savings of enormous expenditures for type and type cabinets.

From the printer's point of view, all this resulted in a great wealth of typefaces. It was cheaper to install a new font of mats than it had ever been to make a new type by hand.

One very important result of this new quality in casting, and the economy of fresh type, was a new emphasis on the cleanness and sharpness of line of a face as printed. After this, there could be no excuse for badly-cut faces, even in the name of "art." The better type thus tended to improve the quality of even routine printing. What Baskerville had started was now fully in effect, and a powerful new tool—the machine—had supplanted the earlier tools such as the pen in influencing type appearance.

The first major typecasting revolution, by which Garamont and others had taken foundering out of the print shop and made a special industry of it, was not being reversed entirely. In the United States, a number of

Process: MONOTYPE COMPOSITION

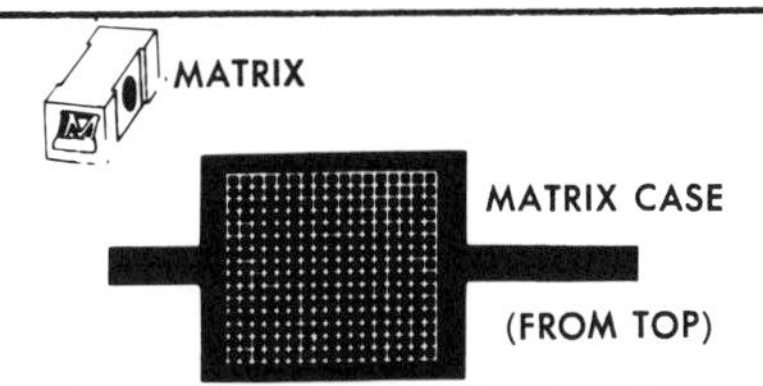

Matrix, shown exact size, has letter punched in end face. Font of these mats, one each of 272 different characters (see Page 61), are locked in together as cells (hence "cellular mats") in a metal frame called a matrix case, about 4 inches square. The matrix case is put into the Monotype casting machine. For larger sizes on other machines, there are "display mats," not unlike the flat hand matrix (see Page 29).

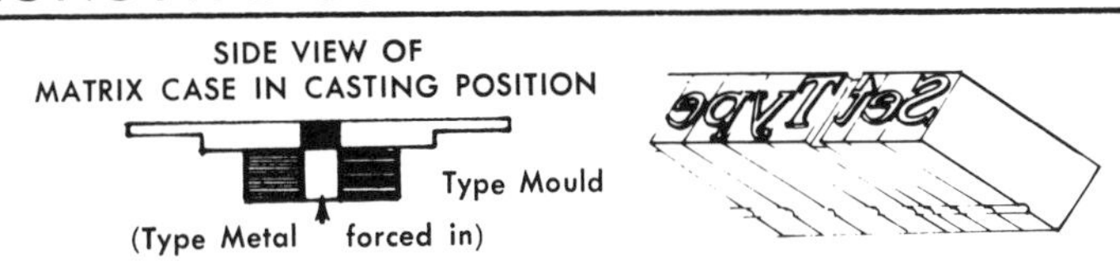

LETTERS ARE CAST SEPARATELY IN SPACED LINE TO SPELL OUT MESSAGE

To cast type, whole matrix case moves for each letter to put particular matrix (shown exaggerated in black) over type mould. Type metal is forced in, and a separate letter is cast. Matrix case then moves to put next needed matrix over mould.

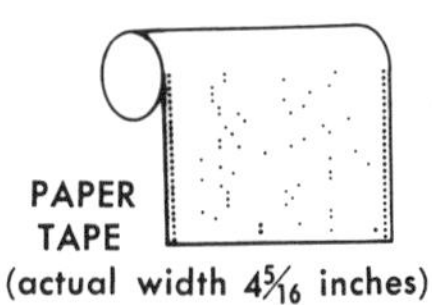

(actual width 4⁵⁄₁₆ inches)

What controls movement of matrix-case is paper tape with holes punched on separate typewriter-like machine. Air pressure through holes moves matrix-case at incredible speeds, also effects spacing between words.

smaller type foundries merged to become the giant American Type Founders (ATF), and, in effect, existing foundries such as Stephenson Blake in England and Bauer in Germany did the same thing and grew even more important. But their emphasis now was on new styles of display type packaged in small "fonts" (see Page 61) for various printing jobs, to give each customer some novelty or distinctiveness.

The availability of small "job" fonts of foundry type, of highest quality and an exact match to earlier purchases of the same face, also meant that a printer could have much more variety of type at his disposal. (Foundry type, more expensive because of the harder metal and more careful precision, as well as the fact that it is usually bought only in the display sizes, is normally saved and re-used.) The introduction of printing papers with different surfaces and inking qualities required this greater range of typefaces. The result was that the printers bought more mats and type as more faces became available, and dropped the old idea of concentrating on one kind of typeface—getting rid of an outdated style as new ones arose and were demanded by customers. Now, printers began building up a *range* of typefaces to offer and attract customers.

NEW TYPEFACES

By the beginning of World War I there were four kinds of typecasters: single cast, hand-set type (foundry); single cast, machine-set (Monotype); hand-set, slug or line cast (Ludlow and competitors) and machine set, line cast (Linotype and its competitor, Intertype). While each found a place, all nevertheless were in hot competition, developing and promoting the sale of new typefaces. The production of mats repesented an important part of the business of the machine manufacturers.

Since the composition-machine companies and type foundries operated in England, Europe and the U.S., there was an international market again for typefaces as there had not been since the 17th century. More-

Process: LUDLOW COMPOSITION

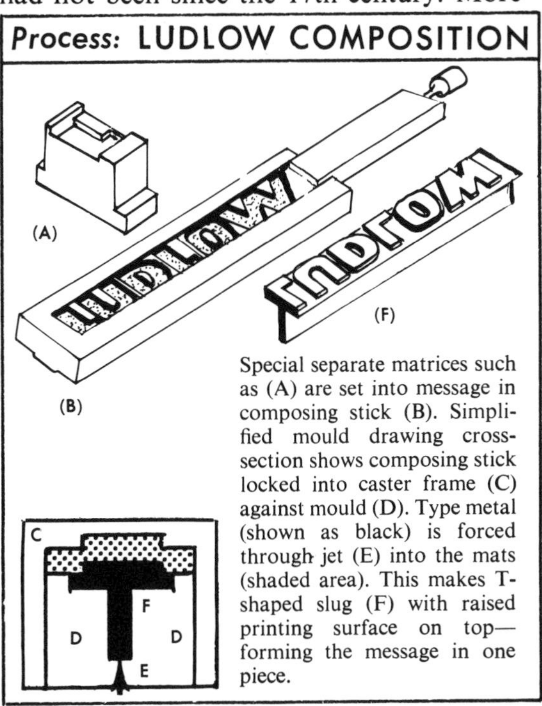

Special separate matrices such as (A) are set into message in composing stick (B). Simplified mould drawing cross-section shows composing stick locked into caster frame (C) against mould (D). Type metal (shown as black) is forced through jet (E) into the mats (shaded area). This makes T-shaped slug (F) with raised printing surface on top—forming the message in one piece.

over, the companies took to copying each other's best typefaces. Sometimes this was by contract, as between Monotype and American Type Founders, when it seemed in the best interest of both to have matching faces for machine-set body type and foundry display type. In such instances, they used the same name for the typeface. But sometimes one firm simply pirated another company's typeface, perhaps changing the letters and the name just enough to constitute a "legal" innovation. Sometimes rival firms honestly thought they improved on the design. The result has been confusion, to say the least.

Another effect of the typecasting revolution was that certain specific mechanical requirements of the two new body-type processes forced type design to change. Thus began a continuing redesigning to produce typefaces *reworked* for new processes—really a part of the development function noted on Page 48.

The Linotype had perhaps the most serious type design problems to overcome. It could not accommodate any kerns. The whole face had to be cut into the edge of the matrix, so that another matrix could fit next to it. This meant that the small f, in particular, had to be designed—as in the case of a standard typewriter—so it would not need a kern and the gap in the "fit" of the letters would be minimized. This was not always good for the design of the f, as you can see:

fa	f a	fa
Kerned f and a	**Same f, not kerned**	**Redrawn, unkerned f to avoid gap**

There was also a problem with the "second alphabet" which the Linotype made possible by putting two different letter forms on the same mat—a companion italic or bold face. Ordinarily, an italic would be narrower than the roman. Left in its natural width, there would be too much space between letters. as (3) shows:

(1) abcdefghijklmnopqrstuvwxyz

(2) *abcdefghijklmnopqrstuvwxyz*

(3) *a b c d e f g h i j k l m n o p q r s t u v w x y z*

(4) *abcdefghijklmnopqrstuvwxyz*

(1) roman lowercase (Garamond); (2) handset italic, close set; (3) handset; letterspaced to width of roman; (4) Linotype italic, close set, designed to same width as roman.

Linotype, therefore, had to widen the companion italics. Some letters were redesigned, others were given looped terminals, and some were given more slant or were turned to fill the space.

One great advantage of old-fashioned type design had been that the width of any given letter could be made whatever seemed best. It is because of such differences that beautiful and legible typefaces are designed. But, to avoid too many different matrix and mould widths, all of the mechanical typesetting systems reduced the potential number of widths from perhaps 90 to as few as 12. However, this has proved flexible enough.

In fact, by careful and sensitive work, virtually all of the potential design problems were overcome. The original fear that machines would forever corrupt good typeface design and printing proved almost entirely unjustified. In another way, as will be seen in later chapters, the manufacturers were soon going to more than make up for whatever changes they forced on type design.

ETAOIN SHRDLU

Actually, these are the letters on the first two vertical rows of the Linotype keyboard. In the old days, the easiest way to correct a noticed error in the midst of setting was to fill in the line of matrices with any letters whatsoever, then cast the line and throw it in the "hell-box" for remelting. The operator had only to run his finger lightly down the keyboard and the matrices would fall out quickly and fill up the space. In this way, ETAOIN SHRDLU would get set into type. Unfortunately, sometimes that defective line of type did not get "pulled" out, but ended up in print, in the middle of something else.

Today, however, the Linotype has an automatic way of solving the problem. So ETAOIN SHRDLU is seen less and less, and soon may be seen no more.

CHAPTER 10

The invention of the type family

AT FIRST, TYPEFACES had been identified only by their sizes (see page 48), although sometimes also vaguely linked to their designers. During the typeface explosion of the 19th century, they first were named according to a general style, such as Egyptian, and then began getting specific names, often exotic or fanciful. Many of these new names, it turned out, were misleading. What was needed was some understanding of relationship between the faces.

First to be seriously affected was the new manufacturing giant, the American Type Founders, that was being formed in 1892 out of a merger of more than 20 foundries. ATF had the problem of making sense and system out of all the typefaces and standing type inherited from the separate companies. The man who got the job was Morris Fuller Benton, son of the inventor of the pantographic punch-cutter. With an invention of his own, the idea of a *family* of typefaces, the fat faces and many other seemingly wild variations of type suddenly found niches.

A family of type consists of a number of typefaces which have a common family resemblance, but also show variations that might be expected in a family: one member is short and heavy, another is tall and thin, yet all have the same large ears or bright red hair or whatever else is the "family trait."

The family trait is seen in unique style elements that the designer gives the basic typeface. For instance, the chief characteristics of today's Bodoni faces are: very thin, flat serifs; vertical stress of thicks and thins, mechanically or geometrically curved, with the thins equal in weight to the serifs and just about hairline thickness. The basic design is then modified by "variables" (such as thicker stress, or a slanted position) to create the "variants" in the Bodoni family.

The point which Benton recognized was that the Thorne fat face and similar faces which followed were really not wildly different from the Modern style which had preceded them. They could be seen as variant members of the Bodoni family. Benton thus proceeded to sort out all the inherited ATF typefaces into families. Later he helped create some new families, notably Goudy, Cheltenham, Century, Cloister and Stymie. The first family to gain popularity, Cheltenham (1904) was the first to be available both in foundry (hand) type and machine-casting type (Linotype).

& Bodoni **Ultra Bodoni Italic** *Bodoni Book Italic* **Ultra Bodoni** &

Bodoni Bold Italic

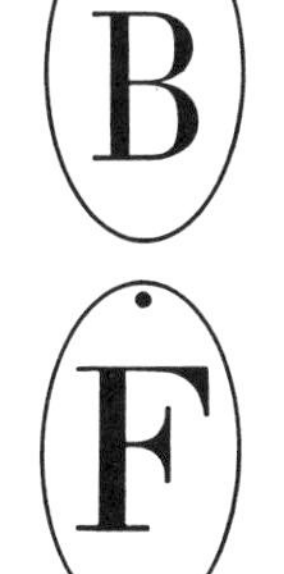

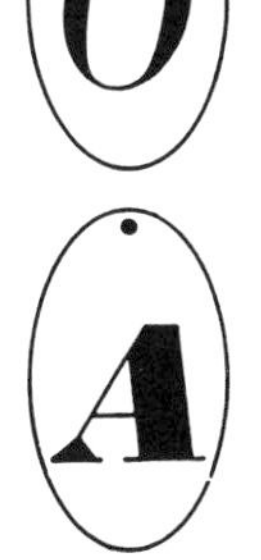

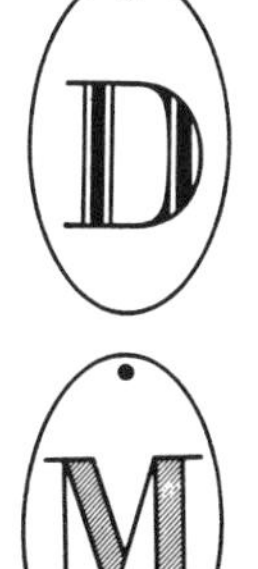

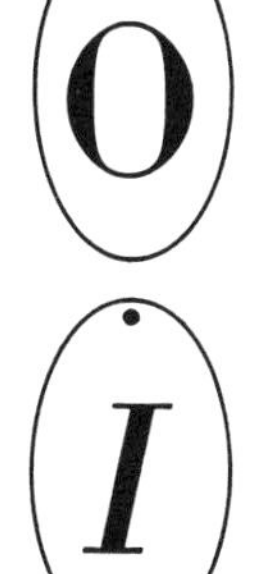

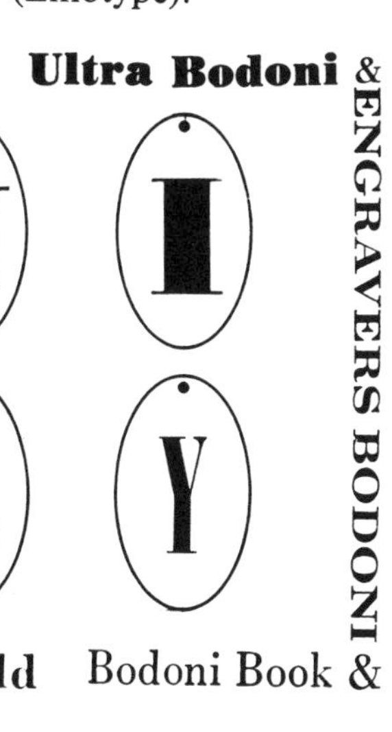

ENGRAVERS BODONI

& **Bodoni Bold Condensed** *Bodoni Italic* **Bodoni Bold** Bodoni Book &

TYPEFACES AND FAMILY FACES

To understand fully what a family is, we first have to agree exactly on what a typeface is. It is not simply the printed letter on a piece of paper, but a particular design for a whole alphabet of letters for printing. It must be available by some setting process, with letters created to fit with one another in any order required. It must have unique characteristics that distinguish it from others.

The original typeface *begets* families; one face is not in itself a family. Beatrice Warde, who discovered that the so-called Garamonds of the 20th century were based on the later cuttings of Jannon, adapted from Garamont, rather than Garamont's own design, suggested using the term "model" for a typeface which is made into families. Each manufacturer uses a model to produce a family; there is an ATF Garamond family, a Monotype Garamond family, etc., all taken from the Jannon model. Each of these families has minor differences, but presumably all have the same certain basic characteristics that make the Jannon model different from the original Garamont, or from the Bodoni model. (The Ludlow Garamond, incidentally, *was* taken from the original Garamont model, by R. Hunter Middleton.)

The term "family" is sometimes used instead of style or class—for instance, the "Gothic family." Obviously, this is confusing and should be avoided.

The major variables among family members are:

WEIGHT VARIABLES—referring to "blackness" or "lightness" in print, as a result of the different thicknesses of the lines of the faces. The Standard British Nomenclature recommends that the relative weights be known as extra-light, light, semi-

Light **Black**

light, medium, semi-bold, bold, extra-bold and ultra-bold (with "medium" normally meaning the regular roman face as originally designed and therefore not appearing as such in the name). A lot of other terms are used, however—such as "book," in the case of Bodoni, to mean light; "demi-bold," as more or less semi-bold; "broad," "heavy," "black" (and in England, sometimes "Clarendon") to mean extra-bold or ultra-bold.

WIDTH VARIABLES—the proportionate narrowness or wideness of *all* the letters (that is, not in the sense of an M being wider than an I). Again in the common nomenclature, these range from ultra-condensed,

Condensed **Extended**

through extra-condensed, condensed, semi-condensed, medium, semi-expanded, expanded, and extra-expanded to ultra-expanded. However, "extended" or "wide" are often used instead of expanded, and "elongated," "narrow" and "compressed" are sometimes used instead of condensed.

SIZE VARIABLES—Some faces have SMALL CAPITALS on the standard body size and some have "titling" variants, which are all-capital versions that can be full-size on the type body and thus much larger "for their size," as shown here:

All three are technically the same size

POSTURE refers to whether the letter as a whole is upright or slanted (and, if slanted, whether to the left or right, and to what degree). The slant to the left is usually called "backslant," and the normal slant to

Backslant *Italic*

the right is usually called "italic," although technically "oblique," "sloped" or "slanted" are more correct for those variants which are virtually the same as the upright letter.

TREATMENT. Sometimes typefaces are incised, shadowed, or decorated. Thus, there is Bodoni Open, Bodoni Shaded, etc. Also, they can be given "swash" (flourished) beginnings or endings. While these typefaces can be considered variant members of the family, they are in a sense "disowned" as standard faces because they are useful for special purposes only. (There is even "right-reading" or reversed type, to print backwards, for special purposes.)

ALIGNMENT. Usually, the various members of a family "align," that is, the bottom or "base" line of the basic letter is the same

CENTURY Light **with Bold**

in all cases, so that italics and bold, for instance, can be used on a line with the regular version without any trouble. Of course, the titling letters do not align with the others.

ABCDEFGHIJKLMNOPQRSTUVWXYZ

12345678901234567890

"Lining" in 12-pt. Lining Cairo Bold, above, means the smaller print sizes shown are available on the 12-pt. body, "lining" (aligning) on same base line, for setting together without trouble of mixing different body sizes.

SERIES, SIZES AND FONTS

Once a typeface variant is pin-pointed—once you have specified Bauer Bodoni Extrabold Italic, for instance—you come to the "series." A series is simply the range of sizes of that particular variant of that particular family, e.g., 6, 8, 10, 12 point, etc.

All the characters in any given assortment of any one size of one variant of type comprise a "font." Most foundry type fonts are assembled by what is called a "fonting scheme," a formula worked out on the basis of average use so that the printer gets the right number of each letter he will need. In a font, there may be 6 A letters, 8 E letters, and 2 Z letters, because those have proved over the years to be about the right proportions. The size of a font, therefore, is usually indicated as 6-A, 12-a, 6-1, meaning there are 6 capital A, 12 small a, and 6 of figure 1, with all other characters in proportion. Here is such a cap font, complete:

AAAAAABBBCCCCDDDDEEEEE
EEEEEFFFGGGGHHHHIIIIIIIJJJJ
KKKLLLLMMMMNNNNNNNOO
OOOOPPPPQQRRRRRRSSSSSSTT
TTTTTTTUUUUVVVWWWXXYY
YZZ&&.......,,,,,,,,---:::;;;!!!???''''$$
$$1111112222223333344444555555
6666667777788888899999000000000

A character of another font, mixed in, is called "w.f.," or wrong font.

"Font" is also used to indicate which different characters are included, especially in terms of the assortment of matrices used in a type composition machine. This is shown in specimen books as follows:

ABCDEFGHIJKLMNOPQRSTUVWXYZ
ABCDEFGHIJKLMNOPQRSTUVWXYZÆŒ
abcdefghijklmnopqrstuvwxyzfiflffffifflæœ
£1234567890 .,:;!?'"-()[]—&ÆŒ
ABCDEFGHIJKLMNOPQRSTUVWXY
abcdefghijklmnopqrstuvwxyzfiflfffiffilæœ
£1234567890 ,:;!?'"()[]&ÆŒ

THE SEVEN ALPHABETS

For setting convenience in using different faces together, a font of matrices will usually include more than one variant of a face (for instance, the normal roman face and its related italic or bold-face). The term "alphabet" has been applied to each different set of letters in the font. On the Monotype, it is possible to get seven such alphabets in the same matrix case, usually as follows:

1 ABCDEFGHIJKL
2 ABCDEFGHIJKLMNOP
3 abcdefghijklmnopqr
4 *ABCDEFGHIJKLM*
5 *abcdefghijklmnopqrstu*
6 **ABCDEFGHIJKL**
7 **abcdefghijklmnop**

UNIVERS: THE PLANNED FAMILY

To provide a full range of completely compatible variants, planned in an orderly degree of difference, a Swiss designer, Adrian Frutiger, in 1957 designed a new kind of family. It has a progression of different weights and different widths, in both upright and oblique, all designed from the same basic set of characteristics. To avoid the confusion of such terms as "bold," "demi-bold," "semi-bold," etc., the variants were first identified only by a series of numbers. However, the usefulness of names for variants proved too much, and now there are Univers Bold, Univers Bold Condensed, etc.

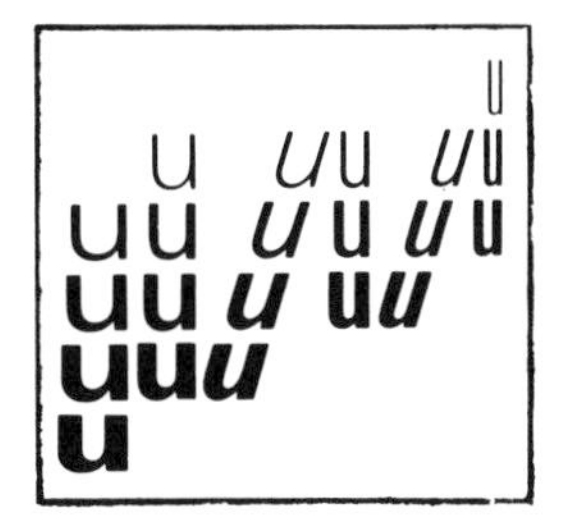

CHAPTER 

The invention of evocative printing

OUT OF THE 19th century, as it ended, came a movement that had tremendous effect on typefaces and printing. It was started by William Morris, an English poet and social reformer with a lifelong drive to restore beauty and craftsmanship to all phases of life in resistance to the machine-stamping mediocrity and conformity resulting from the Industrial Revolution. Printing had suffered along with all other arts and crafts. Morris's method was to start a private press in 1891, in the Hammersmith district of London—what has become the famous Kelmscott Press, whose influence has shaped modern typographic design increasingly to this day. His masterpiece was "The Works of Geoffrey Chaucer," usually called the "Kelmscott Chaucer."

The book created such a stir and had such repercussions that we can properly date much of our 20th century interest in the art of printing from 1896, when it appeared. Morris clothed an English literary epic in a grandeur that befit it, lavishing on it a dazzling combination of type, woodcut illustration, initial letters, hand-made paper, perfect press craftsmanship and an elegant binding. In all, the Kelmscott Press produced 53 books with comparable excitement.

What has simply been called "Morris's spirit" might be termed "evocative printing." As such, it was the fifth of the great ways of handling the alphabet. First, there had been the Roman capital for oral reading. Then, with the invention of the book, came the glorification of the beautiful page as a work of love—"fine printing," in the Incunabula. Third was the invention of letter forms to serve silent reading. And fourth, the opposite, was the typeface that spoke in marketplace terms, to move goods and the minds of men. Now, Morris combined into a new kind of expression some elements of all the previous styles, in order to convey great literature with the potency of visual design. His work *uses* beauty to evoke a desired effect, not simply to grace a page. Morris found value and purpose in creative design and craftsmanship; the *art* of printing was reaffirmed to offset a natural tendency on the part of the machine to make printing more uniform and less human (and thus less meaningful).

Morris's first type, called Golden, was basically a revival of the first roman face—Jenson's. His later face, called Troy and Chaucer in its two sizes, was a revival (updated) of the Old English black letter or spire Gothic. By our standards, these are hardly great typefaces, but the Chaucer type did catch the spirit of the manuscript itself perfectly. This emphasized the primary importance of an appropriate typeface, and this idea became central in the whole

type, in black and red. 425 paper copies to be printed, at Twenty Pounds. 13 on vellum, of which 8 are for sale at 120 Guineas (7 of these have already been subscribed for). To be published by William Morris at the Kelmscott Press. Half holland. All paper copies sold.

Off one that was faire and fre,
And felle in his fighte;
His righte name was Percyvelle,

William Morris, with his Golden type (left) and Chaucer type revolution in typography. Henceforth, type had to be well designed and appropriate to its purpose, as well as highly legible.

Other private presses started up, not only in England, but in Europe and America. And in a short time the Morris message had reached his intended audience, the commercial printers.

From a practical standpoint the movement —as it developed after Morris—worked to encourage improvement in printing of all kinds, even and especially commercial printing, since all good printing is "evocative" while bad printing destroys the message. Good layout, good paper, good presswork, and especially a good type, were wanted, and ornate printing for the sake of "prettifying" a book was definitely out. Morris had made good printing a matter of public importance, giving every literate person a stake in knowing and appreciating type, paper, design and painstaking craftsmanship.

As his example permeated printing circles, at least at the higher levels, and made good printing important, it either caused or hastened the following effects:

It made type designers rethink their purposes, and create much better typefaces.

It made typefounders and typecasting matrix manufacturers likewise redirect their attention to quality typefaces, and create posts for full-time type designers, scholars of type and printing history, and articulate spokesmen for the best in printing.

It set art schools to including typography and graphic design as essential parts of their curricula.

Also the idea of evocative printing, as such, led directly to one new class and two new styles of typefaces:

PERSONAL STYLE

The first new style was based on the idea that an individual human touch is needed along with beauty and legibility. If a type designer is "in tune with the times," his faces will serve typography evocatively. The Personal Style, paradoxically, retained the basic letter forms and even the all-important quality of *im*personality that distinguishes a *type*face, but introduced personal variations,

Style: PERSONAL

AEGMRST
adegmpty

A book face, (1) often eclectic in letter forms, (2) with a freer-flowing line and more expressive serif treatment reflecting a human touch more than a tool; (3) and combining some essence of "its own day" with a feeling of "rightness" as a universal design. (Compare with new style and calligraphic style, on Page 64.) Faces in which the personal touch is too distracting for silent reading do not belong here. They are usually special [mannered] faces. Shown: *Goudy Modern.*

Class: Book Faces (Small Serifs)

including a freer flow of line, sometimes bordering on the calligraphic. (Some faces, of course, cross the border and do become calligraphic, introducing another class.)

Frederic W. Goudy (1865–1946), an American, was the first and perhaps greatest type designer in the Personal Style. Directly inspired by Morris—even to the point of maintaining his own private press, the Village Press—he became the first full-time type designer in history. In all, he cut some 125 faces, for ATF, then Lanston Monotype, and finally as an independent designer and founder at his Village Letter Foundery. He was a personal craftsman, combining beauty with function, an individual expressing himself as a human being against the pressures moving us towards an "ant society," working in the medium of printing because it is the art preservative of all the arts. He went back to the Renaissance for humanistic inspiration for many of his faces, and being a modest man, ruefully observed, "Those old fellows stole all our best ideas."

There was a time when more than half the advertisements in newspapers and magazines on any given day in the United States were set in some Goudy face. Obviously, Goudy was "in tune with the times." But after his death, "times changed," and his popularity

–A. Burton Carnes –©Monotype Co. Ltd. –Guillermo Rodrigues

GOUDY MORISON ZAPF

declined. Many of Goudy's faces have a timelessness about them, even so, and have gradually made a comeback.

Other Personal Style type designers paralleled or have followed Goudy. Among them are W. A. Dwiggins, Bruce Rogers, Jan Van Krimpen, Emil Rudolf Weiss, and Hermann Zapf. The last-named, still comparatively young, is turning out a prodigious number of typefaces himself.

NEW STYLE

Almost the reverse of the Personal Style, and in effect a reaction to it, the New Style is a letter form which seems to be made with tooled precision—but which even so avoids being mechanical, has a broad humanity about it, a nobility, with grandeur, dignity and permanence. Its tool is rather like that of the stone-cutter for incising lasting inscriptions. Given proper page design, with emphasis on the display sizes, this type style says that the message is of majestic importance, worth reading, worth preserving.

The prototype face is Perpetua, designed by Eric Gill in England in 1925. The face which gives New Style its name, however, is Times New Roman, cut in 1932 for *The Times* of London by the Monotype Corporation, under the direction of Stanley Morison. Conceived originally as a newspaper body face, its smaller sizes in particular have earned it great popularity in book work (as in the text of this volume, for instance) as well as in utility printing.

CALLIGRAPHIC ROMANS

The new type class consists of those roman faces which have gone beyond the limits of traditional type forms and legibility to convey the full feeling of hand-lettering and handwriting ("calligraphy"—beautiful writing) so that they cannot be considered standard typefaces, much less book faces. This does not make them any less beautiful or effective in other uses, however, and they have certainly enriched our typographic heritage in the past several decades.

Class: CALLIGRAPHIC

AEGMRST
adegmpty

Usually by intent rather than ineptness, these otherwise standard faces go beyond the strict (and somewhat cold) line quality of the true typeface to convey the feel of calligraphic lettering. (Distinguished also from cursive and [other] hand-letter styles, Page 68.) Shown: *Lydian.*

Category: Simulates (Special Faces)

Style: NEW STYLE

AEGMRST
adegmpty

A 20th-century style, austere and impersonal with clear but gradual differentiation between thick and thins, wide but short and unemphasized capitals, a large x-height, generally old-style stress in eclectically combined letter forms, smallish and quite sharply-cut (vs. expressive) serifs, and a hint of the authoritativeness of stone incising in its quality of line. Shown: *Perpetua.*

Class: Book Faces (Small Serifs)

CHAPTER 

The invention of the Typorama

In the early years of the 20th century, there were at least seven influences at work on type designers, and out of their interaction has come the "Typorama."

These were the influences:

- 19th century type-cutters had demonstrated that type does not have to tie itself down to any particular style.
- The pantographic cutting machine now allowed complete flexibility.
- Monotype and Linotype needed redesigned faces to fit their mechanical (width and kerning) requirements.
- A whole range of new printing processes brought different problems and requirements for type.
- In particular, a greater range of printing papers with different surfaces required different typefaces.
- The arbiters of taste in printing, at the higher levels at least, were becoming interested in better typefaces, as the result of the private press movement.
- Evocative printing had shown that a range of typefaces was needed because different ones had to be used to make different messages effective.

The type designers and manufacturers still had to make body type legible and familiar enough to avoid rejection for being too peculiar, but within those limits they were free to create new typefaces.

Morris and his followers were against the machine, because they thought beauty could come only out of handcraft. But the other side has won—at least to date. The pantographic punch-cutter allowed more designers to participate; talents were uncovered which could never have emerged if punch-cutting skill had been required along with design ability. Charm was not the only beauty, and beauty did not have to be built on a series of accidents—it could be created by genius, or at least talent, with direct intent, once the capabilities of the new machines were understood and employed. Where hand methods would inevitably limit production to small quantities at high prices, the new punch-cutting and type-casting machines with their limitless quantity at much reduced prices, brought new beauty to the whole public.

One spectacular victory for the machine came in the mid-20's, when British playwright and philosopher George Bernard Shaw, then a personage of godlike stature, refused to have his works set on the Monotype, as being inferior to hand-set. Shown two specimens, one hand and one Mono, he made a decisive choice—only to find that he had preferred the Mono, after all!

The new freedom added to the competition among manufacturing giants and created a tremendous profusion of typefaces. In time there came a conscious awareness of the Typorama—the idea that it is not only possible but very useful to offer designers and printers a whole range of faces at all times, from the thinnest to the fattest, from the earliest historical model to the latest *avant-garde*, from the plainest to the fanciest, in body sizes and display sizes.

To get this range, and to keep expanding it, national lines were crossed without regard, until type design and type production became fully universal. Today, we can print anything we can envision and put down on paper, limited only by the taste and skill of designers.

The idea may seem simple now, and we certainly take the result for granted. But it took almost 500 years of type production to bring this about.

THE TYPE REVIVALS

At first, the machine-composition manufacturers simply copied on to their matrices the typefaces then in use in hand type, just as the first printers copied hand letters for their typefaces. But continuing sales depended on constantly introducing *new* faces.

With a cue from William Morris's recutting of Jenson, the first big effort by the machine-composition manufacturers was to revive faces from the past, by cutting versions for the machine, rather than seek out wholly new designs (a much riskier business). The lead in revivals, however, was taken by ATF and Morris Benton (see Page 59), with Cloister, Bodoni and Garamond among others. Benton is perhaps the most prolific and neglected giant in type history.

But even reviving typefaces was something very unusual and new. The first and only important revival in history, except for Morris's Jenson face, had come in 1840, when Caslon, after its eclipse by Baskerville, was used again; it took 10 years to restore it to wide use among book publishers and jobbing printers. It was not until 1899 that Theodore Low De Vinne, a scholarly American printer, published "Plain Printing Types," the first work describing and classifying typefaces, thus giving some direction to the manufacturers and founding the present-day study of typefaces.

Goudy cut a display face, Forum Titling, in 1911 for Lanston Monotype, the first original machine-composition face based on ancient forms, in this case the stone inscriptions of Roman monuments:

FORUM

The first book face ever designed specifically for mechanical composition was Imprint, fundamentally a smoother and rounder version of Caslon. It was cut in 1912 by the English Monotype Works, especially for a new journal on printing art, *The Imprint*.

While the journal lasted only nine issues, it introduced 24-year-old Stanley Morison to the typographic world. He rapidly became the acknowledged leading scholar in the field, with enormous influence over typeface design and acceptance. In due course, he became typographic adviser to the Monotype Corporation, giving them a really breathtaking revival program based on very impressive historical research. (The British Monotype became a separate corporation from Lanston in 1931.)

Starting in 1922, with a recutting of the Jannon model called Garamond, Monotype's program has included Centaur (from Jenson's face), Poliphilus (Aldus's second face), Bembo (Aldus's first face), Plantin (16th century Dutch), Van Dijck (17th century Dutch), Ehrhardt (17th century German), Fournier (18th century French), Caslon, Baskerville, Bell and Fontana (18th century English), Scotch Roman (early 19th century English), Bodoni (early 19th century Italian), Walbaum (18th century French-German), New Clarendon (mid-19th century English), Century (late 19th century American), and Modern Extended (19th century English).

While these are revivals, they are not literal copies. The crudities of the originals (some say the charming variations) are gone. The new book faces are much more legible, and have a different effect than the originals —not necessarily worse or better, but reflecting modern needs and standards, and taking into account width requirements and

Style: UTILITY FACES

AEGMRST

adegmpty

A style keeping only the absolutely necessary elements of the letter (including the serifs) for maximum legibility and "workhorse" usefulness, with no pretensions to beauty or personal expressions. Stress is modern (vertical) but dazzling effect of Didot and Bodoni is avoided by making thick-thin contrasts moderate and gradual, with bracketed serifs somewhat blunt. Shown: *Cheltenham.*

Class: Bracketed (Strong Serifs)

Style: LEGIBILITY FACES

AEGMRST
adegmpty

Newspaper face for maximum legibility despite mechanical problems (high speed printing, cheap paper, runny ink blurring and filling in some faces) and reading handicaps (e.g., poor light on moving vehicles, failing eyesight of older persons). Thus, letters have large x-height; somewhat condensed but with open counter treatment; bracketed serifs strong but not dominant; no eccentricities; modest thick-thin contrast; vertical stress, generally modern style letter form. Shown: *Corona.*

Class: Clarity Faces (Small Serifs)

Style: READABILITY FACES

AEGMRST
adegmpty

These faces add a touch of grace or style to the legibility designs, to gain interest by freshness and life—call it motivation—for what may be lost in optical recognition as such. Also, generally they have more open white spaces to take prominence over the black lines as such, as with New Clarendons and New-Grots (see Page 71). Serifs usually slightly thinned. Shown: *Century Schoolbook.*

Class: Clarity Faces (Small Serifs)

the needs of modern papers and printing processes. It was natural for Monotype to concentrate on book faces, since book-setting is the ideal use for its process.

NEWSPAPER FACES

For newspaper work, Linotype is preferred since full-length slugs of metal are easier to handle under fast deadlines than separate letters. Linotype participated in the revival of classic faces, but concentrated instead on a line of newspaper faces called "the Legibility Group"—Ionic, Excelsior, Paragon, Textype and Opticon. (The rival Intertype developed similar faces in a "Flexibility Group"—Ideal, Rex and Regal.)

These faces were designed especially to meet the conditions of newspaper printing: they must not break when made into curved stereos from papier-mâché matrices; they had to withstand wear on high-speed presses; they had to avoid filling in the eye of the e, for instance, when pressing thin inks on to porous, rough newsprint. They had to provide the greatest possible legibility on the one hand, and the maximum in words per inch on the other. A new class of face!

NON-LATIN FACES

In recent years, especially, both Monotype and Linotype have put great effort into developing matrices for non-Latin alphabets. Monotype, for instance, now has matrices for some 200 alphabets around the world.

DISPLAY TYPE

The foundry-type manufacturers, painfully aware that their major customers—the big book publishers, magazines and newspapers—were not going to use hand-set type when they could use machine-setting, turned to creating the most intriguing styles of display type for the growing demands of advertisers.

They created at least two kinds of line—brush and stencil letters—and revived a

New Lines: Brush, Stencil

Two kinds of letter with a different "feel" came in during the 1930s—the brush and stencil styles. Brush strokes offer informality and an almost completely free line, so that some designs approach the illegible while others have led to new letter forms. Stencil allows a new way of breaking up strokes, leading to decorative faces such as Futura Black. Shown: *Brush* (left) and *Stencil.*

Style: ANTIQUE

AEGMRST
adegmpty

"Antiqua" is German term for roman letters; "antique" was first name for Egyptians, is still often used (especially in England) for all strong serifs. However, it can be delineated more precisely to cover strong-serif bracketed faces, with old-style thick-thins and (usually) slightly exaggerated beaked serifs and a normal weight somewhat heavier than book faces but used as such. Shown: *Bookman.*

Class: Bracketed (Strong Serifs)

group of other faces, primarily in display sizes, which led to a whole category of typefaces best called Residuals—faces which recapture the feeling of the best of the various pre-printing hands, the "residue" of all the early experimentation with letter forms. Besides this, the foundries continued to develop novelty display faces in imaginative variety.

Class: CURSIVES

AEGMRST
adegmpty

Covers all cursive or separately formed (and yet flowing) handwriting letter forms except italic, which is a separate special class. Besides the positive element of a flowing feeling is a negative one: joining or linking letters are not cursives, but scripts. Shown: *Lydian Cursive.*

Category: Residuals (Special Faces)

Class: HAND LETTER

AEGMRST
adegmpty

Technically, a skilled letterer can do by hand even a typeface letter; such a hand letter is called "built-up" or carefully filled in with many strokes and touches. Faces based on letters drawn the usual way, with one stroke for each stroke of the letter, constitute the Hand Letter class (except for the Calligraphic class, based on classic forms). Thus the Hand Letter is usually a free form, often with great individuality. Distinguished from Cursives and Scripts, hand *written* letters. Shown: *Studio.*

Category: Simulates (Special Faces)

The Morris evocative style carried to its literal extreme of using a typeface to create a mood, became popular for a time in the 20's as "allusive typography." Unusual typefaces could make a printed piece look like a historic period piece from, say, Araby or Ancient Greece. This, in turn, stimulated more and more exotic typefaces.

Class: SCRIPTS

AEGMRST
adegmpty

Class imitates handwriting of various styles; increasingly limited to letters which join or "link" to form continuous "writing." (Non-joining "written" letters are called cursives; see class box at left.) Many faces have cursive caps and script l.c. Shown: *Brush.*

Category: Simulates (Special Faces)

Style: GEOMETRIC SANS

AEGMRST
adegmpty

Here, letter forms are constructed geometrically, without personal touches as in Styled Sans Serif (see Box). Not really: letters are altered to meet optical illusion, but intent is to make letters *appear* geometric and uniform in pattern—to give unity to the typeface as a whole and thus avoid conflict in the eye from clashing different geometric shapes and proportions. Shown: *Futura Medium.*

Class: Modern Sans (Sans Serifs)

Style: STYLED SANS

AEGMRST
adegmpty

Advocates of a geometric sans serif urged a pure form but its first version was literally *styled*, meaning personal or faddish touches departing in different ways from strict geometric design. In Metro (shown above), note, for instance, slanted terminals in some letters but not in all, a non-geometric a as different from Futura a, a noticeable thinning of the short stroke of the y and the bar of the e. Shown: *Metro Bold.*

Class: Modern Sans (Sans Serifs)

MODERN SANS SERIF

In the mid-20's, a bold challenge was issued to the whole concept of classical type design and treatment. Carrying the idea of evocative printing to its logical (not literal) extreme, this movement, called the "New Typography," developed very emphatic ideas about how typeface and design can best express our modern technological period. In 1923, the Bauhaus, a German school of design, claimed that the modern style should be functional, based on the dynamics of machinery—movement, as opposed to the concepts of elements at rest. No frills, no elaboration of ancient ideas and traditions. Typefaces must be completely simplified to match modern tools and methods. The "New Typography" did away with such "frills" as serifs, with traces of the human hand, with thick and thin lines in typefaces, and (for a time at least) even with capital letters. (Actually, the revolt was more against the spire Gothic—at that time still the German standard type—and the German habit of capitalizing all nouns.)

abcdefghijklmn
opqrstuvwxyz

In 1925, Herbert Bayer in Germany took sans serif to the extreme. His "Universal type" was to serve *all* lettering purposes with the simplest, basic letter form—and without caps, since "we do not speak with a capital A and a small a." The innovation was not notably successful.

The movement prompted a new class of typefaces called "Modern Sans Serifs." Futura (with which you started this book) was one of the earliest—and the most successful.

The new idea was not so new, of course. The same point had been made in the 1850's to reflect the Industrial Revolution. In fact, sans serif goes back to the earliest lettering. The Kabel face (or Cable) was actually shown by Rudolf Koch, its designer, to have been derived from ancient Greece.

GREEK KOH KABEL KOH

The earlier sans serifs had not died out; on the contrary, they had gained permanent acceptance—still today called "grotesques" in England and much of Europe, and "gothics" in America.

Modern sans serif is more graceful than the grot-gothics, as it uses Roman pro-

Style: STRESSED SANS

AEGMRST
adegmpty

For all the recurrent popularity of sans serif faces, many designers have felt a need to make the class of letter more like the traditional roman forms. The first way this was done was by giving a stress—thick and thin contrast in lines—to the normally monotone or monoline sans serif letter, moving the structure and proportions of the letters somewhat toward classical roman forms. Shown: *Radiant Bold.*

Class: Romanized (Sans Serifs)

Style: SOFTENED SANS

AEGMRST
adegmpty

Another way of romanizing the sans serif letter (see Box, left) is the "softening" of the severe, often-mechanical lines of the sans faces. This is done by adding a touch of grace to the quality of line, and more specifically by flaring the terminals of the stems to suggest serif endings even though there are none. At the same time, the letters are given a basically roman shape and proportion, going beyond the Stressed Sans. Shown: *Optima.*

Class: Romanized (Sans Serifs)

portions and rounds. It certainly does reflect the times (in many aspects), fits well with modern architecture and abstract art,

Jakob Erbar started the modern sans serif vogue (Erbar, 1922), but England points to Edward Johnston's design in 1916 for the London Underground as the precurser, and Rudolph Koch in Germany (Kabel, 1927) and Eric Gill in England (Gill Sans, 1928) were the first fully-successful styled sans serif. Paul Renner's Futura (1927) was the first geometric sans serif.

and is by now considered a standard display face. But its supporters insisted on it for body type as well, and this is where the greatest controversy occurred. Opponents insisted it was not readable in large bodies of text, because the serif serves three functions —to cut down the reflection of light from around the letter into the reader's eye (halation), to link the letters in a word, and to help distinguish one letter from another. In this connection, note the problem of such a word as Illinois!

As T. M. Cleland put it, "Cutting the serifs off roman letters in the name of 'simplicity' may well be compared to simplifying a man by cutting off his hands and feet!"

The stark sans serifs have been softened, as early as 1927 in Middleton's Stellar and more recently (1958) in a face by Hermann Zapf, called Optima, which almost accomplishes the function of serifs for readability by thickening the ends of the letters:

OPTIMA

Nor is readability the only consideration: except for a few faces only technically sans serif, such as Optima, they are monotonous and non-human. Sans serif used exclusively gives the cold feel of an automated factory.

Style: NEW CLARENDONS

AEGMRST
adegmpty

A dominant recent theme in art—the relationship of one shape to another—has moved into typography increasingly since World War II, in a paradoxical way reversing prior emphasis on the shape of the letter's lines. Now, with quite subtle and sophisticated changes of the letter forms, emphasis is on the white space, to make it more powerful to the eye than the lines themselves, creating an excitement even while it achieves the harmony and unity a typeface needs to *be* a readable typeface. Clarendon was first to be reshaped. Shown: *Clarendon* (Haas).

Class: Bracketed (Strong Serifs)

Style: NEW-GROTESQUES

AEGMRST
adegmpty

The same new sophisticated and subtle emphasis on white space in the New Clarendons has been applied to the Grot-Gothics, the simple lines allowing great opportunity for opening up the counters and the space around the letters. One general effect has been widening—even squaring—of letters. (The geometric sans and the slab serifs have not yet been given the "new" treatment, perhaps because the geometric principles behind these letters seemingly do not allow even the subtle reshaping involved.) Shown: *Helvetica.*

Class: Grot-Gothics (Sans Serifs)

THE SLAB SERIFS

Some designers saw the strong serifs—particularly the slab-serif versions (such as Beton and Girder, the latter an apt name for the purpose) as equally expressive of the machine age—and better as the representative type style, since they do not have all the illegibility problems of the sans serifs.

Style: SLAB SERIFS

AEGMRST
adegmpty

Slab serifs, often confused with the English Egyptian style (and thus bearing Egyptian-sounding names), are really geometric sans serifs with a slab (unbracketed, geometric) serif added. Based on English Modern structure, Egyptians are as stressed as possible (often not much); slabs are completely monotone or monoline except in a very few unavoidable junctions in the heavier weights. Sometimes called square serifs, though not all slabs *are* square. Shown: *Memphis Bold.*

Class: Unbracketed (Strong Serifs)

They proved particularly useful for adaptation into typewriter faces, to equalize the width of letters, and the way the typewriter in turn made them familiar to the eye helped to establish them as standard faces.

As it turned out, they seemed to be a compromise that neither side wanted.

However, the occurrence of fads and cycles in the use of typefaces is becoming increasingly pronounced. What holds true today in type taste can be overturned tomorrow—at least for awhile—and long-despised faces become popular again.

In any event, with the invention of the Typorama, we are no longer limited in our choice of typeface, for the next fad or for any distinctive use. And, we have a tradition that can welcome new designs without the kind of battle that broke Baskerville's heart.

Or so it is to be hoped! This book introduces a new "upstroke" principle: what is good for the hand may not be good for the eye. Based on handwriting, typefaces have a heavy downstroke. But this pulls the eye down in reading. Heavy *up*strokes (in small serif faces) would let the eye skip along more easily on the *top* of letters. The first printed book use of the upstroke letter is the M logotype on the title page of this book.

CHAPTER R

The invention of cold type

QUEER AS IT MAY SEEM, after such a wealth of type had been developed, the next steps in printing progress threaten to eliminate type entirely.

For hundreds of years, printing had consisted solely of pressing a piece of type against paper. During the 1930's, however, an entirely different printing principle was perfected called photo-offset, photolithography, or more familiarly "offset" or "litho," which can supplant type.

The idea is old: lithography was invented in 1796 and photography in 1824, and almost from the beginning there were efforts to combine the two. Lithography makes printing possible by the fact that oil and water do not mix (see p. 46). In the modern system, an image is transferred by a photographic system on to a flat metal plate that is chemically treated so that printing parts of the surface will attract oil (printing ink) whereas the non-printing parts will pick up water as separate inked and water-wetted rollers pass over the plate. Then paper stock is pressed against the plate and takes off the ink to make a print.

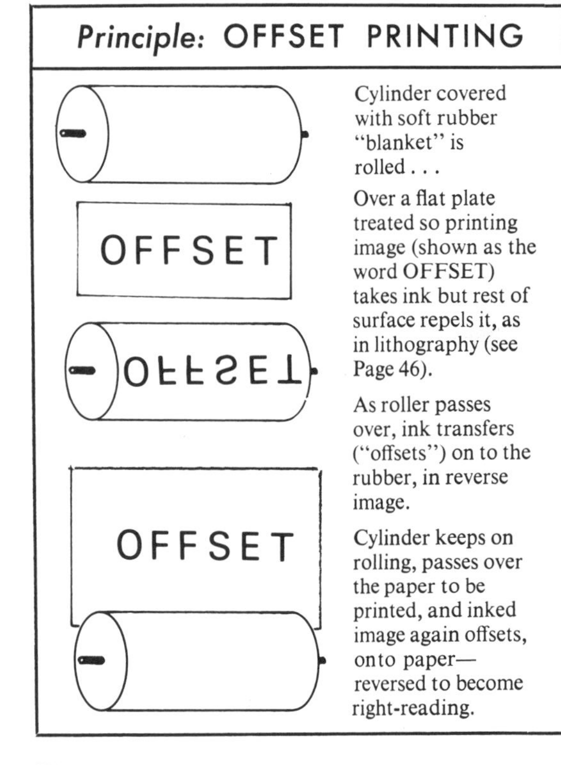

Principle: OFFSET PRINTING

Cylinder covered with soft rubber "blanket" is rolled . . .

Over a flat plate treated so printing image (shown as the word OFFSET) takes ink but rest of surface repels it, as in lithography (see Page 46).

As roller passes over, ink transfers ("offsets") on to the rubber, in reverse image.

Cylinder keeps on rolling, passes over the paper to be printed, and inked image again offsets, onto paper—reversed to become right-reading.

However, this takes pressure, and paper is rougher and more abrasive than you might think, so the photographic image would be worn off after a few impressions. Therefore, a soft rubber blanket is rolled over the inked plate and then over the paper. This blanket takes the ink from the plate without much pressure and with no wear, then "offsets" or prints the ink on to the paper, again with no wear.

What is important from our point of interest here, typefaces, is that anything can be printed by offset which can be photographed. This means that a handwritten message, a typewritten sentence, or a piece of previously printed matter (say, a newspaper clipping or a map) can be copied and printed exactly. Printed letters can be cut out of a newspaper, for instance, pasted to form a particular heading across a typewritten page—and the whole thing can be printed as though both were truly type.

This is called "cold type," to differentiate it from true printing type, which is made from molten (very *hot*) metal.

Offset printing, which has in many ways proved more versatile, simpler and cheaper than letterpress printing, especially in reproducing illustrations, has also made cold-type production an important part of the printing industry. In fact, giving matters a reverse twist, the advantages of cold type have proved so great that letterpress manufacturers have now invented ways to use cold type in producing new kinds of raised-letter plates.

INGENIOUS MACHINES

The first cold-type processes were for display sizes of lettering or type, as obviously these were easier to handle. The usual way was for a phototype maker to get "proofs" or prints of type and photograph them, so as to have negatives of each letter in the alphabet in stock. Then a photographic print of a word could be made to the desired size, and this print could be pasted down as "copy" for the plate-making camera.

From this, it took just a few ingenious steps for a machine to be invented that could also reshape the letters in various ways—make them grow taller or shrink, stretch out or squeeze up, curve, taper off into perspective, or slant forwards or backwards to any angle, change a straight line into a wavy line, etc., in an amazing variety of ways. There are perhaps more different cold-type processes than hot-metal processes today.

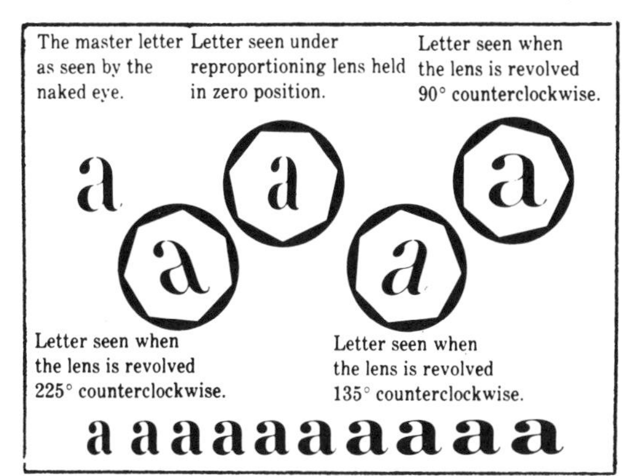

You will recognize that the photographic squeezing and stretching can create new letter forms that are, in effect, additional family members of a typeface. Trick photography, then, is a truly potent tool for creating typefaces: thus one can make a literally infinite number of family variants, and broaden the Typorama considerably.

But this is not all that machines can do: Give them any kind of hand-lettering and they can make a set of negatives of the alphabet for photo-setting—in other words, instant typeface matrices. In fact, they have made many thousands of new "typefaces" in just a few years, perhaps as many as were created in the whole history of metal type.

Similar development, but not yet quite so bizarre, has occurred in body-size type composition. The manufacturers of hot-metal typecasting composition machines—Monotype, Linotype, and Intertype—along with new competitors are now also making photo-setters which use negatives instead of moulds. They turn out copy for platemaking either in strips or sheets on paper or in photographic negative form. That is, they produce letters that look exactly like type without use of metal type.

At the start, they used the standard typefaces for their photographic designs, again reminiscent of the first printers using hand letters to copy, and the composing machine makers first copying foundry faces. Gradually they are making improvements in these typefaces. For instance, they can fit letters together better, and can handle the kerning problem more easily. Thus the reworked faces continue to grow (see Page 58). Also, new "typefaces" are being designed especially for photosetters and computers.

SOME INTERESTING QUESTIONS

Naturally, all this has raised some interesting questions. Letterpress printers are reluctant to call the photo-set alphabets "typefaces." But just because printing can now be done without a piece of metal type, would it not be ironic, to say the least, to refuse to call a photo-set letter a typeface, especially if the original face has been improved thereby?

However, there *is* an opposite extreme: a hasty scrawl made into a set of negatives is not a typeface and a typewriter face does not suddenly become a true typeface because it can be used for cold composition.

Snobbery aside, some lovers of type as an art form and an efficient means of communication are truly worried to think what the floods of photo-copied "typefaces" and their distortions will do to our painfully built-up heritage of true type design. In all the welter of bad, untested, and fleetingly popular cold-type alphabets, how can good typefaces—old and new—be recognized and preserved?

One answer, of course, lies in books like this. If a broad public educational campaign can be launched with perhaps some direct attention in the schools, our true type heritage can be saved. The movement has so far been left in the hands of the old-line typefounders and the composition-machine manufacturers, and a few schools of design, with the help of printing hobbyists and private printers. The ranks are growing by the thousands as the printing hobby spreads. But, there is a long way to go when most people do not know one typeface from another, and would guess (as you probably did when you started this book) that Baskerville, Bodoni and Garamont are names of towns.

Many cold-type operations are now being performed by persons without a background in printing and type, coming to their jobs from photographic or other training. They use different terms, and usually measure in inches (or millimeters) instead of printer's points. They often use different names for the parts of a letter form, and for the typefaces themselves (because of commercial limitations on use of the original names).

SOME NEW TERMS

"Cold type" has come to mean so many things that professionals have evolved a set of more specific terms:

Photo-composition (U.S.) or *film-setting* (England): Primarily for justified text, i.e., complete messages set in continuous lines of desired width, with proper spacing between words and lines. Keyboard control (increasingly computerized) of fonts of alphabets on film masters produces the "matter" on film or paper for further processing.

Electronic composition: As above, except formed electronically instead of photographically.

Photo-lettering: Primarily for display matter, in separate letters, words or lines. Hand positioning of separate letters from film master font, spaced as desired by operator, produces copy on film or paper as above. Letters can be any size, shape, slant, etc., as required, from same masters.

Transfer lettering: Generally for same purpose as photo-lettering. Individual user himself applies on to paper, where he wishes, separate pre-printed letters either adhesive-backed for affixing or chemically treated to rub off (as with a decal) on to the paper. Such letters, of course, keep their original size and shape.

Strike-on or *impact composition:* Messages produced on paper by typewriters for photographic copying and plate-making.

CHANGES IN TERMINOLOGY

Some cold-type enthusiasts insist that the whole printing terminology ought to be changed. For instance, they say, what is the use of learning the sizes in a printer's series—6, 7, 8, 9, 10, 12, 14, 18, 24, 30, 36, 48 and 72 points—when photo-setting can respond to inches just as easily? Moreover, they point out, the size of the body of the metal type itself, which is what the printer's point-size stands for, is almost always larger than the size of the face on that piece of type—the whole thing is "old-fashioned." The adoption of the metric system is strengthening the argument; millimeters are likely to be used.

In the same way, widths and weights can be varied almost infinitely. Edward Rondthaler, one of the real pioneers of the cold-type field, reacting to the confusion of meaning for "bold," "condensed," etc., once suggested a grid with 2,300 different coded weight-width combinations as a cold-type standard.

Yet, it is quite clear that the present system of points and general terminology makes sense and is efficient for hot-metal production—and that printing from hot type will continue for some time to come. As for small-scale printing, hobbyists are increasing in such numbers as to ensure that metal type will never die, despite the commercial inroads of offset.

Furthermore, there is good evidence that knowing the traditional heritage of one's work will help anyone substantially, and this is especially true in typography, where such subtle historic differences have continuing meaning and importance. Even though the new users of "type" may know it only for cold setting and not in its original form, the heritage of usefulness, beauty and taste is still in the design as reproduced. It will be more than ironic—it will be disastrous—if the newest invention to enrich that heritage is surrendered to "know-nothings" who will proceed in their ignorance to destroy the delicate but priceless tool that is our time-tested Typorama.

CHAPTER 

Toward a reinvention?

REAL CHANGES in the basic patterns of the letters of our alphabet—as distinct from style changes which the last several chapters covered—last occurred in the 16th century, when the scripts were developed. A question being raised increasingly today is whether our form of alphabet is really good and useful, an efficient way to convey our language. Some educators think that it has too many letter forms (others say not enough), that in some instances letters are so similar as to cause confusion, that there is no consistent relationship between the letters and their sounds—that, in short, spelling and reading (and therefore both childhood happiness and later adult careers) are being needlessly hampered.

One of the most forceful proponents of a new alphabet was George Bernard Shaw. He left in his will a sizeable sum of money to sponsor the creation of a more phonetic alphabet for all the nuances of the English language. A new alphabet of 22 vowels and 26 consonants, conceived by Kingley Read, won the prize over 450 other entries:

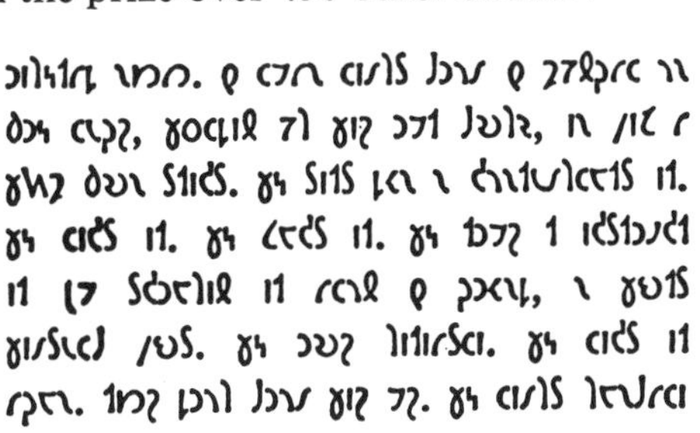

But Shaw was far from the first. Trissino, an Italian author and poet, who made his printers use u and v as distinctly separate letters, for the first time, wanted in 1524 to add some Greek letters to the alphabet. And as early as 1578, Honorat Rambaud wanted to substitute the following for the Latin alphabet:

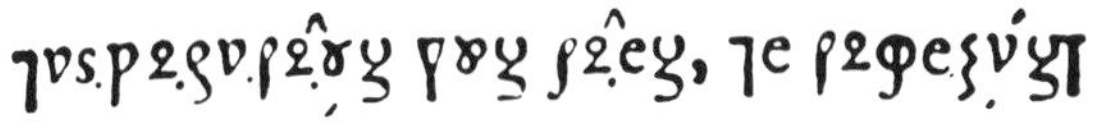

Here are some others as traced by David Abercrombie in *The Monotype Recorder* (Vol. 42, No. 4, Winter 1962–63):

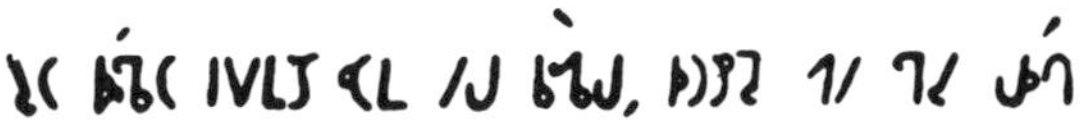

Robert Robinson (c. 1617)

Isaac Pitman (1843)

John Wilkins (1668)

A. M. Bell (1867)

Even Benjamin Franklin, a printer who invented many things, tried his hand at some new letters for the alphabet, the one at the left being for the ng sound as in singing, and the other for the sh as in hush:

For phonetic purposes, as guides in dictionaries, etc., there have long been special letters and symbols, some of them formed by turning existing letters upside down. Three of these have become quite popular in new Latinized writing of African languages:

ɛ ɔ ŋ

A quite different approach is being tried now not only in England, where it originated, but in the United States. This is the Pitman Augmented Alphabet (P.A.A. for short in England and ITA for Initial Teaching Alphabet in the U.S.). Nineteen new characters, based on the standard letter forms, have been added to the standard lower-case alphabet. The new letters keep some resemblance, but are made deliberately differ-

PITMAN ALPHABET

æ b c d ee f g h ie j k l m n œ p r
r s t ue v w y z z wh ch th th sh ʒ
ŋ a a a au e i o u ω ω ou oi

wee ar proud too preesent the pitman i.t.a. in ehrhardt. eech letter has oenly wun sound, and caps ar simply larjer verʒunz of the loewer caes.

ent enough to be clearly apparent to small children.

After the child has learned to read with these letters, he is switched over to standard English letters. The backers of P.A.A. (and of competing systems) claim the results are better than expected, but interest has faded.

A system using new symbols for phonetic purposes, making spelling largely phonetic, was introduced in 1963 by Lucian Bernhard, designer of many typefaces and often considered the "father of the modern poster." It included not only the usual European-language marks, such as the umlaut (ü), the circumflex (ô), the reversed circumflex (ǒ), the macron (ē) and the tilde (ã), but it had also these special new letters, among others:

t g s c

The new t was for th as in the, to distinguish from the th in porthole. The new g was for digit, as distinct from dig it. The new s was for sh, as in sugar and not as in dishearten. The c was for the French derived chic as distinct from chick. Here is how the alphabet looks in use:

Ter is no sûch ting as an exákt fuulpruuf rekórding of spiich-sounds on peper

This has not yet had a notable success either.

Still another kind of alphabet is being worked out, but for a different reason: the need for letters which are clearly distinguishable to an electronic scanning

ABCDEFGHIJKLMNOPQR
STUVWXYZ1234567890

machine. Here is an experimental alphabet created in 1965 by R. C. Miller of Bell Laboratories, New York. (His S is at top of Page 75.)

Readers of this book will recognize substantial reasons why none of these new alphabets have yet been successful in supplanting or even really augmenting the Latin letters—the most important reason being that type's key use is for silent reading, and this has little to do (once learned) with the phonetic sounds the reformers want to capture in print. Conversely—and perhaps exasperatingly!—the phonetic alphabets get more complicated to the eye the more they serve the ear.

But no one should be too sure that the reasons will hold indefinitely, or that some new solution cannot solve the problems. In fact, who is to say that *you*, now that you have an interest in what is certainly an important matter, may not some day invent that solution yourself?

Style: BIFORMS

PEIGNOT TYPOGRAPHIE

MONALPHABET

Biforms are alphabets with caps and l.c. (normal or eccentric) of equal weight and height so they can be mixed at will in any given word. They were inspired by Peignot, a French experiment; by Bayer's Universal alphabet; by increasing use of "alternative characters" in typefaces to add creative differences to printed pieces, and by "monalphabet" suggestions by Bradbury Thompson in the U.S.

Class: Experimental

GETTING DOWN TO CASES

CHAPTER

Classification of typefaces

STUDYING the fine differences among typefaces is much easier if you use a general classification system.

The plan of the first part of the book, therefore, was to give you enough classification (into Standard and Special faces) to get you started through the historic development that changed our letter forms. Then in Part II you were introduced to various kinds of typefaces (including important specific styles, as they were invented) through the entire Typorama—and perhaps even a little bit into the future!

Now you are at the point where you understand the reasons why different faces were developed, and have a feel for different forms of typefaces. You are ready to put all the pieces together into a general classification system.

The key to the whole thing remains the same as at the beginning level: all typefaces were developed for definite purposes.

CATEGORY

In this classification system, faces serving one great purpose or a number of big related purposes are called a "category." As you will see below, the Small Serif faces are one category because they basically serve the one general purpose of silent reading, while the Strong Serif faces are another category, because generally they are not used for silent reading but for utility printing, advertising, promotion, etc.

CLASS

Within each of these categories, there is a second level—a "class"—into which typefaces are divided because they serve separate and specific purposes. Faces which meet a particular purpose tend to have the same general appearance, or at least the same general set of design characteristics. As designers say, "form follows function."

STYLE

Obviously, however, all the typefaces in a given class are not *exactly* alike; on the contrary, there can be dozens or hundreds of very subtle variations within a class—and that is how we get those 10,000 different typefaces in the Typorama. Human talent and ingenuity have worked out slightly different forms to serve the same purpose. These different faces tend to group into a third level of classification, what we have been calling "style" throughout the book. Categories and classes are divided by purposes, but styles are divided according to the different design and lettering techniques that form basically the same general letter shape. Reworked faces (see Page 58) often create new styles.

HELP FOR BEGINNERS

This will be clear to you as you examine the following chart, samples and descriptions. Just a few minutes of study, based on what you have already learned in this book, can show you the relationship of all the categories, classes and styles so clearly that you will soon have the basic knowledge for tracking down virtually any typeface and determining its name and characteristics.

You should know that this classification system is "new" at least in part. In the Standard faces, the styles as listed and described are in most instances those now used by printers and designers. (There is no system on which all agree.) But in making the major division in the first place, between Standard and Special faces, and in the way these faces are divided into classes by function, the system described in this book is new. Years of testing indicate quite strongly that this classification system can help a beginner find a way through a very confused multitude of all kinds of different typefaces.

The full Typorama chart is on the next page. On it, you will also find the most recent "professional" classification system.

The TYPORAMA

STANDARD FACES

SMALL SERIFS

Book Faces

Nuanced

Venetian [*Humanist*]*
Old Style [*Garalde*]
Transitional [*Transitional*]
Personal Style

Regularized

French Modern [*Didone*]
English Modern [*Didone*]
New Style

Clarity Faces

Readability Faces
Legibility Faces

STRONG SERIFS

[*Slab Serifs*]

Bracketed Faces

Antiques
Clarendons
New Clarendons
Utility Faces

Unbracketed Faces

Egyptians
Slab Serifs

SANS SERIFS

[*Lineale*]

Grot-Gothics

Grotesques [*Grotesques*]
New-Grotesques [*Neo-Grotesques*]

Modern Sans Serifs

[*Geometric*]
Geometric Sans Serifs
Styled Sans Serifs

Romanized

[*Humanist*]
Stressed Sans Serifs
Softened Sans Serifs

SPECIAL FACES

RESIDUAL FACES

Roman Capitals

[*Graphic*]
Square Capitals
Rustic Capitals

Cursives

[*Script*]
Humanistic Cursives
Gothic Cursives

Italics [*Italic*]

Unrelated Italics
Related Italics
Matched Italics

Uncials

[*Graphic*]
Calligraphic Uncials
Sans Serif Uncials

Spire Gothics

[*Graphic*]
Textura
Schwabacher
Fraktur
Rotunda
Freeformed

National Hands

Irish
Latin Half-Gothics
Lombardic

NON-LATINS

Foreign Scripts

Finger-Touch

Braille

MANNERED FACES

Special-Form Faces

Altered Extenders
Backslant
Biforms
Chamfered
Concave
Convex
Foreign Face
Interlocking
Non-Aligned
Over-Condensed
Over-Expanded
Overhanging
Rounded
Slanted Variants [*Italic*]
Squared
Thickened

Special-Ending Faces

Copperplates
Flanged
Flared
French Antique [*Slab Serifs*]
Swashed
Tuscan
Wedge Serif [*Glyphic*]

Special-Weight Faces

Blacks
Thins

Treated Line

Actioned
Antiqued
Feathered
Rimpled
Rugged
Varied Line

Reshaped

Curved
Distorted
Monogramed
Perspectived

ADAPTEDS

Decoratives

Enhanced

Embellished
Filigreed
Floriated
Foliated
Ornamented

Initials

Lined [*Inline*]

Chased
Inline
Rimmed

Pictorial

Materiel
Motif

3-Dimensional

Beveled [*Shadow*]
Drop-Shadow
Incised [*Glyphic*]
Outerlined
Projected
Raised
Ribboned
Shadowed
Textured
Tooled or Engraved
Whitetop

Changed-Color Faces

White Letter

Open [*Outline*]
Outline [*Outline*]
Reversed
Shaded [*Inline*]

Toned

Hatched
Patterned
Ruled [*Inline*]
Screened
Two-color

Constructs

SIMULATES

Calligraphic

[*Graphic*]
Sans-Serif
Small-Serif

Hand Letters

[*Graphic*]
Formal Pen
Informal Pen
Formal Brush Ltr.
Informal Brush Ltr.
Freehand Brush Ltr.
Roundball Letter

Scripts

[*Script*]
Ronde
Engravers Script
Commercial Script
Social Script
Informal Pen
Freehand Pen
Informal Brush Script
Freestyle Brush Script
Roundball Script

Imitatives

Engraving
Lithographic
Stencil [*Inline*]
Typewriter
Woodcut

NEWFORMS

Experimental

Monalphabets
Phonetic Alphabets

Non-Optic

Magnetic
Scannals

ABOUT THIS CHART . . .
Here at a glance is the whole classification of the Typorama, starting with the primary divisions in Standard and Special faces (see Page 10), and then distinguishing among the nine categories, 30 classes and some 125 styles, as explained on Page 77. In the following pages, each category and class is described briefly, to fix its role in the Typorama, and each of the styles named is shown in a typeface of that style.

ABOUT THE NAMES IN BRACKETS . . .
*Terms bracketed in italics are categories in the classification system known as the British Standard, based on Maximilien Vox's system of 1954 now widely used in Europe with minor variations. It is also moving into the U.S. As this page shows, the system is far from complete or even systematic—and is quite bewildering to beginners, who need it most.

STANDARD FACES

These are described under their class headings, and then the major styles of each class are shown by a representative face.

SMALL SERIFS

This category of faces resulted from the invention of silent reading, the need for typefaces which would not get in the way of the "mind's eye" moving across the page.

BOOK FACES. As the title of this class indicates, these faces were developed directly for use in setting the "body matter" or "text" of books, although in the display sizes some of them have found other important uses. Hermann Zapf suggests two sub-classes:

1. *Nuanced.* There are subtle variations among the letters, their combination creating a warm, live texture.

Venetian Old Style
Transitional
Personal Style

2. *Regularized.* All letters are uniform in basic characteristics, giving a rigid, austere or mechanical feel.

French Modern
English Modern
New Style

CLARITY FACES. These are designed to be even more readable than the usual book faces, and to meet difficult mechanical printing problems such as "runny" ink on newsprint at high speed.

Readability Faces
Legibility Faces

STRONG SERIFS

These faces meet the need for strong, contrasting, differently-designed type to serve varied styles of printing—yet plain and straightforward enough to be useful in almost any kind of printing without looking peculiar, at least in their medium weights.

BRACKETED FACES. These are the faces which retain a style link with old style faces.

Antiques Utility Faces
Clarendons
New Clarendons

UNBRACKETED FACES. These represent a break toward a more "modern" or mechanical look and feel.

Egyptians
Slab Serifs

SANS SERIFS

Like the Strong Serifs, this category developed in the 19th century from display faces and proved useful for a whole range of printing purposes, especially those considered to need "contemporary" treatment.

GROT-GOTHICS or GROTESQUES. Exclusively in America, these are called "gothic." But in recent years, with the New-Grot style, even Americans have begun calling the class by its European and English name.

Grotesques
New-Grotesques

MODERN SANS SERIFS. This class is the one designed to serve "our contemporary functional society."

Geometric Sans Serifs
Styled Sans Serifs

ROMANIZED. This class is intended to serve between the serifed faces and the starker sans serifs, by adopting most of the characteristics of the serifed faces except the serifs themselves. The purpose is to add grace and human warmth, and in some faces to improve legibility.

Stressed Sans Serifs
Softened Sans Serifs

SPECIAL FACES

The typefaces in this division turn out to be quite easy to separate, too—probably even more than the Standard faces—because each is designed to serve a clear-cut special purpose. Once you know what that special intention is, you can put the typeface in its right place. *Note:* the designer or printer is *not* limited to using the typeface in this particular way.

RESIDUAL FACES

This category is based on the hand-lettering styles of the pre-printing era. Through the centuries they have come to be identified with special feelings, moods and meanings.

ROMAN CAPITALS. This class covers faces which reflect or imitate the hand lettering of ancient Rome.

SQUARE CAPITALS
RUSTIC CAPITALS

CURSIVES. This class reflects the principles, at least, of true cursive handwriting of pre-printing days, with non-joining letters as distinct from the continuous lines of script.

Humanistic Cursive
Gothic Cursive

ITALICS. This class, akin to the cursives in many ways, is often not considered separately, because almost every italic face is identified with some specific type family. The special function of the italics, as developed through the years, is to provide emphasis, grace, harmonious contrast and marked-off matter (as an introduction is marked off from the main text).

Unrelated Italics
Related Italics
Matched Italics

UNCIALS. These are the revivals or modern versions of the writing hand developed in the Dark Ages for Bibles and other revered literature.

CALLIGRAPHIC UNCIALS
SANS SERIF UNCIALS

SPIRE GOTHICS. This class is the Black Letter which became the major hand for much of Europe in the centuries before printing, and which still has special uses in religious printing, diplomas, etc.

Textura Schwabacher
Fraktur Rotunda
Freeformed

NATIONAL HANDS. This class covers those hands which were developed in the particular countries or regions whose names they bear, when the Roman hands were combined with local tastes and styles.

IRISH, GAELIC OR ERSE
LOMBARDIC
Latin Half-Gothics

MANNERED FACES

This category includes faces based on Standard faces, but given a special additional characteristic to make them more effective as display lines, or to convey a special mood or tone as body type, usually by calling attention to themselves.

SPECIAL FORM FACES. This class of typeface achieves its uniqueness by what has been done to the parts or elements of the design, as the style names indicate.

Squared **Rounded**
Altered Extenders **Non-Aligned**
THICKENED **CHAMFERED**
Slanted Variants Convex
Backslant CONCAVE

Over-Condensed OVER-EXPANDED

foreign face BIFORMS

INTERLOCKING

OVERHANGING

For Distorted style see "mangled" faces, P. 45

SPECIAL ENDING FACES. In this class, the serifs, finials or terminals are designed to create an unusual effect in the face as a whole.

Swashed WEDGE

COPPERPLATE

FLARED Flanged

French Antique TUSCAN

SPECIAL WEIGHT FACES. These faces go to extremes in their thickness or thinness.

Blacks Thins

TREATED LINE. This class covers faces which suggest tone or mood by the change in the quality of line.

Antiqued **Rugged**

Feathered

ACTIONED

VARIED LINE

RIMPLED *(does not show well in small sizes)* → R

RESHAPED. Faces which have been changed as indicated:

SIMULATES

This category is intended deliberately to simulate or imitate non-type lettering, such as freehand lettering, typewriting, etc.

CALLIGRAPHIC. The intended effect of this class is a "hand" quality of line.

Small-Serif Sans-Serif

HAND LETTERS. The class includes other faces which clearly are in imitation of letters not basically designed for letterpress printing.

Formal Pen Informal Pen

Formal Brush Letter

Informal Brush Letter

Freehand Brush Letter

ROUNDBALL LETTER

SCRIPTS. As the name indicates, these faces are intended to imitate handwriting, in continuous lines of joining letters.

Engravers Script *Social Script*

Commercial Script *Ronde*

Informal Pen *Freehand Pen*

Informal Brush Script

Freestyle Brush Script

Roundball Script

IMITATIVES. These are intended to imitate letters which are duplicated by some mechanical means other than usual printing:

STENCIL **Woodcut**

Typewriter

Engraving

Lithographic

ADAPTEDS

This category includes those faces purposely made decorative, or given some special shape, or otherwise *changed* in a noticeable way from the ordinary form of type.

DECORATIVES. Here is a class which includes a great variety of treatments of the face, and of the space inside the face (the counters) as well as around the outside of the typeface; it has so many, in fact, that it divides into sub-classes first.

1. *Enhanced.* This sub-class includes those faces which are given "something extra" to make them "fancy," or quaint, etc.

Embellished
Filigreed
FOLIATED
FLORIATED
ORNAMENTED

2. *Initials and capitals.* These are specially decorated or treated typefaces, such as those in the chapter headings in this book, for spot emphasis or decoration.

INITIALS

3. *Lined.* These are faces treated with white lines *not* representing depth (as in 3-D faces) or white or toned letters (see below).

RIMMED CHASED
INLINE

4. *Pictorial.* A sub-class of faces which are decorated or otherwise involved with recognizable pictures or symbolic themes.

Materiel
MOTIF

3-DIMENSIONAL. In this class, the letters are designed to give a feeling of depth (or height) to letters and the printed sheet, or to twist the letters to make them jut out.

Shadowed Tooled
Drop-Shadow
OUTERLINED BEVELED
RAISED
Ribboned
INCISED Textured
PROJECTED
WHITETOP

CHANGED-COLOR FACES. The usual "black" typeface is made a "white letter" (defined by black around it) or a "toned" gray. Toning is by "screening" (fine lines or dots, sometimes called "shaded"); "ruling" (heavier, smooth lines); "hatching" (somewhat coarser lines, as though drawn or scratched); use of patterns, e.g., stipple effect, or by literally printing in two colors using differing pieces of type. Many 3-D faces are basically white. (Note: black and white are colors here, *not* related to spire gothic black letter or "white letter" used early to contrast lighter roman.)

REVERSED
Outline Open TWO
Shaded TWO
Screened HATCHED
RULED PATTERNED

CONSTRUCTS. Designs which are not really faces but rather elements with which the designer or printer can make his own letters.

NEWFORMS

This category of letter forms includes those intended as experiments for improving legibility, capturing the spirit of new eras, or meeting needs of new devices, such as computer scanners, etc.

EXPERIMENTAL. Faces which attempt to improve the basic alphabet for easier reading, better phonetics, etc.

MONALPHABETS

fonétik

NON-OPTIC. This class includes basically roman letters and figures not intended, at least primarily, for reading by the human eye.

1 2 3 4 5 6 7 8 9 0 MAGNETIC

SCANNALS

FINGER-TOUCH. A class of letters which uses perforating type or raised surfaces to serve the blind.

B R A I L L E

Black dots represent raised points "read" by the blind's finger touch

NON-LATINS

In this category are faces intended to serve languages which do not use at least the basic Latin alphabet.

FOREIGN SCRIPTS. Here, "script" is used in a much broader sense to cover all alphabets and styles of the world's languages. A *class* of face to Latin-alphabet users, in each language they may represent a whole Typorama range of standard and special faces. (Printers also call them "exotics.")

• • • the Typorama

Here, then is the Typorama of available faces in a simple classification system which opens the way to studying the more subtle distinctions that give typefaces their particular tone, feel or effect. Not all typefaces fit neatly in one class or even style, precisely because the designer intends to merge two different faces to get a needed or unusual new combination. So, you will find some borderline cases.

After you have studied the various groupings a bit, draw back and try to take an over-all look at the picture. You will perhaps make a remarkable discovery about all the "confusion." You will find that there really is some sense to the total Typorama after all—and that we have been given a quite logical and complete collection of typefaces to serve our different needs, purposes and tastes.

But, of course, the Typorama still grows. Perhaps *you* will add to it some day.

THE 'LAY' OF THE CASE

A standard arrangement or "lay" is used to store type in the cases (see "L. C." box on p. 22). Today, smaller fonts of both caps and l.c. are generally combined in a so-called California case, shown here. Note that important l.c. letters are grouped together to save motions in setting.

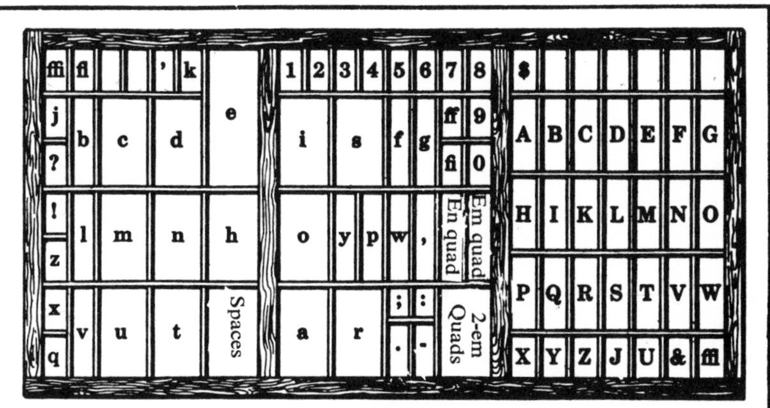

Cap "lay" still shows origin of alphabet: note J, U are at bottom of case, right, not in order, because they were brought into common use long after the lay itself was developed.

CHAPTER U

Best face forward: choosing a suitable type

"Printing should be invisible."

In a speech in 1932, Beatrice Warde dramatically restated the principle underlying silent reading and gave the present generation its highest standard. Mrs. Warde made it clear she meant this principle to apply to display type as well: what held for books was even more true for advertising. "Type well used is invisible *as* type." But type directors and art directors have insisted almost the opposite—that display type should have visual impact and excitement. They have put billions of advertising money on the line to carry out their conviction that a printed piece has first of all to attract attention to itself, then set the tone, support the message, and help create action because, after all, advertising exists to get results.

"The mental eye focuses *through* type and not *upon* it," so that any type which has excess in design, anything that "gets in the way of the mental picture to be conveyed, is a bad type," was Mrs. Warde's answer to that. So the battle was joined.

In between are many shades of difference. Some who lean towards the Invisible school nevertheless continue to hold to the principle of evocative typography, that carefully selected typefaces can set a tone and enhance the message, thus giving it extra potency and effect. In the middle, perhaps, are those who agree on Invisibility where a *mental* picture is involved, but who see many psychological purposes that can be served by using typefaces in a startling, shocking or even irritating way, because man is prompted by emotional and sensory forces as well.

Carrying this last point to a positive approach, some creative individualists believe that printing can be its own justification as an art form, its own kind of self-expression for the artist-printer. Their problem, therefore, is finding the faces they need to do this.

The question boils down, then, by no coincidence, to precisely the same one that controls the design of different typefaces in the first place—the purpose for which the face is intended. No complete catalogue of different purposes has been compiled, but these are among the most important ones:

- attract readers to a message
- duplicate and preserve the message
- encourage the reading of the message
- set the tone or mood of the message
- facilitate and guide the reading
- enhance the reading, by the subconscious setting of beauty, excitement, lushness, historic touch, or whatever may help
- reinforce the message
- prompt the reader to action

The problem is thus to find a suitable typeface for the particular job, one that will do all these things in the appropriate style and at the same time meet the technical requirements of space, printing process, paper, etc. This is precisely why typographers and art directors need both knowledge and talent.

LEGIBILITY AND READABILITY

The chief considerations in determining suitability, along with appropriateness, are legibility and readability. These are not the same thing, even though the distinction is seldom recognized. "Legibility" is based on the ease with which one letter can be told from the other:

bbbbbbhhh

"Readability" is the ease with which the eye can absorb the message and move along the line. The choice of typeface is not the only thing that determines readability. The size of the letter, the spacing between letters and words, the amount of "leading" (spacing) between lines, the width of the line itself, the size of the margins around the type block, the quality of inking, the effect of the printing process used—including the amount of "sock," the texture or finish of the paper stock, the color of paper and ink—all these are involved, both in affecting the appearance of the particular typeface used and in the resulting readability. A poorly designed typeface can be made into a readable page by an expert, and an "ideal" typeface can be mishandled by a poor page designer and printer (see Page 90).

Even legibility in the typeface itself is not a simple matter of clean, sharp lines versus fuzzy lines, for instance. The key element is familiarity. Our "most legible" face today would likely have been difficult indeed for a reader taught in spire Gothic. The typefaces you grow up with are likely to be the most legible for you. Faces similar to them are more legible to you than others.

If some unfamiliar elements in the typeface catch your attention, then the face is less readable—because you are slowed down by this distraction. A conspicuous example is the long s used in England two centuries ago. When it was customarily used, everyone read it automatically as an s. Today, while we know it is an s, we automatically slow down and not only read it as an f, but we usually even stop to *sound* that f.

In more practical terms, the decision as to the suitability of a given typeface rests on a compromise among all these factors. For instance, a telephone directory's type is a fair enough compromise between legibility and the extra costs that would be involved in printing with larger type—but who would be willing these days to read novels set in such type? Similarly, if a book has a monumental message, it has a right to be clothed in monumental format; but such a typeface on a grocery handbill would be ridiculous.

For practical purposes, therefore, suitability is paramount. But beyond some reasonably clear choices, such as given above, there are few guides to follow. Designers' success rests on their imagination, skill and sensitivity to what is suitable, or can be suitable. Studying their efforts can be intriguing, and an amateur's efforts to solve similar problems in his own personal press, for instance, can become very challenging.

(This poses the opposite problem: small, beginning printers, especially, can seldom afford much type. Which fonts to buy? One answer is the "house face," a concentration on different sizes and weights of one typeface —one family—that will best serve the personal taste and the greatest variety of likely uses of the printer, rather than buying a hodge-podge of different styles. Of course, some creative souls like the challenge the other way!)

One thing is certain: there is no definite, single "right" choice for any particular job. W. A. Dwiggins, the designer of Electra and Caledonia typefaces, once summed it up: "What type shall I use? The gods refuse to answer. They refuse because they do not know."

But Mrs. Warde had a different conclusion. An editor, type director or printer, sensitive, creative and concerned about finding the most suitable face for the texts he handles ". . . may spend endless years of happy experiment in devising that crystalline goblet which is to try to hold the vintage of the human mind."

THE UNSUNG SINGERS

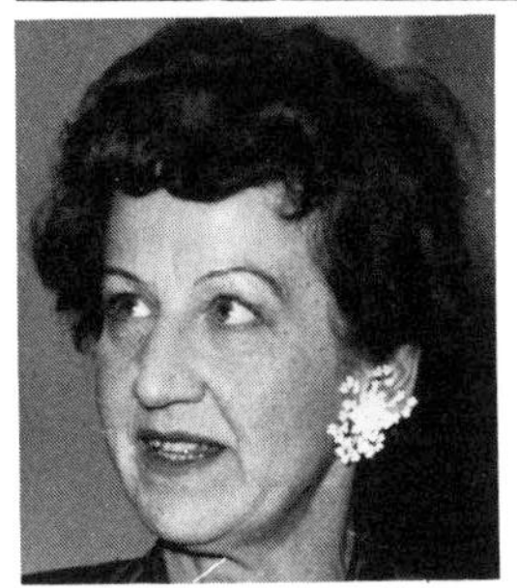

—©The Monotype Company, Ltd. *—A. Burton Carnes*

One unappreciated reason for the high quality of even our ordinary printing today is the educational job the manufacturers did to improve printing taste and build acceptance for better typefaces. The singers of wares are seldom sung. But two of them, deservedly, *did* become legends in their time–Beatrice Warde of Monotype (England) and Paul A. Bennett of Linotype (America). Because it is an effort in its own small way to join in their work, this book has been dedicated to them. (Sadly, both died around the time the first edition of this book was published.)

Prominent faces: friends everyone ought to know

STILL UNKNOWN to the general public, certain typefaces nevertheless are particularly prominent in designers' and printers' thinking and usage. These are not necessarily the "best" faces, but rather the ones which are most-often used or referred to as representing a certain class of letter. It can be argued that an educated person ought to know most of these typefaces at least as well as he knows paintings by Picasso and Van Gogh.

Opinion can differ as to which faces can be included in this group. The ones shown below would almost certainly make anyone's list; fault might be found with faces omitted This applies particularly to the grotesques and slab serifs, which have been placed together by style in the Appendix, making comparison easier. To have attempted to do them justice here would have more than doubled the size of this chapter. Also, some other important faces, including scripts, decoratives, etc., have been omitted here because they are distinctive enough not to need special clues to recognition.

The display lines which head the description of each face include what printers call "earmark" letters, those which provide special clues to the identification of the different faces. ("Earmark" comes from herdsmen branding ears of livestock for identification.)

The style of each face below is shown in brackets following its name, and the page number refers you to the style box that will refresh you on the *general* characteristics of the face. Where an earmark letter in the description is followed by other letters in parentheses, e.g., B (D, E) under Baskerville, the other letters have the same earmark.

More details about each typeface—who designed it and when, who makes it now, what other faces are similar, etc.—are contained in the headings to the type specimens beginning on Page 99. You will find it rewarding to study the whole alphabet shown there in conjunction with the information here. You may find it even more rewarding to examine these typefaces in their body sizes beginning on Page 125.

Note that alternate characters which are less distracting for reading are sometimes substituted for precisely the most obvious earmarks, e.g., this S for S in Palatino. Also, reworking (see P. 58) may change letters.

BCEJKQTagt *Jw*

BASKERVILLE [transitional book face, p. 40] is wide, with open counters, feeling of grace, precision of line; medium weight, medium thick-thin contrast, based on Caslon letter forms in general, with stress a bit more vertical. B (D, E) curves up in bowl where bottom stroke meets main stem. C serifs nearly close bowl, but some versions have no lower serif. E lower bar extends unusually to right. J descender especially long (or large) with ball terminal. K tail (lower arm) extra long and strong. Q has special flourish. T arms extra wide. a bowl slants up. g loop does not close, t crossbar thin, off-center. *J* has swash effect, as does *w* (also *N, T, Y, v, z* in most versions). Pronounced BAS-ker-vill.

AEKMQTadefms*gky*

BEMBO [old style book face, p. 38] has comparatively small x-height; capitals shorter than ascenders; feel of quiet elegance, yet undistracted readability. A is flat at top (apex). E top, middle arm same size, with nearly-touching serifs; bottom arm longer. K arms both curved. M splayed slightly, center counter especially wide. Q tail almost straight. T top serifs spurred and slant out from already-wide arms. a has very small, almost flat bowl. e crossbar very high, thin. m (n) right stroke bent. *a* bottom arc stays flat. *g* loop almost a triangle. *k* upper arm is looped. *s* lower arc flat thickening terminal. *y* tail nearly straight, hairline serif. Pronounced BEM-boe.

CGJQTWcgy*fkvw*

BODONI [French modern book face, p. 42] formal, precise, in most versions (except Bauer) quite severe; long ascenders, descenders, each 2-7th of total face. C counter very open, serifs far apart. G bar low on widened support. J tapers to hairline (usually left, but right in Bauer) with ball terminal. Q tail centered, tapering curve. T arms seem part of long, tapering serifs. W has one long hairline serif over all but right stroke. c has one ball terminal. g bowl small and thus high, to align at x-line; y has continuous hairline in descender, ending in ball. *f* especially long descender. *k* top arm droops into ball. Bauer *v*, *w* left stems curve in. Pronounced buh-DOE-nee.

BEQSTagmty

BOOKMAN [antique strong serif, p. 68] has heavy, even color in body sizes, very large x-height. Spurs above cap line make face as whole easy to spot. B bowls wide, flat. E (F, L, Z) have characteristic long arms, serifs angling up (or down) to widen curve of bracket. Q tail weak, curls up. S, with beaked serif, seems snake ready to strike. T has E-like serifs but shorter and with spurs, making the bracket an arc to the vertical stroke; a top terminal thickens to tear-shape and droops almost to touch bowl, which is low and flat. Loop of g is flat, with bottom line thin. m top arcs unusually flat. t has tall filled-in bracket on cross-bar. y descender wide, flat, curves up. Pronounced BOOK-man.

CDERYagity*Ty*

BULMER [transitional book face, p. 40] based on Baskerville; ATF recutting virtually a softened English modern style face, brilliant and sharp but avoiding cold precision by making thick-thin contrast more gradual. Face has elegant appearance. Capitals not to height of ascenders. C lower serif slightly concave. D bowl seems to dip below base line. E, most other letters have Baskerville proportions. R widened curled tail close to English modern. Y stem quite short. Top of a droops beyond left of bowl. g bowl is off to left, making letter seem tilted. Dot of i at top of cap line. t stroke thickens on way down. *T*, other letters follow Baskerville swash effect. *y* bowed to right. Pronounced BUHL-mur.

AELQTZacs*Ack*

CASLON [English old style book face, p. 38] full of imperfections that add up to what some consider the perfect face. Letters simple, honest; light over-all color unless socked into paper; small x-height. Many versions change weight, tidy up the imperfections. A has concave jutting side of apex, great thick-thin contrast. E has long serif across middle arm. Arm of L quite long. Q tail a short stub. T serifs taper out from thin arms which seem lower at center. Z has longer bottom arm. a bowl small, tucked in under overhead stroke. c stress heavier, quite low. s very light, seems above base line. *A* leans far to right. *c* very narrow. *k* arm has large loop, tail small. Pronounced KAZZ-lun.

BCGJKQRbefk

CENTURY SCHOOLBOOK [readability face, p. 67] widened and slightly graced version of earlier Century—a regularized English modern, almost a Clarendon. Light weight with large x-height; strong, square-cut serifs; short descenders but not cramped; open counters, evenness of line, simplicity of letter forms make it highly legible, hence its name. B lower bowl a little droopy. C terminals almost close counter, barb serif slopes slightly. G spur pointed down. J lining or ranging on base line. K tail attached to arm. Q inner loop formed by tail. R tail curled like English moderns. b has spur at lower left pointing out. e eye seems extra large loop, riding high.

AGHRSegs*epy*

CHELTENHAM [utility strong serif] is a perennially popular workhorse with high legibility, little aesthetics. Contrast between thicks, thins is slight; texture in mass is even, dull; basic characteristic of thickish stems, with vertical stress thinned matter-of-factly suggests mechanical precision which in fact is missing, so face has same kind of individual faults as Caslon. A main stem juts out at apex. G has spur. H, other letters are wide. R bowl (like others) is wide; tail joins far from stem. S lower arm longer than top one. e bar is high. g has unique open loop. s ends in balls, is weak, seems tilted. *e*, *p* bowls not closed. *y* descender curves up evenly. Pronounced CHELT-en-HAM, or called "Chelt."

ABCGJKQRakm

CLARENDON [bracketed strong serif, pp. 46, 71] is English Modern book face given bold weight as companion to the normal book face. Crisp, elegant and authoritative styling with slight thick-thin contrast; serifs long, heavy, cleanly bracketed; capitals tall as ascenders, only slightly heavier than l.c.; x-height large. A flat on apex. B overhand typical of serifs. C (c, e) lower terminal moving outward. G has matching spurs. J is lining. K arm joins low, tail joins at point to balance it. Q curled tail makes inner loop. R tail characteristic English modern. a bowl slopes to allow oval terminal at top fit in. k has full serif atop arm. m serifs almost close counters. Pronounced CLARE-en-dun.

ABEGMQWafgjt*A*

FUTURA [geometric sans serif, p. 69] is geometric typeface without apparent eccentricity: monotone, with no stress; uniform in sizes of circles and arcs, and treatment of joining stems and apexes. Letters do not follow roman proportions. A crossbar low. B top bowl much smaller than lower one. E (F) center bar longer than arms. G quite wide, with jutting point at bar. M splayed, apexes, vortex pointed. Q tail straight line with diagonal shearing. W seems turned up M, but is wider. a (etc.) has straight stem overlapping circle, but lines thin at crotches. f top arc very small. g tail arc differs from bowl above. j, t have no tails or hooks. *A*, other italics simply oblique roman. Pronounced few-TURR-uh.

ACDGMNTW*ahp*

GARAMOND [French old style book face, p. 38] has elegance, grace, freshness, restful legibility; thick-thin contrast not great; smallish x-height; short caps; descenders long; over-all color light. A bar high; slightly concave serifs typical. C flattened top and bottom; sheared terminals also typical. D thickening at lower stem almost triangular; G stem, bar short; lower counter almost flat. M splayed left side only. N (most designs) goes below base line with diagonal stroke. T has perhaps most famous earmark in typography: left serif slants, right one vertical. W center strokes cross. a (e) bowl very small. *h* almost a b; *p* top of bowl stroke starts to left of stem. Pronounced GARE-uh-MUND.

ADLNPQip*ahmv*

GOUDY OLD STYLE [personal style book face, p. 63] is basically an old style with grace, warmth, richness, soft sparkle, achieved by slight curving of many strokes, subtle styling of serifs. A top terminal has hint of barb; bottom one sheared. D has curved effect where bowl meets stem. L (etc.) arm has graceful curved thinning terminal; top serif also typically slightly concave. N left stroke slants outward slightly, as does M. P narrow, bowl not closed. Q has typical Goudy tail. i has diamond dot, as do punctuation marks. p serif not symmetrical. *abc* show unusual roundness of italics. *hmn* right stroke slopes out. *v*, *w* have looped starting terminal. Pronounced GOW-dee.

AEGMRaj*cgkw*

JANSON [old style book face, p. 38] has more contrast between thicks, thins than most old styles; many serifs hairlines. Some versions thicken these. Cut in Holland, has basic capital forms used later by Caslon, but narrower. A apex has very sharp point. E (F) serif across bar is long hairline, faintly bracketed. G has hairline spur. M is splayed, with left main stroke filling into serif past thin stroke. R bowl large, makes letter dumpy. a top terminal virtually a ball. j stroke tapers to point at descender curve. *c* not as slanted as other letters. *g* bowl narrow vertical, loop wide horizontal. *k* loop narrow. *w* (*v*) has swash starting terminal. Pronounced JANN-sun.

BCPUaefgiprt

KABEL [styled sans serif, p. 69] is basically geometric, monotone, but with many "relics" of other letter forms. Thus a is roman, not geometric; e has Venetian sloped bar; f reverses long s, half a bar at right; U has uncial right stroke with its own terminal. Terminals are cut obliquely, not straight and sharp. B bowls equal, makes top one seem larger. C flattens beyond arc of circle. P typifies many very narrow letters in contrast to C, has long bowl. g has open loop. i, j dots are diamond, carried to punctuation marks. p shows extremely short descenders. r very narrow. t quite wide, especially considering narrow f,r, and proportions of other letters. Pronounced KAY-bull.

AEOWafghmty*Rfko*

MELIOR [mannered small serif; see p. 80] is almost squared in effect, but elegant instead of just boxy. Stress is vertical, thick-thin contrast is not great in basic weight; stroke-ends are slightly rounded off. A has high bar, flat top. E almost symmetrical; vertical serifs characteristic. O shows basic squarish shape. W center strokes meet to flat top, no serif. a counter almost closed. f quite small button-hook top. g link between bowl, loop almost straight line. m feet almost like Clarendon. t top terminal has diagonal cut. y left stroke cuts off instead of merging into descender stroke. *R* tail like English modern. *f* tapers to thin terminal. *k* tail half imitates *R*. Pronounced MEE-lee-ORE.

ADKSSYaefghy*ak*

PALATINO [personal style book face, p. 63] is almost calligraphic in style; letters wide, open, graceful, fresh. A has high bar, is unusually wide at feet. D bowl seems to flair to right. K arm, tail long with only a suggestion of serifs. S unusual curve of spine is Palatino's key hallmark, but has been recut as too individualistic (both shown). Y has calligraphic left arm, no top serifs. a top terminal tapered. e bowl open, slanted cut at right. f thickens above cross bar. g bowl, loop large, close together. h (m, n) have only half serif on final stroke. y left stroke does not fuse into descender. *a* typical of calligraphic italic l.c. *k* arm curves to bottom of main stroke. Pronounced PAL-uh-TEEN-oh.

AEIOUacfgqr*Bfgqr*

PERPETUA [new style book face, p. 64] dignified, monumental, with feeling of authority especially in larger sizes; curves precise and cold; x-height small but letters generally wide; caps little heavier than l.c. Italic basically oblique roman. A top flat. E arms almost equal. I thin, short, full-bracketed serifs typical. O is circle, vertical stress. U is uncial. a terminal hooked, pointed. c top terminal sheared, thin barb. f wide at top, obliquely pointed terminal. g ear flat out from bowl. q top is flat, no serif. r ear calligraphic. *B* (*DPR*) has thin curved half-serif at top. *f* wide with flared, sheared terminals. *g* is script form. *q* (*p*) has upstroke half-serif on descender. Pronounced purr-PET-chew-uh.

AEMNWbgjt

PLANTIN [old style book face, p. 38] is based on 16th century forms but with heavy face, large x-height to serve for all reproduction processes with economy of space. Stress diagonal; line slightly irregular; serifs sturdy. Italic is a very regularized Granjon. A main stroke goes beyond thin stroke at apex, and has flat top. E top arm and bar nearly equal, bottom arm longer. M splayed, and thin strokes end below apex. N has top of strong main stroke even further to left of thin stroke (as A, M). W middle strokes cross in caps, not in l.c. b (etc.) ascender top serif virtually a triangle. g rides high. j has short tapered descender. t very narrow. Pronounced **PLAN-tin.**

ABFIKQRTik*flv*

SCOTCH ROMAN [English modern book face, p. 43] looks punch-cut rather than precisely drawn; letters wide, serifs thin and sharp but bracketed; thick-thin contrast strong but not abrupt. A bar is low. B inside top bowl has no softening of corner. F upper left shows too-strong version of upper B serif treatment. I cupped serifs typical. K long arm starts low with slight curve; tail joins high. Q loop at left side. R tail loop modern, but tail itself more slanted. T beaks slant out very slightly. i (j) dots quite heavy. k arm curves, accentuates low tail. *f* bar quite high. l (etc.) horizontal top half-serif contrasts with typical hooked terminals. v (w) has vertical serif on swash terminal.

ABEJQRTWbc*gkv*

TIMES NEW ROMAN [new style book face, p. 64] has large x-height, sturdy parts, large counters, simplified and strengthened forms for mass production use, yet also has basic new style characteristics. A quite wide, bar somewhat low. B lower bowl seems smaller. E top serifs nearly touch, lower arm and serif extend out. J is lining; upturn is small. Q tail small, pointed. R tail long, spreads at bottom. T arms thicker than thin strokes. W middle main stroke cuts off left thin stroke. b bowl line spears main stroke. c (e) bottom arc stress nearly horizontal. *g* bowl seems almost roman over italic loop. *k* tail starts low, has graceful curl. *v* (*w*) right stroke curves back.

CHAPTER 

Practical problems of type identification

THE FINAL APPEARANCE of type in print is all that really counts, and a number of factors can change that final appearance from what the designer envisioned it to be. Type designer, typographer and type-identifier, therefore, have to take such factors into account in settling upon a particular typeface. Here are the key ones:

Paper stock. Soft paper, which embeds the types (giving a feeling of texture or "bite" in impression), makes a typeface look thicker. Hard paper makes it thinner. Porous paper (such as newsprint) makes it especially thick because the ink soaks up and spreads. Shiny (coated, gloss, art) paper makes it look even thinner because of the way the light reflects around it. The color or shade of paper, too, can make a difference—often unpredictable. Rough paper affects the sharpness of line.

Printing process. Dampened paper (usually soft) printed letterpress spreads the face and thickens it. Bad offset printing can soften the edges and widen the letters slightly. Gravure process printing thickens the face and fuzzes the edges very slightly. Poor stereotypes or electrotypes make the letters thicker. And, of course, there is "sock." (See Pages 39, 40, 85.)

Inking. Over-inking makes the face darker and thicker, fuzzes up the clean outlines of the letters, and blunts any sharp terminals, etc. Under-inking makes the face lighter and thinner, and drops out more delicate details altogether. Over-inking also fills in the small counters, as in the e of some faces. Wrong kinds of ink for the paper or process will affect appearance, much like over- and under-inking. The color of ink used, like the color of paper stock, can make substantial differences in appearance.

Condition of type. Worn-down type makes a thicker face; battered or really worn-out type changes the shape, loses the crispness of the edge.

Size of typeface. Designs often are changed in different sizes in the same series, deliberately, to keep the same optimal effect. Smaller sizes are relatively thicker than larger sizes. If you measure microscopically, stereotyping (used commonly on newspapers) shrinks the type from its original size. Type made into a photoengraving (cut) or used in cold-type processes can be enlarged or reduced in size drastically, and this sometimes also changes appearance drastically, usually very much for the worse.

(1) a (2) a (3) a (4) a

(1) true size (2) reduced from 72 point;
(3) true size (4) blown up from 12 point.

Spacing. Leading between lines, spacing between words, letterspacing (putting thin spaces between all letters within a word), optical spacing, and even differing "set" of the letters can make typefaces look different.

Reversed and toned letters. Various processes can also change the color of the faces in more drastic ways, making them "reversed" or "drop-out" white letters on black or toned gray. (See Page 82.)

Tight setting. Cold type is so completely flexible in spacing that the kerning problem of hot metal can be all but eliminated by slight typeface design changes. This has spawned a fad of crowding letters so tightly together that their near-touching sides result in literally new *kinds* of letters as seen by the eye (the ascenders of a d and b, for instance, seem to make a separate mark, parallel lines, in some typefaces set quite close). Ugly and hard to read, this also may throw you off in identifying typefaces—even in hot metal, because some shops mortise type to match the fashion.

NOTE: Many of the above elements, not just tight setting, get into the broader question of design of the whole printed piece. This book, about typefaces as such, has only touched on the way typeface and graphic design as such affect each other, and has not attempted to go into the design question of how best use to use the Typorama. You will find graphic design another fascinating field to learn abc ut.

NOW THAT YOU KNOW

CHAPTER

Hobby interests that can start with type

IF YOU PURSUE typefaces further, whole new worlds of quietly pleasurable or exciting activities await you. There are many ways for you to tie your interest in type to some of your existing interests and career possibilities.

Here are some of the principal hobby activities:

Type lore itself. You can continue beyond where this book leaves off. There are literally hundreds of books on the subject, and more coming out every year. Just collecting books about type has become an important avocation. You don't have to be wealthy to build a good collection.

Printing history. Broadening out from type lore, you can find the history of printing itself a fascinating field to explore. (See Page 96.)

Book collecting. The collecting of incunabula printing, fine printing of any period and especially of private presses such as Kelmscott and Doves, specimens of personal press work (e.g., ephemera, prop cards), books about printing, is another type of collecting.

Collecting specimen sheets. Type specimen sheets (and books) are printed examples of different faces available from particular typefounders or printers. Through the centuries, these have been produced in tremendous variety and quantity in all sizes and shapes. The earliest ones are now museum treasures almost beyond price but enough material both old and new, as issued by printing houses and type manufacturers, exists to make the collecting interesting and challenging.

Collecting type. Collecting type (metal or wood) itself, especially antique type, is an increasingly popular hobby. Collecting the different "pin marks" or identifying symbols which old-time foundries cast into the sides of their type characters is a special but intriguing sub-hobby, as are collecting initial letters, electros and cuts.

Calligraphy. The art of beautiful hand-

THE TYPE-LORE 'SHINGLE'

IN 1957, BRADBURY THOMPSON produced as a cover for *Westvaco Inspirations* this stylized California Job Case, a splendid Mondrian-like abstract with letters filling the type compartments. It blossomed immediately on home and office walls, proclaiming the occupant's interest in type.

Spurred by this, a custom grew by which a type "aficionado" produces his own typecase "shingle."

This can be a decorated actual wooden type case, with letters pasted in from cutouts, or hand lettered; wood-type letters are often mounted in. At least one printer, to get his nursery-school son interested in letters, pasted in rhymes and drawings from an ABC book.

More often, the shingle is a hand-drawn lay of the case (see Page 83), in whatever size and style one wishes. Professional calligraphers have made truly beautiful wall adornments. But even beginners, using a little imagination and picking unusual printed letters to paste down or copy, have done most interesting shingles.

If you would like to try your own hand at it, the lay on Page 83 will give you proportions and arrangement.

writing—out of which printing itself came—is having a rebirth both for professionals and amateurs. Some want to learn how to write in calligraphic styles so they can produce beautiful calligraphic works, and many belong to an international society. You do not have to be an artist to master the skills. Museums are beginning to recognize that there can be a true art manifested in calligraphy.

Manuscript illumination. This is another ancient craft which is gaining new interest, particularly in connection with calligraphy. There is a special push towards illumination with pure gold, an immensely satisfying—and peculiarly difficult!—skill to learn, and not nearly as expensive as it sounds.

Type designing. With new photo-setting companies interested in buying good new type designs, there is profit in developing a new idea for a typeface. Specifically, if you have a private press, you may want to follow in the Morris tradition of having your own private typeface. At least, you can design your own special initial letters. Designing a good face takes the mind of a chess player, a jig-saw puzzle enthusiast, an acrostics fan, and a mathematician—plus, of course, true artistic talent. Or maybe just a new idea.

Typecasting. Actual casting of type as a hobby is now done by perhaps a few dozen persons in the United States, and a few others in England. The advice of these persons is that one should be quite mature and fully knowledgeable before he undertakes this hobby, as it involves casting with molten metal, which has its dangers.

Wood and stone incising. The skills of cutting letters into wood and stone are finding renewed interest among both professionals and amateurs. There is a genuine thrill in inscribing a message to the ages.

Bookbinding. This is, of course, closely related to typefaces from the earliest days. The "stamping" of letters and ornaments on the bindings, or the collecting of bindings (that is, of books with special bindings), is enhanced greatly by one's knowledge of typefaces and type lore.

Printing. If reading about type has made you want to do true printing with real metal printing type, but you have mistakenly thought it was impossibly beyond you, then you should know that the hobby of personal printing is surprisingly inexpensive to start, simple to do, and involves practically no space (at an elementary level). For books with details, see the bibliography, Page 96, "Hobby, Personal and Simple Printing."

Your printing hobby can grow to whatever extent you wish. A fully equipped automatic-inking press, with as many as 25 fonts of type and all the other gadgets and supplies, is housed in many a small apartment living room, bedroom or kitchen!

Of course, you can go on from there to buy for your own use whatever you want of the typefaces this book has told you about.

TYPE-WATCHING: A New Hobby for Any Age or Interest Level

A NEW HOBBY which suggests itself, suitable at different levels for both a nursery school child and the most serious-minded scholar of type design, might be called *type-watching*. It can be done at no cost, or whatever expense one might choose. All one needs to start is scissors, printed matter and adhesive.

In name and simplest form, it is akin to bird-watching. It is also like stamp collecting in a way: collecting printed samples of typefaces cut from magazines, newspapers, etc., either one of everything or specializing in one class of typeface. In due course, no doubt, one can swap a rare Caslon long s for two semi-rare Fournier accented e's!

Beyond that, you can make of it what you will. At a professional level, for instance, it can involve collecting printed books or pamphlets in different body types, with a reference file a resulting dividend. Or it can mean collecting full alphabets of the whole Typorama, again with reference value.

Not that the simple form of the hobby—being always on the look-out for a different printed specimen to add to the collection—is not without its challenge to the sophisticated type man, once the common faces are in. For a beginner, it can have great educational and training benefit as well.

CHAPTER Y

Benefitting from your knowledge of typefaces

KNOWLEDGE OF TYPEFACES will help you in your personal life, in whatever career you are following, and in your education towards a career, especially in the graphic arts. For instance:

Ordering printing. Because printing is so all-important a part of our society at every level of activity, sooner or later everyone who participates in business, government, church, educational, civic, social, political or recreational activity finds himself responsible for getting something printed. Even a slight knowledge of type design can result in more appropriate printing.

Personalized printing. The joys of individualism in your own personal printed materials (stationery, greeting cards, etc.) will come with a knowledge of type. You can order something to your own taste from the local printer—and get it, without undue trouble or expense—if you know how to show him what you want.

Education. Learning about type develops appreciation for an art form, trains the eye to be perceptive of forms and styles, helps otherwise reluctant or halting readers to identify with the printed word and develop motivation, creates friendly familiarity with letters of the alphabet in ways that help spelling and the reading process itself, and can become the starting focus of a core curriculum in the visual arts in the elementary grades of school.

Because our typefaces carry the whole heritage of man, our entire intellectual history, the mainstream of our arts, and the substance of our knowledge and wisdom in printed pieces, the study of type is a legitimate and potent addition to the school curriculum.

Aesthetic satisfactions. Type is an art form, giving great pleasure to the knowledgeable observer. As T. M. Cleland translated the observation of Viollet-le-Duc, the French writer on architecture: "A civilization cannot pretend to possess an art unless that art shall penetrate everywhere—unless it makes its presence felt in the commonest of works." Great typefaces are in constant use all around us, for civilized man to appreciate.

Pre-training. In the communications field, knowledge of typefaces is of great value in advertising, journalism, printing, proofreading, editing, publishing and, of course, graphic design. George Bernard Shaw maintained it was even helpful for an author to know type and printing. Certainly he made it his business!

GRAPHIC ARTS STARTING JOBS

Obviously the sooner one starts to get the "feel" for typefaces, and know their history and development, the better off one is in a graphic arts career. Printing and publishing form the sixth largest industry in the United States, and are almost as important in Britain. Top positions to aspire to are those of printer, type director, production manager, type designer, art director, sign writer, film and television graphics managers. Not directly involved in communication are positions in architecture, exhibition design and retail store display, activities in which typefaces are used. There are career opportunities at all levels—and an interest in typefaces, with some knowledge to back it up, gives you a head start over others who come in without it. Among the starting jobs are:

Production assistant. In a graphic arts department, working with printers, there are many jobs for the beginner in helping prepare materials for press. If a beginner has artistic talent, he can go up the ladder quickly.

Secretary-clerk in graphic arts. There are many interesting jobs, and it helps to know the special language and have a feel for the subject.

Printer's apprentice. Printing apprenticeships are sometimes difficult to obtain, but the printing craft is most interesting and useful, well worth aspiring to.

PROFESSIONAL CAREERS

Among the professional jobs to which the above might lead, the most pertinent is that of typographer. In earlier times, this meant the printer himself. Today, it more often means the man or woman who works with the printer on type, design and production problems. More specifically, it is the person who designs the format of the materials to be printed, providing the actual specifications of typeface, size, etc. which the printer is to follow in production. A good typographer is well paid!

Another career more and more directly involving type design is that of art teacher, whether in a vocational or a general education sense. In both, infusing students with a knowledge of typefaces is a substantial contribution to their growth in perception, pleasure in art forms, and ability to live and produce with a sense of style—and perhaps with creativity. To quote a pungent observation by Bradbury Thompson: "[Printers] make art a language, for all to understand."

ACKNOWLEDGMENTS

The following experts in England and the United States read the basic manuscript of this book and made valuable contributions: Paul A. Bennett, Eugene W. Ettenberg, Horace Hart, Emil Klumpp, Dr. Robert L. Leslie, R. Hunter Middleton, James Moran, James Mosley, Frank Powers, Edward Rondthaler, Martin K. Speckter, Beatrice Warde and Steve Watts.

The basic classification which is central to the book has been developed through the years in discussions (not always in complete agreement!) with Ephram Benguiat, Paul A. Bennett, Jackson Burke, John S. Carroll, Eugene W. Ettenberg, Willard and Douglas Morgan, Frank Powers, Jack Rau, Edward Rondthaler, Herbert W. Simpson, Martin K. Speckter, Beatrice Warde, Steve Watts and Hermann Zapf among others—including the memberships of the Moxon, Goudy, and Westchester Chappels of private press proprietors, whose lively appreciation of the need for more general information about typefaces led to this book. Messrs. Benguiat, Carroll, Rau and Rondthaler were particularly helpful on the classification problem while the first edition (1967) was being prepared. Messrs. Zapf and Bradbury Thompson were especially helpful with this second edition, as was Charles H. Klensch.

However, none of the individuals named here or in the other more specialized acknowledgments should be held responsible in any way for this book as it finally appears. The type field has many divergent opinions and in reconciling them or stating new ones, the author often had to go contrary to one or more of the authorities he consulted.

The art work profusely illustrating the book was executed almost entirely by Jack Rau, who also made many important contributions to their conception, and did much of the detailed research involved. He also offered up for mutilation (where photo-copies could not hold the detail) his extensive collection of type specimens, gathered through many decades, to provide the precisely right type examples where needed. This book could not have been so produced without his unstinting assistance.

The style specimens of Chapter T (pp. 77–83), requiring settings in more than 100 different styles of typefaces covering the whole range of the Typorama, were supplied through the courtesy of Mr. Rondthaler and Photo-Lettering, Inc., one of the very few organizations with broad enough resources to do the job.

Most of the caption material was set by Terry Linotyping, Inc., with Terry Halpine giving his personal attention to a demanding project.

A. Burton Carnes, D.J. Culver, John De Pol, Stuart C. Dobson, Guillermo Rodrigues and Lisl Steiner provided photographs, drawings and other illustrative materials.

In this second edition John Dreyfus was most helpful with material on the Monotype Corp.

Many reference authorities gave substantial assistance in the first edition, notably the New York Public Library Rare Book Division; the St. Bride Printing Library, London; the Grolier Club, New York; the Typographic Reference Library of The Composing Room, Inc., New York, and the Advertising Typographers Association of America. In particular, the personal assistance of Lewis Stark and his staff at the N.Y.P.L., James Mosley at St. Bride, and Dr. Robert L. Leslie, president of the Composing Room, is gratefully acknowledged.

Finally, and in this instance it is no perfunctory matter, the assistance of Elizabeth K. Lieberman, the author's wife, and Lina Sarah Haddon, their daughter, is acknowledged, in researching the type specimen headings (Pages 99-122) and preparing the index.

[See also Special Acknowledgments on Page 98]

CHAPTER 

Books and other sources for learning more about typefaces

BOOKS ABOUT TYPE AND related subjects are much more numerous than might be suspected. On the other hand, the literature is hardly as great as the importance of the field deserves. What makes the matter worse is that because of the close connection between type and printing, and a fine printing tradition of small editions, many of the best writings on the subject are virtually unavailable to the general reader because of their limited press runs and their present location in special library and private collections.

Thus, for instance, The Typophiles of New York have produced a series of more than 50 magnificent "chapbooks" to date, under the inspiration, editorship and management of Paul A. Bennett until his death, and then under Dr. Robert L. Leslie, covering the whole field in depth. The work is one of the real monuments of typography. But with rare exceptions for special reasons, fewer than 1,000 copies of each book have been produced—and in many instances it has been fewer than 500—with an average of no more than 50 going to libraries, and to specialized libraries for the most part, at that.

There has been compelling reason for this kind of limitation, not only with the Typophile Chap Books but The Fleuron, The Dolphin, The Colophon, Motif, Signature, and Alphabet and Image, other notable and rare series of publications about type, books and printing. But the result is that these volumes are safeguarded in special collections, available to the more serious, qualified reader. In a real sense, this means there are special treasures that will open up to you when you reach the more sophisticated levels of interest and knowledge—and meanwhile, you ought at least to know of the existence of the specific series noted above.

There is no point, however, in listing such works in a general bibliography. In fact, for our purposes here, it seems desirable to limit a recommended reading list even more —to books at the level you, the new reader in the subject, have now reached with the completion of this book. The works listed below will take you in whatever direction you now find yourself interested in going, and since most of these books have their own bibliographies, they in turn will guide you to the stages beyond.

GENERAL

ABOUT ALPHABETS: Some marginal notes on type design, by Hermann Zapf. 1970. M.I.T. Press, Cambridge, Mass., and London. An insightful commentary on type for our time.

BOOKS AND PRINTING, by Paul A. Bennett. 1951. World Publishing Company, New York and Cleveland. (Paperback edition, 1963, Forum Books, New York.

FIRST PRINCIPLES OF TYPOGRAPHY, by Stanley Morison. Fleuron vii, 1930; revised reprints in various forms.

FIVE HUNDRED YEARS OF PRINTING, by S. H. Steinberg. 1955. Penguin Books, Middlesex, England.

INTRODUCTION TO TYPOGRAPHY, by Oliver Simon. 1945. Faber and Faber Ltd., London. Pelican edition, rev. 1954.

LETTERING FROM A TO Z, by Clarence P. Hornung. Revised edition, 1954. Wm. Penn Publishing Corp., New York. Paperback, Tudor Publishing Co., New York.

ON DESIGNING AND DEVISING TYPE, by J. van Krimpen. 1957. The Sylvan Press, London. A personal statement by one of our century's great typographers.

ON TYPE DESIGNS PAST AND PRESENT, by Stanley Morison. Revised edition, 1962. Ernest Benn, London.

THE ALPHABET and ELEMENTS OF LETTERING, by Frederic W. Goudy. Reprint edition, 1963. Dover Publications, Inc., New York.

THE BOOK, THE STORY OF PRINTING AND BOOKBINDING, by Douglas C. McMurtie. 1937. Oxford University Press.

THE CRYSTAL GOBLET, by Beatrice Warde. 1956. World Publishing Company, Cleveland and New York.

THE TYPOGRAPHIC ARTS and THE ART OF PRINTING, by Stanley Morison. Combined reprint, 1949. The Sylvan Press, London.

TYPE FOR BOOKS AND ADVERTISING, by Eugene M. Ettenberg. 1947. D. Van Nostrand Company, Inc., New York; Macmillan & Co., Ltd., London.

POPULAR INTRODUCTIONS

AN APPROACH TO TYPE, by John R. Biggs. Second edition, 1961. Blandford Press, London.

PRINTING TYPES: An Introduction, by Alexander Lawson. 1971. Simple, brief, well illustrated. Beacon Press, Boston.

THE SHAPING OF OUR ALPHABET, by Frank Denman. 1955. Alfred A. Knopf, New York.

THE 26 LETTERS, by Oscar Ogg. 1948. Thomas Y. Crowell Company, New York.

HISTORY

A TALLY OF TYPES, by Stanley Morison, revised edition edited by Brooke Crutchley. 1973. Cambridge University Press, Cambridge, England. A classic of typographic history and practice, emphasizing the (British) Monotype contribution.

AN INTRODUCTION TO THE HISTORY OF PRINTING TYPES, by Geoffrey Dowding. 1961. Wace & Co., Ltd., London.

GOUDY'S TYPEFACES, by Frederic W. Goudy. Second Edition, 1978. The Myriade Press, New Rochelle, N.Y. One of history's greatest type designers tells the story and purpose behind his typeface designs, with specimens of almost all of them.

XIXTH CENTURY ORNAMENTED TYPES AND TITLE PAGES, by Nicolette Gray. Second edition, 1976.

PRINTING TYPES, THEIR HISTORY, FORMS, AND USE, by Daniel Berkeley Updike. 1962. Third edition. The Belnap Press of Harvard University Press, Cambridge, Mass.

THE ALPHABET: A Key to the History of Mankind, by David Diringer. Two volumes. Third edition, 1968. Funk & Wagnalls, New York. A comprehensive coverage (with Volume II being illustrations entirely) of the whole subject, worldwide, from the beginning.

THE INVENTION OF PRINTING IN CHINA AND ITS SPREAD WESTWARD by T.F. Carter and L.C. Goodrich. Second edition, 1955. Ronald Press, New York.

TYPE DESIGNS, by A. F. Johnson. Second edition, 1959. Grafton & Co., London.

ENCYCLOPAEDIAS

THE ENCYCLOPAEDIA OF TYPE FACES, by W. Pincus Jaspert, W. Turner Berry and A. F. Johnson. Fourth edition, 1970. Blandford Press, London. *The* encyclopaedia on the subject to date, surprisingly comprehensive despite disclaimer to contrary, highly authoritative if slightly British oriented.

PRACTICAL HANDBOOK ON DISPLAY TYPEFACES, by Kenneth B. Butler and George C. Likeness. 1959. Butler Typo-Design Research Center, Mendota, Ill. A quite comprehensive informal encyclopaedia of typefaces from American point of view. Unfortunately out of print, but probably available in most good libraries.

TREASURIES, SURVEYS, SHOWINGS

A BOOK OF SCRIPTS, by Alfred Fairbank. 1947. Third edition, 1952. Penguin Books, Middlesex, England.

A BOOK OF TYPE AND DESIGN, by Oldrich Hlavsa. 1960. Peter Nevill, London.

ABC OF LETTERING AND PRINTING TYPES, by Erik Lindegren. Vol. A, Lettering and type design; collection of the work of renowned graphic designers, 1964. Vol. B, Outstanding type faces used today in the printing of books and advertising typography, 1965. Vol. C, A survey in word and picture of the development of lettering and the history of printing, 1966. Museum Books, New York. AN ABC BOOK, 1976, Pentalic, Inc., New York, is a one-volume shortened version.

AMERICAN WOOD TYPE, 1828-1900, by Rob Roy Kelly. 1969. Van Nostrand Reinhold Company, New York. History, commentary, splendid specimens.

DOVER PUBLICATIONS, Inc., New York, is producing a remarkable set of collections of typefaces, lettering, borders and pictorial archives, etc., in paperback. Check bookstores for titles.

THE WESTERN HERITAGE OF TYPE DESIGN; A MANUAL OF DECORATED TYPEFACES; A MANUAL OF SANS SERIF TYPEFACES; A MANUAL OF EGYPTIAN TYPEFACES, by R. S. Hutchings. 1963–1966. Cory, Adams & Mackay Ltd., London; Hastings House, New York.

TREASURY OF ALPHABETS AND LETTERING, by Jan Tschichold. 1966. Reinhold Publishing Co., New York.

TYPE & LETTERING, by William L. Longyear. Fourth ed., 1966. Watson-Guptill Publications, Inc., New York.

TYPE AND TYPOGRAPHY, by Ben Rosen. 1963, Reinhold, New York. Splendid specimens.

TYPOGRAPHIC VARIATIONS, by Hermann Zapf. Second Edition, 1978, The Myriade Press, New Rochelle, N.Y. A remarkable showing of the classic faces of Zapf and others in use, imaginatively, colorfully and impeccably.

CRAFT AND LEARNING AIDS

MECHANICK EXERCISES, by Joseph Moxon. 1683–84. In new edition, edited by H. Davis and H. Carter. 1958. Oxford University Press, New York.

THE HISTORY AND TECHNIQUE OF LETTERING, by Alexander Nesbitt. 1957. Dover Publications, Inc., New York.

THE USES OF TYPE, by John R. Biggs. 1954. Blandford Press, London.

WRITING AND ILLUMINATING AND LETTERING, by Edward Johnston. 1932. Sir Isaac Pitman & Sons, Ltd., London.

TYPE RECOGNITION AND SELECTION AIDS

A.T.A. TYPE COMPARISON BOOK, by Frank Merriman. 1965. Advertising Typographers Association of America, Inc., New York.

ALTERNATE TYPE FACES, by Harold E. Waite. Second edition, 1951. The Technical Publishing Co., Ltd. London.

HOW TO RECOGNIZE TYPE FACES, by R. Randolph Karch. 1952. McKnight & McKnight Publishing Co., Bloomington, Ill.

PRINTING TYPES AND HOW TO USE THEM, by Stanley Hlasta. 1950. Carnegie Press, Pittsburgh, Pa.

HOBBY OR PERSONAL PRINTING

PRINTING AS A HOBBY, by J. Ben Lieberman. Third edition, 1978. The Myriade Press, New Rochelle, N.Y.

PRINTING FOR PLEASURE, by John Ryder. 1955. Phoenix House Ltd., London. Charles T. Branford Co., Boston.

Of the books listed above, the author wishes to acknowledge the special importance of the Jaspert-Berry-Johnson encyclopaedia, the Butler handbook, Oldrich Hlavsa's book, the Hutchings series of books, the ATA Type Comparison Book, and Professor Alexander Nesbitt's lettering book in the preparation of this book. They do not always agree with one another, but they each represent great achievements in making available the kind of information summarized in this book.

HINTS FOR FURTHER LEARNING

Beyond the reading list suggested above, there are many other ways the interested beginner can learn more. Here are a few, simply as a starter:

Collect samples of interesting printing, and try to identify them. Organize them in ways that will be useful to you later for reference.

Compare different editions of the same book, such as a Latin classic (a suggestion by Updike), to see how printers in different countries produced the book during the same era, and how printers of different eras produced the book. Learning why their formats are so different will be not only fascinating but instructive.

If you have a particular interest in the fine arts, try matching typefaces to the styles of different artists.

Take adult education courses dealing with typography.

Design, and keep redesigning, the "perfect typeface." Or try reconstructing existing ones. If you do happen to hit upon one which is different and useful, there is a market for it. (But it has to be good.)

Join the American Printing History Association (APHA, Box 4922, Grand Central Station, New York, N.Y. 10017) or the Printing Historical Society (PHS, St. Bride Printing Library, Bride Lane, London, EC 4, England), for information about meetings, courses, new books, exhibits, lectures, etc., and for contacts, fellowship and inspiration. Write them for details.

APPENDIX I

THE BASIC TYPORAMA OF MACHINE-CAST TYPEFACES

DISPLAY SPECIMENS
with listings of other typefaces in similar styles

THIS IS THE FIRST systematic, comprehensive compilation and showing of the whole Typorama ever presented in compact form—the *basic* Typorama, a collection of the faces that are the most important and most representative of our Twentieth Century Typorama, which started more or less with the advent of mechanized type composition.

These are the faces of the past which were preserved and put into modern production because they proved their worth. And these are the new faces which were added to fill gaps and to serve new purposes and new tastes in book, periodical, job and advertising printing, and which reflect (and help create) new styles in design of clothes, automobiles, interior decoration, even architecture.

The collection may be used simply to browse through, for the excitement of the great array of different designs, or to learn the appearance of a typeface mentioned in the main body of the book. However, it offers much more as well to readers who may deal with type in their work, studies, hobbies or further reading in the field.

For these readers, the following explanation of how the Basic Typorama was compiled will be useful:

- The intent was to include those faces in the unaccented Latin alphabet, from whatever country, that made and make typographic conversation and history, except privately-held faces. But there was no attempt to include *all* faces ever cast. There may be, regrettably, inadvertent omission of some faces properly belonging here. And some other omitted faces can be argued for inclusion, obviously. Later editions will attempt to make improvements indicated meanwhile by readers.
- The showings are of the most commonly-used version of a face, in general. There is no effort here (it would take a full encyclopaedia) to cover all sizes and variants, much less technical variants with different-size descenders, etc.
- At least one typeface has been included of every basic style in current use in every class using the Latin alphabet as such, based on the chart on Page 78.
- Specimens are shown in 24-point size where possible, unless otherwise indicated, so that details can be seen. If a body size is shown as well, because of its importance, it is in 12-point, unless otherwise indicated. Where only a body size is shown, the face has no display sizes or they are seldom used. A "D" after the point size indicates Didot measurement.
- Full alphabets are shown of all key faces, except in cases where a few letters were omitted for space reasons. For interesting but less central faces, only partial (but fully indicative) showings are made, again to save space. The same technique is used for important faces which have so distinctive a character that seeing a partial alphabet will serve to recognize the missing letters as well. (This is particularly true of the initial letters shown on Page 122.)
- Considerable attention was given to the problem of different trade names for substantially the same face. The detailed information in the specimen headings is the result. With a few necessary exceptions, only one typeface of a given "model" is shown, usually the first of its kind. However, if you wish to know the general style of a face that is not listed in the headings, simply use the index listing of the name you have, and if it is in common use, the index will refer you to the showing of the face which is similar to it. The code mark ¶ will tell you just *how* similar. (See top of next page for explanation of the codes.) Some faces with only technical style similarities are included after the ¶ mark as at least suggesting the general character of the face, e.g., that it is a script, say, instead of a roman or black letter. This allows inclusion of at least basic information about many faces which could not be shown separately in any collection short of an encyclopaedia.
- Note especially that this index-reference system will show you which names are used for more than one kind of face, e.g., Spartan as both a modern sans serif and a copperplate gothic. They are kept separate by use of manufacturers' code initials.
- In the grot and slab serif styles, in particular, various versions of faces are shown. However, even these could not be more than suggestive of the total range of faces and variants within those families. Neither the inclusion nor omission of the faces concerned, nor for that matter the inclusion or omission of names of any of the faces shown as "similar" throughout the headings, should be taken in any way to imply that the faces not shown in specimens are unwarrantedly close copies of those shown. What may seem inconsequential differences to the beginner may well be valid departures fully justifying the claim to constituting a quite separate typeface. To underscore all this, listing of similar faces is in alphabetical order, not by date of issue or any judgment as to importance.
- Unless indicated otherwise, the specimen shown is the one in capitals at the beginning of the heading, from the first founder or manufacturer as listed. Where more than one face is listed as shown, they are presented in order, left to right or top to bottom.

KEY TO SYMBOLS AND ABBREVIATIONS USED

A, ATF, etc.—indicates manufacturer of the type or matrices; see list immediately below for full names and addresses.
¶—indicates faces named to right of the symbol are not as similar in appearance to the specimen shown as those to the left, but are within the same general style.

A—Tetterode (formerly Lettergieterij) Amsterdam, 163 Bilderdijkstraat, Amsterdam-W.

ATF—American Type Founders Company, Type Division, 200 Elmora Avenue, Elizabeth, New Jersey 07202, USA

BB&S—Barnhart Brothers & Spindler, now ATF.

BG—Bauersche Giesserei [Bauer Type Foundry], Frankfurt-am-Main, West Germany. Now defunct. NB continues about half of faces.

Ba—Baltimore Type and Composition Co., 15 S. Frederick St., Baltimore, Md. Now defunct.

Be—H. Berthold AG, Mehringdamm 43, Berlin S.W. 61, West Germany

D&P—Fonderies Deberny et Peignot, Paris. Now defunct. Stempel and Haas have mats.

E—Joh. Enschéde en Zonen, Haarlem, Netherlands

FTF—Fonderie Typographique Francaise, 10 avenue Guynemar, Champigny (Seine), France

FTN—Fundición Tipográfica Nacional, C.A., Tomàs Breton 47, Madrid, Spain

G—Richard Gans, Princesa 61, Madrid, Spain

H—Haas'sche Schriftgiesserei AG [Haas Typefoundry], Gutenbergstrasse 1, Basle-Münchenstein, Switzerland

I—Formerly Intertype Co., now Harris Systems Division of the Harris Corporation, P.O. Box 1030, Winchester, Virginia 22601, USA

JW—J. Wagner, Roemerstrasse 35, Ingolstadt, Donau, West Germany

K—Klingspor Typefoundry, Offenbach-am-Main, West Germany. Now defunct. Stempel continues designs shown.

L—Mergenthaler Linotype Co., Mergenthaler Drive, Plainview, New York 11803 USA; L(F) Linotype, Frankfurt; L(L) London; L(M) Mergenthaler U.S., where face is special to one.

Lu—Ludlow Typograph Co., 2032 Clybourn Avenue, Chicago, Ill. 60614, USA

L&M—Ludwig & Mayer Typefoundry, Hanauer Landstrasse, 187, Frankfurt am Main, West Germany

M—Monotype. M(E) when only the Monotype Corp. Ltd., Salfords, Redhill RH1 5JP, England. M(L) in code indicates Lanston Monotype, now defunct. Most of its cellular mats up to 12 pt. are now made by Hartzell Machine Works, Market and Bethel Road, Chester, Pennsylvania 19014. Hartzell also is U.S. distributor for all M(E) mats.

N—Societá Nebiolo, Via Bologna 47, Turin, Italy

NB—Fundición Tipográfica Neufville, S.A., Traveserade Gracia, 183 Barcelona 12, Spain

O—Fonderie Olive, 28 rue Abbè-Ferraud, Marseilles 5, France

S—D. Stempel AG, Hedderichstrasse 106-114, Frankfurt-am-Main 70, West Germany

SB—Stephenson Blake & Co. Ltd., Sheffield 3, Yorkshire, England

Sim—Off. Simoncini S.p.A, Bologna-Rastignano, Italy

SS—Stevens Shanks & Sons Ltd., 89 Southwark Street, London S.E.1, England

W—C. E. Weber Typefoundry, Stuttgart. Defunct; Stempel and Wagner have mats.

Wa—Fonderie Warnery et Cie., Paris XIV, France. Defunct; mats at Stempel, Wagner

(This list was updated for this edition by Vincent Giannone, Vice President, Typefounders of Chicago, and by Hermann Zapf.)

SPECIAL ACKNOWLEDGMENTS

The information in the headings of the specimens was compiled and cross-checked from the author's own files, conversations in England, Europe and the U.S. with many of the persons involved, the general literature concerning type and more specifically those reference books indicated in the Bibliography (Page 95), as well as information supplied on request by the various manufacturers.

To further make these headings as accurate and complete as possible, the entire working draft of the first edition (1967) was checked by each of the following representatives of the manufacturers and suppliers, shown as of that time:

Richard K. Ansell, Executive Vice President, Amsterdam-Continental Types, Inc., New York

Whedon Davis, Sales Manager, Type Division, ATF, Elizabeth, N.J.

Horace Hart, President, Lanston Monotype Co., New York

A. D. B. Jones, Publicity Manager, The Monotype Corporation Ltd., London

Emil Klumpp, Executive Vice President, and Vincent Giannone, Sales Manager, Bauer Alphabets, New York

R. Hunter Middleton, Director, Department of Typeface Design, Ludlow Typograph Company, Chicago

Michael Parker, Director of Typographic Development, Mergenthaler Linotype Co., Brooklyn

Hans Schneider, Type Director, Lanston Monotype Co., Philadelphia

Edwin W. Shaar, Art Director, Intertype Co., Brooklyn

These men did a most conscientious job, and provided not only data but helpful advice, nearly all of which could be accepted. They thus made a very substantial contribution to "The Basic Typorama," which the author and publisher are pleased to acknowledge. *However*, none of them are necessarily in agreement with the final presentation here, even as to the listings of typefaces produced by their own companies. This is because the nature of the material and the book required some arbitrary judgments by the author, occasionally in the face of one or more of the authorities just named.

In addition, Hy Needleman of King Typographic Services Corp., and Frank Powers, type consultant to King, read the manuscript and made important suggestions.

The type specimen showings were, for the most part, also supplied by these men and their organizations—Mr. Jones and the Monotype Corporation being particularly generous with specimens set especially for the book's requirements. In addition, specimens were provided by Murray Berger, Howard O. Bullard, Inc.; Peter W. Jedrzejek, Matrix International, Inc.; and Dr. Robert L. Leslie, The Composing Room, Inc., all of New York. Once again, Jack Rau's comprehensive collection of typeface specimens was enormously helpful when the author's own files and other resources proved insufficient on faces hard to find, at least in 24-point alphabets.

Robert Foster, designer of the Pericles faces, was kind enough to lend his personal font of the type for making a repro proof.

Much of the painstaking and time-taking detailed work involved in finding and assembling the specimens, organizing them, checking sources, and cross-referencing the information was done by the author's wife, Elizabeth K. Lieberman, and their daughter, Lina Sarah Haddon.

[*See also the general acknowledgments on Page* 94]

AD LIB. Freeman Craw, 1961, ATF. Shown: 18 pt.

ABCDEFGHIJKLMNOPQaabccdeeffgghijkllmmnoop12345678

ADMIRAL SCRIPT. R. H. Middleton, 1953, Lu.

ABCDEFGHIJKMabcdefghijklmnopqrstuvwxyz12345

ALBERTUS. Berthold Wolpe, 1932, M(E).

ABCDEFGHIJKLMNOPQRSTUVWXYZ&
abcdefghijklmnopqrstuvwxyz1234567890

ALDUS BOOK. Hermann Zapf, 1954, S; also L(F)

ABCDEFGHIJKLMNOPQRSTUVWXYZabcdefghijklmnopqrstuvwxyz1234567*ABCDEFGabcdefghij*

ALLEGRO. Hans Bohn, 1937, L&M.

ABCDEFGHIJKLNOPQRSTUVWXYZabcdefghijklnopqrstuv123

ALPHA and BETA. K. F. Bauer and Walter Baum, 1954, BG. Two lowercase alphabets share the same capitals.

abcdefghijklmABCDEFGabcdefghijkl12345

AMERICAN UNCIAL. Victor Hammer, c 1953, K; now S, and also called New Hammer Uncial by S; ¶ Hammer Uncial by S; Solemnis, Be. Shown: 18 pt. with companion Initials, capitals.

abcdefghjklmnopqrstuvwxyz
ABCDEFGHIJKLMNOPQRSTUVWXYZ1234567890
abcdefghijklmnopqrstuvwxyz

ANTIQUE OLD STYLE. Based on face by A. C. Phemister, c. 1860. Now general. M uses same name. Others: Antique No. 1, I, L; Bookface, I; Bookman, ATF, M(L); Bookman, Lu. Shown: M(E) 161.

ABCDEFGHIJKLMNOPQRSTUVWXYZ&
abcdefghijklnopqrstwxyz*abcdefghijklnopqrst*
*ABCDEGHIJKLMOPQRSTWXYZ*123456789

ARIADNE INITIALS. Gudrun Zapf-von Hesse, 1954, Stempel.

ABCDEFGHIJKLMNO LRVZ

ARISTON. Martin Wilke, 1933, Be. Shown: Ariston Medium.

ABCDEFGHIJK abcdefghijklmnopqrstuvwxyz 123

ARRIGHI ITALIC. Based on a script of Ludovico degli Arrighi. Frederic Warde, 1925, Plumet; 1931, M. ¶ Bembo Condensed Italic, M(E); Blado Italic, M(E) (See Centaur for showing).

ARTSCRIPT. Based on Spanish cancelleresca hands of late 18th century. Sol Hess, 1940, M(L).

ABCDEFGHIJKLMNOPQRSTUVWXYZ&
abcdefghijklmnopqrstuvwxyz ffifflffiffl aemt gggy 1234567890

ASTER. Francesco Simoncini, 1958, SI; also L&M.

ABCDEFGHIJKLMNOPQRSTUVWXYZ abcdefghijklmnopqrstuvwxyz*abcdefghijklmno*12345

ASTUR. Produced by FTN.

ABCDEFGHIJKLabcdefghijk12345

AUGUSTEA ROMAN. Alessandro Butti and Aldo Novarese, 1951, Shown: 18 pt. For Augustea Roman Inline, see Page 122.

ABCDEFGHIJKLMNOPQRSTUVWXYZ&123456789

AURORA. Newspaper face fitted to teletypesetter composition. Jackson Burke, 1960, L.

ABCDEFGHIJKLMNOPQRSTUVWXYZ& abcdefghijklmnopqrstuvwxyzfiflffffiffl 1234567890$£,.:;'-'?-!—()*/@℔%
ABCDEFGHIJKLMNOPQRSTUVWXYZ& abcdefghijklmnopqrstuvwxyzfiflffffiffl 1234567890$£,.:;'-'?-!—()*/@℔%

BALLÉ INITIALS. Maria Ballé, BG. (See Page 122).

BALLOON or LASSO. Max R. Kaufmann, 1939, ATF. Shown: Extrabold with sampling of Light and Bold.

ABC ABC ABCDEFGHIJKLMNOPQRSTUVWXYZ123456789

BANK GOTHIC. C. 1900, ATF; also L. Commerce Gothic, Lu; Stationers Gothic, M(L); Agency Gothic, ATF; DeLuxe Gothic, I. Poster Gothic, ATF, is condensed
Shown: 12 pt. No. 18, ATF.

ABCDEFGHIJKLMNOPQRSTUVWXYZ1234567890

BANK SCRIPT. James West, 1911, ATF. Bond Script, ATF; Commercial Script, ATF ¶ Cantate, BG, is bold; Youthline Script, SB.

ABCDEFGHIJKLMNOPQRSTUV

WXYZ& abcdefghijklmnopqrstuvwxyz 1234567890

BASKERVILLE. Based on face by John Baskerville, c.1750; now general. D&P uses original punches; M.F. Benton, ATF, designed first revival, 1915; S, close to D&P, 1924; M(E), regularized version, 1924, with I, similar; L, 1931, orig. except for machine modifications. BG version is Baskerville Antiqua, called Bauer Classic in U.S.
Shown: (1) Original Baskerville. S, 28D pt.; (2) M(E) No. 169; (3) ATF.

(1) ABCDEFGHIJKLMNOPQRSTUVWXYZ
abcdefghijklmnopqrstuvwxyz1234567890 *NTVY*
ABCDEFGHIJKLMNOPQRSTUVWXYZAJK
abcdefghijklmnopqrstuvwxyz abcdefghijklmnopqrstuv
(2) ABCDEFGHIJKLMNOPQRSTUVWXYZ& wxyz
ABCDEFGHIJKLMNOPQRSTUVWXYZ& 1234567890
abcdefghijklmnopqrstuvwxyz abcdefghijklmnopqrstuvwxyz&! 9
(3) ABCDEFGHIJKLMNOPQRSTUVWXYZ$12345678

BAUER TOPIC. Paul Renner, 1953, BG. Also called Steile Futura. Condensa, M(E), similar to italic.

ABCDEFGHIJKLMNOPQRSTUVWXYZabcdefghijklmnopqrstuvw
xyz1234567890 ***abcdefghijklmnopqrstuvwxyzQRSTUVWXYZ&***

BELL. Based on face by Richard Austin, 1788, for John Bell. Recut, 1932, M. Oxford, ATF.

ABCDEFGHIJKLMNOPQRSTUVWXYZ&abcdefgh
ijklmnopqrstuvwxyz1234567890*abcdefghijklmnopqrstuvw*
ABCDEFGHIJKLMNOPQRSTUVWXYZ&123456

BELL GOTHIC. Designed especially for use in telephone directories. 1938, L; also I,M Shown: 6 pt. L, Light; 8 pt. I, Bold.

ABCDEFGHIJKLMNOPQRSTUVWXYZ abcdefghijklmnopqrstuvwxyz 1234567890 **ABCDEFGHIJKLMNOPQRSTUVWXYZ abcdefghijklmnopqrstuvwxyz 1234567890**

BEMBO or ALDINE BEMBO. Based on face by Francesco Griffo, 1495, for Aldus Manutius. Recut 1930, M. Dante, M(E); Romanee, E. Shown with Italic and Bold.

ABCDEFGHIJKLMNOPQRSTUVWXYZ& 1234567890
abcdefghijklmnopqrstuvwxyz *abcdefghijklmnopqrstuvwxyz*
ABCDEFGHIJKLMNOPQRSTUVWXYZ& 1234567890
ABCDEFGHIJKLMNOPabcdefghijklmnopqrstuvw

BERNHARD CURSIVE. Lucian Bernhard, 1925, BG. Also as Madonna, SB; light called Madonna Ronde, SB. ¶ Liberty, ATF; Lotus, I; Mayfair Cursive, Lu. Shown: bold

ABCDEFGHIJKLMNOPQabcdefghijklmnopqrstuvwxyz12345

BERNHARD FASHION. Lucian Bernhard, 1929, ATF, also I. ¶ Groteskfeiler, JW; Vogue, SB. Banjo D&P similar but with very wide and very narrow alternate caps.

ABCDEFGQRSW&abcdefghijklmnopqrstuvwxyz123456

BERNHARD MODERN. Lucian Bernhard; Roman cut in 1937, bold 1938, ATF. Shown: Bold.

ABCDEFGHIJKLMNOPabcdefghijklmnopq1234567

ABCDEFGHIJKLMNOPabcdefghijklmnopqr1234567

BERNHARD TANGO or AIGRETTE. Lucian Bernhard, 1934, ATF; also A, as Aigrette. Bernhard Aigrette Initials are matching.

ABCDEFGHIJKLMOPQRSTWabcdefghijklmnopqrstuvwx

BIFUR. A. M. Cassandre, 1929, D&P. (See use as initial on Page 122.)

BLADO ITALIC. Used with Poliphilus. Cut in 1923 by M(E). based on a formal hand of Vicentino (Ludovico degli Arrighi). See Poliphilus.

BODONI. Based on face cut by Giambattista Bodoni, 1789. Redesigned by M. F. Benton, 1907, ATF. Now general. Shown: (1) M(E) 135; (2) Bauer Bodoni Bold; (3) Bodoni Book, M(L) 875.

(1) ABCDEFGHIJKLMNOPQRSTUVWXYZ&1234567890

abcdefghijklmnopqrstuvwxyzabcdefghijklmnopqrstuvwx

ABCDEFGHIJKLMNOPQRSTUVWXYZ&123456789

(2) ABCDEFGHIJKLMNOPQRSTUVWXYZ&1234567890

abcdefghijklmnopqrstuvwxyabcdefghijklmnopqrstuvwxyz

ABCDEFGHIJKLMNOPQRSTUVWXYZ 1234567890

(3) ABCDEFGHIJKLMNOPQRSTUVWXYZ ABCDEFGHIJKLM

abcdefghijklmnopqrstuvwxyz abcdefghijklmnopqrstuvwxyz

BODONI EXTRA CONDENSED. A variant in most Bodoni families, but some have special names: Bodoni Campanile, R. H. Middleton, 1936, Lu. ¶ Amati, W; Arsis, A; Elongated Roman, SB; Figura K.; Jeannette, S.; Liliom, FTF; Mondial Bold Condensed, S.; Olympic, D&P; Onyx, ATF, M; Poster Bodoni Compressed, L; Romain Ideal, H; Slim Bodoni, I; Slimblack, D&P; Vertical, H. Shown: Campanile, Lu.

ABCDEFGHIJKLMNOPQRSTUVWXYZ&abcdefghijklmnopqrstuvwxyz123456789

BOLOGNA. 1946, SB; also ATF. Verona, ATF. ¶ Freehand, ATF; Motto, ATF; Rembrandt, BG; Runnymede, SB.

ABCDEFGHIJKLMNOPQRSTUabcdefghijklmnopqrstuvwxy

BRUSH. Robert E. Smith, 1942, ATF. Wave, Lu

ABCDEFGHIJKLMNOPQRSTUVWXYZ&

abcdefghijklmnopqrstuvwxyz 1234567890

BULMER. Based on face cut by William Martin, c. 1790. M. F. Benton, 1928, ATF; also I, M(L).

ABCDEFGHIJKLMNOPQRSabcdefghijklmnopqrst1234567

ABCDEFGHIJKLMNOPQRSTabcdefghijklmnopqrst123456

CALEDONIA. W. A. Dwiggins, 1938, L. Called Cornelia, L (F), S.

ABCDEFGHIJKLMNOPQRSTUVWXYZ&12345678

abcdefghijklmnopqrstuvwxyzabcdefghijklmnopqrstuv

CALIFORNIAN. F. W. Goudy, 1938, as private face for the University of California Press; made generally available 1958, M(L).

ABCDEFGHIJKLMNOPQRSTUVWXYZ abcdefghijklmnopqrstuvwxyz 1234567890

ABCDEFGHIJKLMNOPQRSTUVWXYZ abcdefghijklmnopqrstuvwxyz 1234567890

CALYPSO. Roger Excoffon, 1958, O.

ABCDEFGHIJKLMNOPQRSTUVWXYZ

CANCELLERESCA BASTARDA. Jan Van Krimpen, 1934, E. Based on 15th century humanistic cursive. Shown: 18 pt.

ABCDEFGHIJKLMNOPQRSTUVWXYZabcdeffghhijklmnopqrstuvwxyyz

CARTOON or FRESKO. Howard Allen Trafton, 1936, BG. ¶ Studio, A.

ABCDEFGHIJKLMNOPQRSTUVWXYZ

CASLON with italic and swash. Based on face cut by William Caslon, c. 1726. Now general. Shown: (1) M(E) 128; (2) ATF 540; (3) Linotype Caslon No. 3; (4) True-Cut Caslon, Lu.

(1) ABCDEFGHIJKLMNOPQRSTUVWXYZ&12345678
abcdefghijklmnopqrstuvwxyz*abcdefghijklmnopqrstuvwxyz*90
ABCDEFGHIJKLMNOPQRSTUVWXYZ&123456789

(2) ABCDEFGHIJKLMNOPQRSTabcdefghijklno
ABCDEFGHIJKLMNOPQRSTabcdefghijklnop

(3) **ABCDEFGHIJKLMNOPQRSTabcdefghijklm**

(4) ABCDEFGHIJKLMNOPQRSTabcdefghijklmnopqrst

CASLON ANTIQUE. C. 1897. BB&S as Fifteenth Century, now ATF. Powell Bold, Lu; Plymouth, M(L).

ABCDEFGHIJKLMNOPQRSTUabcdefghijklmnopqrstuvwxy

CASTELLAR. John Peters, 1957, M(E).

ABCDEFGHIJKLMNOPQRSTUVWX

CENTAUR. Based on face cut by Nicolas Jenson, 1470. Bruce Rogers, 1914, private, redesigned 1931, M. ¶ Bauer Text or Schneidler Old Style, BG; (M shown with Arrighi Italic.)

ABCDEFGHIJKLMNOPQRSTUVWXYZ& 1234567890
abcdefghijklmnopqrstuvwxyz *abcdefghijklmnopqrstuvwxyz*
ABCDEFGHIJKLMNOPQRSTUVWXYZ& 1234567890

CENTURY. L. B. Benton and T. L. De Vinne, 1894, ATF. Adapted as Century Expanded, c. 1901, by M. F. Benton, with whole family following, including the readability version, Century Schoolbook, 1926, ATF, and most recently, Century Nova, by Charles E. Hughes, 1964, ATF. Century families now by I, L, Lu, M. Lu calls its readability version Century Modern. ¶ Augustea, Be. (1) Century Expanded, ATF; (2) Century Schoolbook, M; (3) Century Nova, ATF.

(1) ABCDEFGHIJKLMNOPQRSTUVWXYZ1234567
abcdefghijklmnopqrstuvwxyz*ABCDEFGHIJKL*
MPQRSTUVWXYZabcdefghijklmnopqrstuvwxyz

(2) ABCDEFGHIJKLMNOPQRSTUVWXYZ
abcdefghijklmnopqrstuvwxyz*abcdefghijklmnopq*

(3) ABCDEFGHIJKLMNOPQRSTUV abcdefghijklmnopqrstuvwx

CHAMFER GOTHIC. Based on 19th century chamfer-cornered grot-gothics. Lu uses name; Herald Gothic Extra Condensed, ATF, I; Gothic No. 14, L. **Shown: 30 pt., Lu.**

ABCDEFGHIJKLMNOPQRSTUVWXYZ& 1234567890

CHAMPLEVÉ or SYLVAN. Bernard Naudin, D&P, also SB; A as Sylvan. (See Page 122)

CHELTENHAM. Bertram G. Goodhue, designed 1896 for L; cut 1902, ATF, 1906, L, Lu. Now general. Other families: Bodonia, N; Cheltonian, I; Gloucester, M(E); Sorbonne, Be; Winchester, SB. **Shown: (1) Lino Bold Condensed; (2) Cheltenham Old Style, Lu; (3) ATF Cheltenham Bold; Cheltenham Cursive, Lu.**

(1) **ABCDEFGHIJKLMNOPQRSTUVWXYZabcdefghijklmnopqrstuvw**
1234567890 ABCDEFGHIJKLMNOPQRSTUVWXYZ&
abcdefghijklmnopqrstuvwxyz*abcdefghijklmnopqrstuvwxyz*
(2) **ABCDEFGHIJKLMNOPQabcdefghijklmnopqr123**
(3) *ABCDEFGHIJKLMNOPQRSTUVWX*

CHISEL and CHISEL WIDE. Inline version cut by SB and E. **Shown: Chisel and Latin Bold Condensed, 30 pt., Chisel Expanded and Wide Latin, 18 pt., all SB.**

ABCDEFGHJ **ABCDEFGHIKLM** **NOPQR** NOPQR

CITY. Georg Trump, 1930, BG. **Shown: Medium and Light.**

ABCDEFGHIJKLMNOPQRSTUVWXYZabcdefghijklmnopqrs
ABCDEFGHIJKLMNOPQRSTUabcdefghijklmnpqrstuvwxyz tuvwxyz1234567890
ABCDEFGHIJKLMNOPQRSabcdefghijklmnopqrstuvw

CIVILITÉ. Based on French 16th century hand as cut by Robert Granjon, but "modernized" for legibility. M.F. Benton, 1922, ATF (Shown). La Civilité, D&P, is close to original.

ABCDEFGHIJKLMNOPQRSTUVWXYZ
abcdefghijklmnopqrstuvwxyz 1234567890

CLARENDON. Based on Caslon Foundry's Ionic of 1842–43 and Robert Besley's Clarendon, 1845. Now general. Recut in New Clarendon style, first by Hans Eidenbenz, 1951–53, H; called Haas Clarendon but now simply Clarendon; also L, S. Antique No. 3, SS; Consort, SB; Craw Clarendon, ATF and M(L); Egizio, N; Fortuna [Fortune] or Volta, BG; New Clarendon, M(E). **Shown: (1) Haas, S, L; (2) Consort, SB; (3) Fortuna [Fortune] Light, BG; (4) Eigizio Bold, N, 14 pt.; (5) Craw Clarendon, ATF.**

(1) ABCDEFGHIJKLMabcdefghijklm1234
ABCDEFGHIJKLM abcdefghijklmno
(2) ABCDEFGHJKLMNOPabcdefghijklmnopqrst
(3) ABCDEFGHIJKLMabcdefghijklmnopqrst
(4) **ABCDEFGHIJKLMNOPQRSTabcdefghijklmnopqrstuvwxyz 1234**
(5) **ABCDEFGHIJKLMabcdefghijklmnopqrst**

CLARITAS. The 4¾ pt. size of Times New Roman (*q.v.*), especially developed for classified ads or small announcements in newspapers.
ABCDEFGHIJKLMNOPQRSTUVWXYZabcdefghijklmnopqrstuvwxyz1234567890*ABCDEFGHIJKLMNOPQRSTUVWXYZ abcdefghijklmnopqrstuvwxyz 1234567890£$*

CLAUDIUS. A Fraktur in freshened line. Paul Koch, 1937, K; now S.

ABCDEFGHIJKLMNOPQ1234567890
RSTUVWXYZ&abcdefghijklmnopqrſstuvwxyz

CLEARFACE. M. F. Benton, 1907, ATF. Also I, L, Lu, M, SB. Shown: Lu.

ABCDEFGHIJKLMNOPQRSTUVWXYZ&12345678
abcdefghijklmnopqrstuvwxyz *ABCDEFGabcdefghijkl*

CLOISTER BLACK. M. F. Benton, 1903, ATF. ¶ Caslon Text, L; Engraver's Old English, ATF, I; Lino Text, L; Old English Text, Lu; Wedding Text, M(L) SB. Shown: (1) Linotype Cloister; (2) Cloister Bold, M 295; (3) L, 12 pt.

ABCDEFGHIJKLMNOPQRSTUVWXYZ
abcdefghijklmnopqrstuvwxyz 1234567890

CLOISTER INITIALS. F. W. Goudy, 1918, ATF; also M(L). (See Page 6)

CLOISTER OLD STYLE. Based on face cut by Nicolas Jenson, 1470. Redesigned by M. F. Benton, 1913, ATF. Also I, L, M. ¶ Benedictine, L; Eusebius, Lu; Italian Old Style, M(L); Jenson, ATF; Verona Roman, SB; Veronese, M(E). Shown: Cloister Old Style and Cloister Bold.

ABCDEFGHIJKLMNOPQRSTUVWXYZabcdefghijklmnopq
rstuvwxyz *ABCDEFGHIJKLMNOPQRSTUVWXYZ&1234567*
abcdefghijklmnopqrstuvwxyz **ABCDEFGHIJKabcdefghijklmnop**
ABCDEFGHIJKLMNOPQRSTUVWXYZ& abcdefghijklmnopqrstuvwxyz *abcdefghijklmnopqrstuvwxyz*

COCHIN. 1913, D&P; also M. Shown: M(E) 165.

ABCDEFGHIJKLMPQ *ABCDEFGHIJKLM*
abcdefghijklmnopqrstuvwxyz *abcdefghijkwxyz* 1234

CODEX. Georg Trump, 1954–56, W.

ABCDEFGHIJKLMNOPQRSTUVWXY
abcdefghijklmnopqrstuvwxyz Z

COLUMBIA. Walter McKay, 1957, A; also I. Shown: 18 pt.

ABCDEFGHIJKLMNOPQRSTUVWXYZ abcdefghijklmnopqrstuvwxyz
ABCDEFGHIJKLMNOPQRSTUVWXYZ abcdefghijklmnopqrstuvwxyz 1234567890

COMSTOCK. C. 1860. BB&S, now ATF. Astoria, B. ¶ Gill Sans Shadow Line, M(E).

ABCDEFGHIJKLMnopqrstuvwxyz12345

CONSTRUCTS. Separate pieces of type with lines, curves or solids to be put together by printer to construct various letters. Alpha-Blox, ATF. (See Page 122 for letters formed by Alpha-Blox.)

COOPER BLACK. Oswald B. Cooper, 1921, BB&S, now ATF. ¶ Goudy Heavy, M; Ludlow Black, Lu; Pabst Extrabold, L; Rugged Black, I.

ABCDEFGHIJKLMNOPQRSTUVWXYZ
abcdefghijklmnopqrstuvwxyz1234567

COPPERPLATE GOTHIC. F. W. Goudy, 1901, ATF uses name, now general. Special names: Atalante, N; Plate Gothic, W; Spartan, M(E) and SB; Steelplate Gothic, ATF Shown: Heavy Extended No. 79, ATF.

ABCDEFGHIJKLMNOPQ12345

CORNELL. George Trenholm, 1947, I. Shown: 10 pt.

ABCDEFGHIJKLMNOPQRSTUVWXYZ abcdefghijklmnopqrstuvwxyz **1234567890** *abcdefghijklmnopqrstuvwxyz*
ABCDEFGHIJKLMNOPQRSTUVWXYZ **ABCDEFGHIJKLMNOPQRSTUVWXYZ abcdefghijklmnopqrstuvwxyz**

CORONET. R. H. Middleton, 1937, Lu. Shown: Coronet Bold.

ABCDEFGHIJKLMOPQRST abcdefghijklmnopqrstuvwxyz1234

CORVINUS. Imre Reiner, 1929–34, BG; M(L) as Glamour. ¶ Coronation, SB; Eden, Lu; Keyboard, SB; Mondial, S. Shown: Medium, Light and Bold.

ABCDEFGHIJKLMNOPQRSTUVW abcdefghijklmnopqrstuv wxyz *ABCDEFGHIJKLMNOPQRSTUV abcdefghijklmnopqrstuvwxyz* 123

ABCDEFGHIJKLMNOPQRSTUVWXYZ abcdefghijklmno

ABCDEFGHIJKLMNOPQRS abcdefghijklmnopqrstuvwxyz *ABCDEFGHIJKLMNOPQRST abcdefghijklmnopqrstuvwxyz*

CORVINUS SKYLINE. Typical of extra-condensed variants of softened or stylized Didot-like letters (e.g., Corvinus). Also Greenwich, Lu; Spire, M(L). Shown: 18 pt.

ABCDEFGHIJKLMNOPQRSTUVWXYZ abcdefghijklmnopqrstuvwxyz 1234567890

CRAW MODERN. Freeman Craw, 1958; Bold, 1959; italic, 1966, ATF. ¶ Card Mercantile, ATF, older version. Shown: 18 pt.

ABCDEFGHIJKLMNOPQRSTUVWXYZ
abcdefghijklmnopqrstuvwxyz *1234567890*
ABCDEFGHIJKLM abcdefghijklmnopqrstuvwxyz

CRAYONETTE. A remnant of 19th century lithographic lettering, ATF. Shown: 18 pt.

ABCDEFGHIJKLMNOPQRSTUVWXYZ
abcdefghijklmnopqrstuvwxyz1234567890$

CRISTAL. Rémy Peignot, 1955, D&P.

ABCDEFGHIJKLMNOPQRSTU123456789

De ROOS. S. H. De Roos, 1947, A. Also ATF, I.

ABCDEFGHIJKLMNOPQRSTUVWXYZ abcdefghijklmnopq rstuvwxyz *ABCDEGHJKLMNOPQRSTUVWXYZ* 123456789
abcdefghijklmnopqrstuvwxyz ABCDEFGHIJKLMNOPQRST abcdefghijklmnopqrstuvwxyz *ABCDEFGHIJKLMNOPQRST abcdefghijklmnopqrstuvwxyz*

DE VINNE. Based on Elzevir, a basic French old style face. Gustav Schroeder, 1894, ATF; also I, L, M. Linotype De Vinne is a modern face; also I.

ABCDEFGHIJKLMNOPQRSTUVWXYZ& abcd efghijklmnopqrstuvwxyz $1234567890

DEEPDENE. F. W. Goudy, 1927, Continental; now M.

ABCDEFGHIJKLMNOPQRSTUVWXYZ&1234567890
abcdefghijklmnopqrstuvwxyz *abcdefghijklmnopqrstuvwxyz*
ABCDEFGHIJKLMNOPQRSTUVWXYZ&1234567890

DELIA. Francesco Simoncini, 1962, Sim. Designed for small advertisements in newspapers. Shown: 6 pt. and Bold.

ABCDEFGHIJKLMNOPQRSTUVWXYZ abcdefghijklmnopqrstuvwxyz 1234567890 **ABCDEFGHIJKLMNOPQRSTUVWXYZ abcdefghijklmnopqrstuvwxyz 1234567890**

DELLA ROBBIA or WESTMINSTER OLD STYLE. T. M. Cleland, 1903, ATF; now also D&P, I, M(L), SB. Canterbury, M; Korinna, I.

ABCDEFGHIJKLMNPQ abcdefghijklnopqrstu123

DELPHIAN OPEN TITLE. R. H. Middleton, 1930, Lu.

ABCDEFGHIJKLMNOPQRSTUVWXYZ&

DELPHIN I and II. Georg Trump, 1951–55, W. Shown: I and II.

ABCDEFGHIJKLMNOPQRSTUVWXYZ*abcdefghijklmnopqrstu*

*vwxyz&dgs1234567890*ABCDEFGHIJKLM*abcdefghijklmnop*

DIDOT ORNAMENTED INITIALS. Cut by Pierre Didot Sr., c. 1820; now E. (See Page 122)

DIETHELM ROMAN. Walther Diethelm, 1948–50, H; aso L(F)

ABCDEFGHIJKLMNOPQRST *ABCDEFGHIJ*

abcdefghijklmnopqrstuvwxyz*abcdefghijklmnop*

DIN-GROTESQUE ITALIC. Based on mechanical drawing lettering, usually from templates. Cut by S.

ABCDEFGHIJKLMabcdeffghijklmnopqrsſtu123456

DIOTIMA. Gudrun Zapf-von Hesse, 1948–54, S.

ABCDEFGHIJKLMNOPQRSTUVWXYZ1234567

abcdefghijklmnopqrstuvwxyz*ABCDEFGHIJKLM*

NOPQRSTUVWXYZabcdefghijklmnopqrstuvwxyz

DOM CASUAL and DOM DIAGONAL. Peter Dom, 1951–53, ATF; also A, as Polka; Trend, Ba. Dom Bold matches Dom Casual. First cold-type face to be put into hot metal.

ABCDEFGHIJKLMNOPQRSTUVWXYZabcdefghijklmnopqrstuvwxyz12345678

***ABCDEFGHIJKLMNOPQRSTUVWXYZabcdefghijklmnopqrstuvwxyz*ABCDEFG**

DOMINO. Produced by L&M.

ABCDEFGHIJKLMNOPQRSTUVW

abcdefghijklmnopqrstuvwxyz12345

DORCHESTER SCRIPT. 1938, M(E). ¶ Grosvenor, M(E).

ABCDEFGHIJKLMNOPQRSTUVWXYZabcdefghijklmnopqrstuvwxyz12345

DUTCH INITIALS. Based on 16th-18th century calligraphic initials; ATF. (See Page 122)

ECLAIR. Maximilien Vox, 1935, D&P.

ABCDEFGHIJKLMNOPQRSTUVWXY&Z12345

EGMONT. S. H. De Roos, 1932, A; also I. For Egmont Decorative Initials based on Egmont Medium, see Page 122.

ABCDEFGHIJKLMNOPQRSTUVWXYZ12345678

abcdefghijklmnopqrstuvwxyz *abcdefghijklmnopqrstuvwx*

EGYPTIAN. Based on the original Egyptians of early 19th century; recut by M(E), under same name. Other families: Antique Nos. 5, 6, SS; Contact, ATF; Cushing Antique, Lu; Pharaon, D&P; Superba, H. Shown: M(E) 173 and Egyptian Expanded, 22 pt. SB.

ABCDEFGHIJKLMNOPQRSTUVWXYZ&

abcdefghijklmnopqrstuvwxyz**ABCabcd**

ELDORADO. Designed to convey a Spanish spirit for Latin-American readers. W. A. Dwiggins, 1951, L.

ABCDEFGHIJKLMNOPQRSTUVWXYZ abcdefghijklmnopqrstuvwxyz 1234567890

ABCDEFGHIJKLMNOPQRSTUVWXYZ abcdefghijklmnopqrstuvwxyz 1234567890

ELECTRA, ELECTRA ITALIC and ELECTRA CURSIVE. W.A. Dwiggins, 1937, L. Original italic is slightly oblique roman; True italic lowercase called cursive, added in 1944.

ABCDEFGHIJKLMNOPQRSTUVWXYZ& *ABCDEFGHIJKLMNOPQRSTUVWXYZ&* 1234567890
abcdefghijklmnopqrstuvwxyz *abcdefghijklmnopqrstuvwxyz* *abcdefghijklmnopqrstuvwxyz* 1234567890

ELZEVIR. Based on 19th century revival of face used by Elzevir press in the 17th century for its famous small-size books, leading French to call old style (faces) "Elzevir." Now many foundries. ¶ Lorimer with Remson Bold, I; Romana, FTN; Raffaello, N; Romanische Antiqua, I; L Elzevir No. 3 shown.

ABCDEFGHIJKLMNOPQRSTUVWXYZ12345 12345
cdefghijklmnopqrstuvwxyz *abcdefghijklmnopqrstuvwxyz 12345678 12345678*
ABCDEFGHIJKLMNOPQRSTUVWXYZ&

EMERSON. Joseph Blumenthal, 1936 M(E). Shown: 24 pt. and 10 pt.

ABCDEFGHIJKLMNOPQRSTUVWXYZ&1234567890
abcdefghijklmnopqrstuvwxyz *abcdefghijklmnopqrstuvwxyz*
ABCDEFGHIJKLMNOPQRSTUVWXYZ&1234567890
ABCDEFGHIJKLMNOPQRSTUVWXYZ abcdefghijklmnopqrstuvwxyz *ABCDEFGHIJKLMNOPQRSTUV abcdefghijklmnopqrstuvwxyz*

ENGRAVER'S ROMAN, BOLD and SHADED. Based on copperplate engravers' lettering. Family using name designed by M. F. Benton, 1898, ATF; also SB, M. Other families: Bold Face No. 9, I; Copperplate, L&M; Litho Roman, ATF; Noblesse, BG; Orlando, N. Shaded: Azuree, BG; Excellent, BG. **Shown: 24 Engraver's Bold, ATF**; 18 pt. Shaded No. 1, SB, and 12 pt. Engraver's Bold No. 3, ATF.

ABCDEFGHIJKLMNOPQRSTUVWXYZ

ERASMUS INITIALS. S. H. De Roos, 1923, A. (See Page 122)

ERBAR INITIALS. Jakob Erbar, L&M. (See Page 122)

EUROSTILE. Aldo Novarese, 1962, N. Microgramma is earlier capitals, N. **Shown: 24 normal and Bold Extended.**

ABCDEFGHIJKLMNOPQRSTUVWXYZ1234567890
abcdefghijklmnopqrstuvwxyz **ABCDEFGabcdefg**

EVE or LOCARNO. Rudolf Koch, 1922, K; now S. Also called Koch Antique and Koch Cursive (italic). Rivoli, ATF, I. ¶ Paramount, ATF, is a bold.

ABCDEFGHIJKLMNOPQRSTUVWXYZ&abcdefghijklmnopq
rstuvwxyz1234567890 *ABCDEFGHIJKabcdefghijklmnopqrstuvwxyz*

EXTRA ORNAMENTED No. 2. Cut by Figgins, c. 1840, now SS. Called Tuscan Floral or Floradora in U.S. Shown: 30 pt.

ABCDEFGHIJKLMNOPQRSTUVWXY

FAIRFIELD. Rudolph Ruzicka, 1939, L.

ABCDEFGHIJKLMNOPQRSTUVWXYZ& 1234567890 abcdefghijklmnopqrstuvwxyz 1234567890
ABCDEFGHIJKLMNOPQRSTUVWXYZ& 1234567890 abcdefghijklmnopqrstuvwxyz 1234567890

FAT FACE (England) or ULTRA BODONI (U.S.). Based on fat faces of Robert Thorne, other early 19c English typecutters; now usually considered the extra-bold variant of Bodoni, thus general. Most faces, however, still have special names: Bodoni Black, Lu; Bodoni Modern, I; Compact, E; Falstaff, M(E); Normandia, N; Poster Bodoni, L; Thorowgood Roman (the Thorne original), SB; Ultra Bodoni, ATF and M. ¶ Normande, H, Be, differs in having a graceful transition from thins to thicks. Shown: M(E) 120 [Ultra Bodoni].

ABCDEFGHIJKLMNOPQRSTUVWXYZ&
ABCDEFGHIJKLMNOPQRSTUVWXYZ
abcdefghijklmnopqrstuvwxyz123456789
abcdefghijklmnopqrstuvwxyz12345678

FAT FACE OUTLINE SHADOW. Face shown is Thorne Shaded, SB, based on Robert Thorne's fat face cut in 1803. Others: Figgins Shaded, SS, and Verdi, BG, with Elongated Roman Shaded, SB, and Regina, Be, more condensed.

ABCDEFGHIJKLMNOPQRXYZ12

FESTIVAL TITLING. Phillip Boydell & Associates, 1951, M(E). Shown: 36 pt.

ABCDEFGHIJKLMNOPQRSTUVWXYZ&

FIRMIN DIDOT. First modern style face, cut by Firmin Didot, 1784, produced today from original punches held by D&P; L&M version close; also A. ¶ Didot, Neo-Didot are M(E) versions.

ABCDEFGHIJKLMNOPQRabcdefghijklmnopqrstuvwxyz1234

FLASH. Edwin W. Shaar, 1939–40, M(L). Shown: Flash Bold, with sample of Light.

ABCDEFGHIJKLMNOPQRSTUVWXYZabcdefghijklmnopqrs
tuvwxyz1234567890ABCDEFGHIJKLMNOPQRSTUVWXYZ&

FLASH or PARIS FLASH. Crous-Vidal, 1953, FTF. Shown: 18 pt.

ABCDEFGHIJKLMNOPQRSTUVWXYZ

FLORENTINE CURSIVES. R. H. Middleton, 1956, Lu.

ABCDEFGHIJKLMPQRSTUVWYZabcdefghijklmnopqrstu

FLORIATED CAPITALS. Eric Gill, 1932, M(E). In U.S., sometimes called Canterbury Initials. (See Page 122)

FONTANESI. Aldo Novarese, N. (See Page 122)

FORUM TITLE or CAPITALS. F. W. Goudy, 1911, M(L); also SB. Shown: 18 pt.

ABCDEFGHIJKLMNOPQRSTUVWXYZ&1234567890

FOURNIER. Based on face cut by Pierre Simon Fournier, c. 1745. Cut by M, 1925. Barbou, M(E). Shown: E(M) 185, 10 pt.

ABCDEFGHIJKLMNOPQRSTUVWXYZ&1234567890
abcdefghijklnopqrstuvwxy ABCDEFGHIJKLMNOPQRSTUVWXYZ abcdefghijklmnopqrstuvwxyz
ABCDEFGHIJKLMNOPQRSTUVWXYZ abcdefghijklmnopqrstuvwxyz

FOURNIER LE JEUNE. Based on face cut by Pierre Simon Fournier, c. 1746, recut by D&P, 1913. Also A, ATF. ¶ Vogue Initials, ATF; June, SB.

ABCDEFGHIJKLMNOPQRSTUVWXYZ123

FRAKTUR. Based on Fraktur style of Spire Gothic. General. (Lu Fraktur shown).

ABCDEFGHIJKLMNOPQRSTUVW
abcdefghijklmnopqrstuvwxyz 1234567890

FRENCH (or ITALIAN) ANTIQUE. Based on so-called French Antique or Italian Antique faces of early 18th century. Now general: ¶ Figaro, or Old Towne, Showboat, M(E); Hidalgo, A; Playbill, SB; Pro Arte, H; P. T. Barnum, ATF; Trylon, Ba, SB. U.S. foundries call Figaro by such names as Old Towne and Showboat. Magnet, L&M, is an oblique version. Shown: (1) Playbill; (2) Barnum, (3) Figaro.

ABCDEFGabcdefgABCDEFGHIJKLabcdefghijklABCDEFGabcdefg12345

FRY'S ORNAMENTED. Cut by Richard Austin, 1796, for Fry's foundry. Now SB. Also called Colonial. (See Page 122)

FUTURA BLACK and FUTURA DISPLAY. Paul Renner, Display, 1931, BG. Braggadocio, M; Transito, A; similar to Black. Resolut, N, is styled italic. Othello, ATF; Airport Tourist or Airport Display, Ba, similar to Display. (1) is Display, (2) is Black.

(1) ABCDEFGHIJKLMNOPQRSTUVWXYZ abcdefghijklmnopqrstu
vwxyz 1234567890 (2) ABCDEFGHIJKLMNOPQRST
UVWXYZ&abcdefghijklmnopqrst123456789

Makin' Tracks

GARAMOND. Based on face cut by Claude Garamont, c. 1531, via Jean Jannon face cut c. 1615. Designed by M. F. Benton and Thomas M. Cleland, 1914, ATF; also SB. Now general. Lu based directly on Garamont, D&P based directly on Jannon punches. M(L) also has face called Garamont, by Goudy. (See also Granjon.) Shown: M(E) 156; (2) Bold, ATF; (3) Garamont, M(L) 14 pt.; (4) Ludlow Garamond.

(1) ABCDEFGHIJKLMNOPQRSTUVWXYZ&123456789
abcdefghijklmnopqrstuvwxyz *abcdefghijklmnopqrstuvwxyz*
ABCDEFGHIJKLMNOPQRSTUVWXYZ& 12345678

(2) **ABCDEFGHIJKLMNOPQRSTUabcdefghijklmnopqrstv**

(3) ABCDEFGHIJKLMNOPQRSTUVWXYZabcdefghijklmnopqrstuvwxyz *abcdefghijklmnopqrst*

(4) ABCDEFGHIJKLMNOPQRSTUVWXYZabcdefghijklmnopqrs
tuvwxyz *abcdefghijklmnopqrstuvwxyz ABCDEFGHIJKLMNOPQRST*

GEOMETRIC SANS SERIF. First achieved by Paul Renner and BG, 1927, with Futura, after earlier stylized attempts. Other families are Airport, Ba; Atlantis Grotesque, W; Europe, D&P; Simplicitas, Sim; Spartan, ATF, L; Twentieth Century, M(L). I also has Futura. **Shown, in order: Futura Book, Medium, Demi-Bold and Oblique, Bold, Ultra and Ultra Condensed.**

ABCDEFGHIJKLMNOPQRSTUVWXYZabcdefghijklmnopqrstuvw
ABCDEFGHIJKLMnopqrstuvwxyz *ABCDEFGH ijklmnopqrstuv*
ABCDEfghijklm*NOPQRstuvwxyz* ABCdefghij*KLMnop*
ABCDEFGhijklmnopq*rstu VWXYZ* abcdeFGHIJKLM

GEORGIAN INITIALS. Based on 17th-18th century copperplate titles. Clarence P. Horning, 1924, ATF. (See Page 122)

GILL SANS CAMEO and GILL SANS CAMEO RULED. Eric Gill, 1928–36, M(E). Lucina, L&M, similar to Cameo. Cameo Ruled called Airport Relief by Ba, Banner by Los Angeles.

ABCDEFGHIJKLMNOPQRSTUVWXYZ1234

GILLIES GOTHIC (or FLOTT). William S. Gillies, 1935, BG.

ABCDEFGHIJKLMNOPQRSTUVWXYZabcdefghijklmnopqrstuvwxyz123

GOLD RUSH. A holdover from the 19th century, it is an outerlined or reverse Shadow Egyptian; ATF.

ABCDEFGHIJKLMNOPQR123

GONG. Cut 1953, JW.

ABCDEFGHIJKLMNOabcdefghijkl12345

GOUDY MEDIAEVAL. Cut by F. W. Goudy, 1930, at his Village Foundry. One of the many "lost Goudy faces," its punches and mats destroyed by fire, but with enough type already sold to leave a mark in typographic history. Shown 24 pt. and 14 pt.

ABCDEEFFGGHIJKLMNOPQRSSTUVWXYZ .,-:;'?!&
abcdefghijklmnopqrstuvwxyz $1234567890 ff fi fl ffi ffl
ABCDEFGHIJKLMNOPQRSTUVWXYZ& abcdefghijklmnopqrstuvwxyz 1234567890

GOUDY MODERN. F. W. Goudy, 1918, M.

ABCDEFGHIJKLMNOPQRSTUVWXYZ&1234567890
abcdefghijklmnopqrstuvwxyz *abcdefghijklmnopqrstuvwx*
ABCDEFGHIJKLMNPQRSTUVWXYZ&12345678

GOUDY OLD STYLE and GOUDY BOLD. Old Style: F. W. Goudy 1915, ATF; also M. Bold: M. F. Benton, ATF; also M, I, ¶ Goudy Catalogue, ATF, M; No. 11, Lu. Shown: M(E) O.S. 291, Bold 269.

ABCDEFGHIJKLMNOPQRSTUVWXYZ123456789
abcdefghijklmnopqrstuvwxyz *abcdefghijklmnopqrstuvwxyz*
ABCDEFGHIJKLMNOPQRSTUVWXYZ&
ABCDEFGHIJKLMN abcdefghijklmnopqrstuvwx

GOUDY TEXT and GOUDY TEXT SHADED. F. W. Goudy, 1928, M. First called Goudy Black. Shown: Text M(E); Shaded, 36 pt., M(L).

ABCDEFGHIJKLMNOPQRSTUV
WXYZ&abcdefghijklmnopqrstuvwxyz1234567890 ABCabc

GRANJON. Based on Garamond; some consider it closest to original. George W. Jones, 1924–28, L; also M(L).

ABCDEFGHIJKLMNOPQRSTUVWXYZabcdefghijklmnopqrstuvwxyz1234567890 *abcdefghijklmnopqrstuvwxyz*

GRAYDA. F. H. Riley, 1939, ATF.

ABCDEFGHJKLMOPQRSTUWXYZabcdefghijklmnopqrstuvw1234

GRECO (Bold), 1925, G; also Ba. Bristol, SS; Vulcan, L The decorated version by G, shown here with Greco Bold, is Greco Adornado; Rosart, SS, is similar ¶ Ottocento, N; Vesta, Be, in same general style.

ABCDEFGHJKLMNPQRSTUWYZ1234
abcdefghijklmnopqrstuvwxyzABCDEFGH

GROT-GOTHIC (GROTESQUE, England; GOTHIC, U.S.) Based on 19th century English grotesque. Grotesque No. 8 cut c. 1898, SB, has early spirit; other English Grots were recut to be more regular; Grotesque (various numbers), M, SB; Condensed Title Gothic, ATF, M; Doric 12; SB; Franklin Gothic, ATF, I, L, Lu; Headline Bold, M(E); Lining Sans Serif 25, SS; Mercator, A; Monotone Gothic, ATF; News Gothic, ATF, I, M; Railroad Gothic, ATF; Square Gothic, Lu; Trade Gothic, L. Tourist Gothic, M, uses alternate rounded caps; Jefferson Gothic, M(L) is extra condensed. Shown: (1) Grotesque No. 8, SB; (2) Doric No. 1 Italic, SB; (3) Franklin Gothic with Italic, ATF; (4) Square Gothic, Lu; (5) Headline Bold, M(E); (6) Grotesque No. 18, SB.

(1) **ABCDEFGHIJKLMNOabcdefghijklmnopqrst**
(2) ***ABCDEFGHIJKLMNOabcdefghijklmnopqr***
(3) **ABCDEFGHIJKLMNOPQRSTUVWXYZabcde**
fghijklmnopqrstuvwxyz *ABCDEFGHIJKLMN*
abcdefghijklmnopqrstuvwxyz1234567890
(4) **ABCDEFGHIJKLMNOPQRSTUVWXYZ&**
abcdefghijklmnopqrstuvwxyz 123456789
(5) **ABCDEFGHIJKLMNOPQRSTabcdefghijklmnopqrstuvwx**
ABCDEFGHIJKLMNOPQRSTabcdefghijklmnopqrstuvw
(6) **ABCDEFGHIJKLMNOPQRSabcdefghijklmnopqrstuvw**

GROT-GOTHIC CONDENSED. Most makers show this variant under the family name, but ATF calls it Alternate Gothic 1, 2 and 3 by M. F. Benton, 1903, shown below. It is Antique Bold Condensed, FTF; Condensed Gothic, Lu; Grotesque Condensed, M(E). Shown: Alternate Gothic No. 1, ATF 51.

ABCDEFGHIJKLMNOPQRSTUVWXYZ&abcdefghijklmnopqrstuvwxyz1234567890

GROT-GOTHIC EXTRA-BOLD EXPANDED. The blackest (so far) variant of the grots, most makers having them, and keeping more or less to family characteristics. In the U.S., "Black" or "Broad" are sometimes used instead of Extra Bold Expanded. Venus Extra Bold Extended, BG, considered the prototype, is shown in 14 pt.

ABCDEFGHIJKLMNOPQRSTUVWXYZ&123
abcdefghijklmnopqrstuvwxyz 4567890

HADRIANO and HADRIANO STONECUT. F. W. Goudy, 1918; Stonecut by Sol Hess, 1932, M(L).

ABCDEFGHIJKLMNOPQRSTUVWXYZ&

HAUSER SCRIPT. George Hauser, 1936, Lu

ABCDEFGHIJKLMNPQRSTUVWXYZabcdefghijklmnopqrstuvw12

HELLENIC WIDE. Based on 19th century Antiques; cut by Gensche & Heyse as Breite Ionisch, later taken by BG. Shown: 18 pt.

ABCDEFGHJKLMabcdefghijklmopqrs12

HOBO. M. F. Benton, 1910, ATF; also I.

ABCDEFGHIJKLMNOPQRSTabcdefghijklmnopqrst

HUXLEY VERTICAL. Walter Huxley, 1935, ATF; Vernen, Ba. ¶ Phenix, ATF. Shown: 36 pt.

ABCDEFGHIJKLMNOPQRSTUVWXYZ& 1234567890

IMPERIAL. A newspaper face with transitional characteristics. Edwin W. Shaar, 1954, I.

ABCDEFGHIJKLMNOPQRSTUVWXYZ abcdefghijklmnopqrstuvwxyz *abcdefghijklmnop* 12345678

IMPERIAL SCRIPT. Based on Firmin Didot's Anglais, 1809. Cut c. 1880, SB. Anglaise Excelsior, A; Embassy Script, SB; Formal Script, Lu; Graphic Script, BG; Invitation Script, SB; Marina Script, SB; Palace Script, SB, M(E); Royal Script, ATF; Society Script, SB; Typo Script, ATF.

ABCDEFGHIJKLMNOPQRSTUVWXY& Z

abcdefghijklmnopqrstuvwxyz 1234567890

IMPRINT. Based on Caslon Old Face, redrawn by M(E) with help of Edward Johnston and J. H. Mason, 1912. Shown: 10 pt.

ABCDEFGHIJKLMNOPQRSTUVWXYZ abcdefghijklmnopqrstuvwxyz *ABCDEFGHIJKLOPQR abcdefghijklmnopqrstuvwxyz*

ITALIENNE OMBRÉE. Based on 19th century three-dimensional faces. D&P. (See Page 122)

JANSON. From original matrices by Nicholas Kis, Hungarian punchcutter of late 17th century who worked in Holland. Cut by S, which has the original mats; also L, M(L). M(E) has very close version called Ehrhardt, based on early 18th century type in Leipsig, Germany. Shown: 28D, Stempel.

ABCDEFGHIJKLMNOPQRSTUVWXYZ 1234

ABCDEFGHIJKLMNOPQRSTUVWXYZ 5678

abcdefghijklnopqrstuwyz *abcdefghijklnopqrstuvwxyz*

JESSEN. Cut personally in 14 pt. by Rudolf Koch, and completed in 1930 by Klingspor designers as a modernization, in the lowercase, of textura style Spire Gothic. Now S.

ABCDEFGHIJKLMNOPQRSTUVWXYZ&ÄÖÜ

abcdefghijklmnopqrſstuvwxyzäöü1234567890

JIM CROW. A toned, shadowed chamferred or octagonal grot-gothic, first cut around 1850 as Gothic Shade. Its present name is as mystifying as many another type name.

ABCDEFGHIJKLMNOPQRSTUVWXYZ&1234567890

JOANNA. Designed for his own use by Eric Gill in 1930, given general distribution by M(E) in 1958.

ABCDEFGHIJKLMOPQRSTUVWXYZ abcdefghijklnopqrstuvwxyz

ABCDEFGHIJKLMOPQRSTUWXYZ abcdefghijklnopqrstuvwxyz

JUMBO TYPEWRITER. Typefaces imitating typewriter, which imitates type, available for virtually all typewriter styles. This one, ATF, shown to indicate how broad the range is.

ABCDEFGHIJKLMNOPQRSTUVWXYZ&

1234567890.,-'":;!?(

KAUFMANN SCRIPT and KAUFMANN BOLD. M. R. Kaufmann, 1936, ATF. Swing Bold, M, is the same bold. Shown: Bold and Script.

ABCDEFGHIJKLM1234567890abcdefghijklmnopqrstuvwxyz

KENNERLEY OLD STYLE. F. W. Goudy, 1911, M(L), SB. Kentonnian, I.

ABCDEFGHIJKLMNOPQRSTUVWXYZ123456789
abcdefghijklmnopqrstuvwxyz*abcdefghijklmnopqrstuvwxyz*
ABCDEFGHIJKLMNOPQRSTUVWXYZ&1234567

KLANG. Will Carter, 1955, M(E); also SB, with Klang Bold.

ABCDEFGHIJKLMNPQRS*abcdefghijklmnopqrstuvwxy*

KOMPAKT. Hermann Zapf, 1954, Stempel.

ABCDEFGHIJKLMNOPQRSTUVWXYZ .,-:;!?'$
abcdefghijklmnopqrstuvwxyz & 1234567890

LATIN. Wedge-serif form of 19th century Antiques. (Efforts are under way to end use of name for type to avoid confusion with use as name for our basic alphabet.) ATF, I, M, SB. Shown: Condensed, SB.

ABCDEFGHIJKLMNOPQRSTUVWXYZabcdefghijklmnopqrstuvwxyz1234567890

LEGEND or LEGENDE. F. H. Ernest Schneidler, 1937, BG. ¶ Ondine, D&P. Shown: 30 pt.

ABCDEFGHIJKLMNOPQRSTUVWXYZ
abcdefghijklmnopqrstuvwxyz 1234567890&

LEGIBILITIES. Newspaper faces based on 19th century Egyptians, sometimes called Ionics. C. H. Griffith, 1926, designed Ionic No. 5 for L; also M. Ideal, I, similar, came soon after, I; also M, A. (First called Ideal News, I; still called Pressa Antiqua on Continent). Sim has New Ionic. Other similar "legibility faces" by L (the phrase is L's originally) are Aurora, Corona, Excelsior, Opticon, Paragon, Textype. Other I faces are Berlin, Regal, Regent, Rex, Royal, Windsor; The Scotsman Royal, I, is Royal with certain redesigned characters. See Clarendon, p. 103. Shown: (top) Ionic No. 5, L, and Ideal, I, both with bold.

ABCDEFGHIJKLMNOPQRSTUVWXYZ abcdefghijklmnopqrstuvwxyz **ABCDE abcdefghijklmnop**
ABCDEFGHIJKLMNOPQRSTUV abcdefghijklmnopqrstuvwxyz **ABCDE abcdefghijklmnop**

LETTRES OMBRÉES ORNÉES. From face cut by Gillé, 1820; now D&P. (See Page 122)

LIBRA. S. H. De Roos, 1938, A. Shown: 30 pt.

abcdefghijklmnopqrstuvwxyz123

LILITH. Lucian Bernhard, 1930, BG.

ABCDEFGHIJKLMNOPQRSTUVWXYZ
abcdefghijklmnopqrstuvwxyz 1234567890

LOMBARDIC CAPITALS or INITIALS. F. W. Goudy, 1929, M.

ABCDEFGHIJKLMNOPQRSTUVWXYZ

LUCIAN. Lucian Bernhard, 1925, BG. Graphic, Ba; Vulcan, L. Shown: Bold.

ABCDEFGHIJKLMOPQabcdefghijklnopqrstvwxyz12

LUTETIA and LUTETIA OPEN CAPITALS. Jan Van Krimpen, 1925–30, E; also M. ¶ Similar to Open Capitals: Colonna, M(E); Dalia, G; De Roos Inline Initials, A; Egmont Inline Capitals; Fortuna, Genzsche & Heyse, now defunct. Shown: M(E) 255, 28D.

ABCDEFGHIJKLMNOPQRSTUVWXYZ
abcdefghijklmnopqrstuvwxyz 1234567890 YZ
ABCDEFGHIJKLMNOPQRSTUVWX

LYDIAN. Warren Chappell, 1938, ATF; also I. ¶ Czarin, Ba; Offenbach, K; Steel, K; Valiant, M (a bold condensed). **Shown**: 12 and 24 pt., with bold.

ABCDEFGHIJKLMNOPQRSTUVWXYZ&1234567890

abcdefghijklmnopqrstuvwxyz *abcdefghijklmnopqrstuvwxy*

ABCDEFGHIJKLMNOPQRSTUVWXYZ&1234567890

ABCDEFGHIjklmnopqrstuvwxyz ABCDEFGHIJKLMNOPQRSTUVWXYZ
abcdefghijklmnopqrstuvwxyz1234567890

LYDIAN CURSIVE. The name properly distinguishes the true cursive from the italic, above. Warren Chappell, 1938, ATF.

ABCDEFGHJKLMPQRSTUWX YZabcdefghijklnpqrstu

MANDARIN. One of the few "foreign-face" **designs still in use**; originally ATF.

ABCDEFGHIJKLMNOPQRSTUVWXYZ1234567890

MARBLE HEART. Traced back as Gothic Double Shade of the old Boston Type Foundry in the 1870s, and recently recast by ATF. (See Page 122)

MATURA. Imre Reiner, 1938, M(E). Sometimes called Pagoda Bold in U.S.

ABCDEFGHIJKLMNOPQRSTUVWXYZ&

abcdefghijklmnopqrstuvwxyz1234567890

MAXIM or **MAXIME.** Peter Schneidler, 1955, BG.

ABCDEFGHIJKLMNOPQRSTUVWXY

abcdefghijklmnopqrstuvwxyz1234567890

MELIOR. Hermann Zapf, 1952, S., L. ¶ Dominante, Sim. **Shown**: Melior, Italic, and Melior Bold.

ABCDEFGHIJKLMNOPQRSTUVWXYZ

abcdefghijklmnopqrstuvwxyz&1234567890

ABCDEFGHIJKLMNOPQRSTUVWXYZ

abcdefghijklmnopqrstuvwxyz&1234567890

ABCDEFGHIJKLabcdefghijklmnopqrstuvwxyz

MENHART ROMAN. Oldrich Menhart, 1939, BG; also M(E).

ABCDEFGHIJKLMNOPQRSTUVWXYZ

abcdefghijklmnopqrstuvwxyz 1234567890

MERCURIUS BOLD SCRIPT. Imre Reiner, 1957, M(E).

ABCDEFGHIJKabcdefghijklmpqrstuvwxyz

MISTRAL. Roger Excoffon, 1953, O; also A. ¶ Champion, Be. **Shown**: 24 pt. large.

ABCDEFGHIJKLMNOPQRSTUVWXYZ& abcdefghijklpqrstuvwxyz

MODERN. Based on combinations of English and French modern-style faces. Most makers. Shown: Modern No. 20, SB.

ABCDEFGHJKLMNOPQRSTUVWXYZ1234567890
abcdefghijklmnopqrstuvwxyz*abcdefghijklmnopqrstuvwxyz*
ABCDEFGHIJKLMNOPQRSTUVWXYZ123456789

MODERN OPEN FACES. Many families have such a variant. Gresham, SS, is one not recognizable from its name alone. Shown: Bodoni Open, ATF.

ABCDEFGJKLMPQRSTabcdefghijklmpqrstuvwxy12

MODERNE. Sophisticated styling of the 1920s under influence of Cubists and others led to exaggerated curves, distorted proportions, and angular or round-segment accents. The most popular, Broadway, by M. F. Benton, 1928, ATF (also M(L)), is shown. Others: Bristol, A; Parisian, ATF, I, L; Ultra Modern, Lu.

ABCDEFGHIJKLMNOPQRSTUVWXYZ1234567890

MODERNE DECORATED. These added lines and patterns on the face to the basic moderne characteristics. Gallia, shown here, by Wadsworth A. Parker, 1927, ATF, was typical. Others: Boul Mich, ATF; Carlton, A; Chic, ATF; Modernistic, ATF; Vesta, Be.

ABCDEFGHIJKLMNPQRSTWX123

MODERNE FAT FACE. Some of the modernes were extra black, but designed in different ways. Nubian, 1928, ATF, shown below. Others: Sphinx, 1925, D&P (also serifed) and (sans serif) Basuto, SB; Grock, E(M); Koloss, L&M; Meridian, K; Messe Grotesk, Be; Modernique, ATF; Novel Gothic, ATF; Stygian, Lu. Shown: 12 pt. Nubian.

ABCDEFGHIJKLMNOPQRSJTUVWXYZ&
abcdefghijklmnopqrstuvwxyz 1234567890

MOLÉ FOLIATE. Based on design of Molé, French founder, c. 1819. Redrawn by Sem L. Hartz, 1960, E; also SB. (See chapter initial letter on Page 95.)

MONTICELLO. Recutting of 1796 face by Binney of Binney & Ronaldson, Philadelphia; L, 1950. Original design available from ATF as Oxford.

ABCDEFGHIJKLMNOPQRSTUVWXYZabcdefghijklmnopqrstuvwxyz1234567890*abcdefgABCDEF*

MURRAY HILL. Emil J. Klumpp, 1956, ATF. Shown with Murray Hill Bold.

ABCDEFGHIJKLMNOPQRSTUVWXYZ 1234567890
abcdefghijklmnopqrstuvwxyz ABCDEFGHIJ abcdefghijklmnopqrstuvwxyz

NEON, NEON BOLD and NEON OMBRATA. This Nebiolo face should not be confused with Neon by Weber, also a 3-dimensional capital, as black as Ombrata is white.

ABCDeFG**HIJKLMNOP**QRSTUVWXYZ123456789

NEULAND and NEULAND INLINE. Rudolf Koch, 1923, K. ¶ Norway, SB; Othello, M(E).

ABCDEFGHJKLMNPQRSTUWXYZ12345

NEW-GROTS. First was Helvetica, by Max Miedinger, 1954, for H, originally called Haas Grotesque and New Haas Grotesque; now also L, S. Univers, by Adrian Frutiger, 1957, D&P now also ATF, L, M(E), spurred the move with a systematic family of New-Grots. Others now: Adonis, SB; Advertisement Grotesque, H; Annonce Grotesque, A, or Antiques Doubles Larges, D&P; Aurora Grotesk, W, or Cairoli, N; Edel Grotesque, JW; Folio, BG (now also I), or Caravelle, FTF; Information, K, or Reform Grotesque, S; Lessing Grotesque, JW; Mercator, A, I; Normal Grotesque, H, L(F); Permanent, L&M, Sim; Progress, W; Record Gothic, Lu; Standard or Akzidenz Grotesque, Be, I; Venus, BG. Shown: (1) Helvetica and Helvetica Bold; (2) Univers, Light, Medium Expanded, Bold; (3) Folio Extra Bold and Light; (4) Standard Medium Condensed, Extra Light Extended; (5) Record Gothic and Bold.

(1) ABCDEFGHIJKLMNOPQRSTUVWXYZ1234
abcdefghijklmnopqrstuvwxyz**ABCDabcdefg**

(2) ABCDEFG*HIJKLMN*OPQRSTUVW***XYZ&***
abcdefghi*jklmnop*qrstuv**wxyz*****abcdefghijklm***

(3) **ABCDEFGHIJKLMNOPQRSTUVWXYZ12345678**
abcdefghijklmnopqrstuvwxyzABCDEFGHIJKL

(4) ABCDEFGHIJKLMNOPQRSTUVWXYZabcdefghijklmnopqrstuvwxyz1234567890
ABCDEFGHIJKLMabcdefghijklmnopqrstuvwxy

(5) ABCDEFGHIJKLMNOPQRSTUVWXYZabcdefghijklmno
pqrstuvwxyz**ABCDEFghijklmnopqrst*****UVWxyz&***

NICOLAS COCHIN. Based on 18th century engraved letters of Cochin. Cut by D&P; ATF, M(L) have Mazarin, SB.

ABCDEFGHIJKLMNOPQRSTUVWXYZ&
abcdefghijklmnopqrstuvwxyz 1234567890

OLD BOWERY. Another nostalgic face out of the 19th century; ATF. Shown: 30 pt.

ABCDEFGHIJKLMNOPQRSTUVWXYZ&

OLD STYLE. Based on face by Alexander Phemister, c. 1860; now SB and general. Binny Old Style, M; Bruce Old Style, M; Dickinson Old Style, L(L); Old Style Nos. 1, 3, L; Old Style Nos. 1, 7, 9, I; Old Style No. 10 L(L); Period Old Style, I; Ronaldson Old Style, ATF, M. ¶ Monticello is recutting of 1796 face by Binney of Binney & Ronaldson, L, 1950, original still available from ATF as Oxford. Shown: Linotype Old Style No. 7, 24 pt., Lino O.S. No. 1, 12 pt.

ABCDEFGHIJKLNabcdefghijklmnopqrst1234567890
ABCDEFGHIJKLMNOPQRSTUVWXYZ&abcdefghijklmnopqrstuvwxyz 1234567890 1234567890
ABCDEFGHIJKLMNOPQRSTUVWXYZ& abcdefghijklmnopqrstuvwxyz 1234567890 1234567890

OLD STYLE OPEN FACES. Based on 18th century lettering, Old Style Bold Outline, cut by M(E), is typical of technique. Others: Caslon Openface, ATF; Cochin Open, M(L); Goudy Open, ATF, M(L); Gravure, A; Moreau le Jeune, D&P; Old Face Open, SB; Paganini Filettato, N; Ratio Open Capitals, Be, S.

ABCDEFGHIJKLMNOPQRSTUVWXYZ
abcdefghijklmnopqrstuvwxyz 1234567890

OPEN ROMAN CAPITALS. An outline face by Jan Van Krimpen, 1928, E. ¶ Columna, B; Daphnis, K.

ABCDEFGHIJKLMNOPQ RSTUVWXYZ

OPTIMA. Hermann Zapf, 1958, S and L. ¶ Colonia, L&M; Ile de France, FTF; Pascal, A. Shown: Optima and Optima Bold.

ABCDEFGHIJKLMNOPQRSTUVWXYZ1234567890
abcdefghijklmnopqrstuvwxyz*abcdefghijklmnopqrstu*
ABCDEFGHIJKLMNOPQRSTUVWXYZ1234567890
ABCDEFGHJKLMNOabcdefghijklmnopqrstuvwxy

ORNATA. O. H. W. Hadank, 1943; K; now S. (See Page 122)

PALATINO. Hermann Zapf, 1950, S and L. Michelangelo and Sistina, S, are more stylized medium and bold capitals as companion faces. Shown: (1) Palatino, (2) Palatino Italic, (3) Palatino Demi-Bold, (4) Michelangelo, and (5) Sistina.

(1) ABCDEFGHIJKLMNOPQRSTUVWXYZ1234567
abcdefghijklmnopqrstuvwxyz*abcdefghijklmnopqrstuvwxy*
(2) *ABCDEFGHIJKLMNOPQRSTUVWXYZ ABDEJ*
(3) **ABCDEFGHIJKLMabcdefghijklmnopqrstuvwxyz**
(4) ABCDEFGHIJKLMNOPQRSTUVWXYZ 1234567
(5) ABCDEFGHIJKLMNOPQRSTUVWXYZ 1234567

PAPAGENO. Richard Weber, 1958, BG.

ABCDEFGHIJKLMNOPQRSTUVWXYZ
abcdefghijklmnopqrstuvwxyz&1234567890

PARK AVENUE. R. E. Smith, 1933, ATF; also I. Parkway Script, Lu.

ABCDEFGHIJKLMNOPQRSTUVWXYZ

abcdefghijklmnopqrstuvwxyz 1234567890

PARSONS. Will Ransom, 1918, ATF. Shown: Bold

ABCDEFGHIJKLMNOPQRSTUVWXY

abbcddefg hikkllmnop qrstuvwxyz1234567

PEIGNOT. A. M. Cassandre, 1937, D&P. Called Touraine with normal l.c.

ABCDEFGHIJKLMNOPQRSTUVWXYZ 1234567890

abcdefghijklmnopqrstuvwxyz

PERICLES. Robert Foster, 1934, ATF.

ABCDEEFGHIJKLMNOPQRRSTUVWXYZ1234567890

PERPETUA. Eric Gill, 1925–30, M(E). Italic also called Felicity. ¶ Minerva, L(L); Imprimateur or Horizon, BG, I(B). Arena, Be, is a condensed bold. Shown: M(E) with Bold.

ABCDEFGHIJKLMNOPQRSTUVWXYZ1234567890*123456*

abcdefghijklmnopqrstuvwxyz&*abcdefghijklmnopqrstuvwxyz7890*

ABCDEFGHIJKLMNOPQRSTUVWXYZ& **ABCDEFGHIJKLM**

NOPQRSTUVWXYZ&abcdefghijklmnopqrstuvwxyz

PHOSPHOR. Based on Erbar. Jakob Erbar, c. 1925, L&M

ABCDEFGHIJKLMNOPQRSTUVWXYZ123456

PLANTIN. Based on 16th century roman face cut by Robert Granjon. F. H. Pierpont, 1913, M(E); also I, Lu. Shown: M(E) Light with 10 pt.

ABCDEFGHIJKLMNOPQRSTUVWXYZ&

ABCDEFGHIJKLMNOPQRSTUVWXYZ&

abcdefghijklmnopqrstuvwxyz1234567890*123456789*

abcdefghijklmnopqrstuvwxyz ABCDEFGHIJKLMNOPQRSTUVWXYZ abcdefghijkl mnopqrstuvwxyz *ABCDEFG abcdefghijklmnopqrstuvwxyz*

POLIPHILUS. Based on face cut by Francesco Griffo, 1499. Cut 1928, M(E). The italic used with Poliphilus is Blado, cut by M(E) in 1923, based on formal calligraphy of the Roman, Vicentino (Lodovico degli Arrighi). Shown: 24 pt. Poliphilus and 10 pt. Poliphilus and Blado Italic.

ABCDEFGHIJKLMNPQRSTUVWYZ

ABCDEFGHIJKLMNOPQRSTUVWXYZabcdefghi jklmnopqrstuvwxyz 1234567890

ABCDEFGHIJKLMNOPQRSTUVWXYZabcdefghij klmnopqrstuvwxyz 1234567890

POST ROMAN. Herman Post, 1937, Be; also I. Post Mediaeval, Be, is a calligraphic serifed face. Shown: Post Roman Light and Bold.

ABCDEFGHIJKLMNOPQRSTUVWXYZabcdefghijklmno

pqrstuvwxyz*ABCDEFGHIJKLabcdefghijklmnopqrstuvwxyz*

ABCDEFGHIJKLMabcdefghijklmnopqrstuv*123456789*

PRIMER. Rudolph Ruzicka, 1951, L.
ABCDEFGHIJKLMNOPQRSTUVWXYZabcdefghijklmnopqrstuvwxyz*abcdefghijklmnop*1234567890

PRISMA. Rudolf Koch, 1931, K; now S.
ABCDEFGHJKLMNPQRSTUVZ1234

PROFIL or PROFILE. Eugen and Max Lenz, 1946, H. ¶ Sculptura, H, is a condensed roman grot.
ABCDEFGHIJKLNQRST12

RAFFIA INITIALS. Henk Krisger, 1952, A. (See Page 122)

RECHERCHÉ. Face of earlier French heritage, produced by SB.
ABCDEFGHIJKLMNOPQuRSTUVWXYZ
abcdefghijklmnopqrstuvwxyz 123456789&

REINER SCRIPT. Imre Reiner, 1951, A; also ATF. ¶ Pepita, M(E).
ABCDEFGHIJKLMNOPQRSTUVWXYZ abcdefghijklmnopqrstuvwxyz 1234567890

RHAPSODIE or RHAPSODY. Based on Schwabacher Spire Gothics. Ilse Schuele, 1949, L&M.
ABCDEFGHIJKLMPQRSTUVWXYZabcdefghijklnopqrstuvwxyz1

ROMANTIQUES. These have various numbers and names; many of them were cut c. 1870 by FTF. Ornamented Outline, SS, is FTF No. 1, shown as P-Z here.
ABCDEFGHIJKLMNOPQRSTUVWXYZ

RONDO. Stefan Schlesinger and Dick Dooijes, 1948, A.
ABCDEFGHIJKLMNOPQRST
UVWXYZabcdefghijklmnopqrstuvwxyz1234567890

ROSART. J. F. Rosart, 1759, E. Prototype for tooled roman capitals.
ABCDEFGHIJKLMNOPQRSTUVWXYZ

RUSTIC. A theme variously executed through the years. This one, cut c. 1850, was reissued recently by Typefounders (Arizona).
ABCDEFGHIJKLMNOPQRSTUVWXYZ 123456789

SALTINO and SALTA. Karlgeorg Hoefer, 1952–3, K; now S. These faces share the same lowercase; Saltino is the more regular capital face. Shown: 20D pt.
ABCDEFGHIJKLMNOPQRSTUVW
XYZ 123 ABCDEFGHIJKabcdefghijklmnopqrstuvwxyz

SAMSON. R. H. Middleton, 1940, Lu. ¶ Jacno, D&P.
ABCDEFGHIJKLMNOPQRSTUVWXYZ&
abcdefghijklmnopqrstuvwxyz 1234567890

SANS SERIF LIGHT. A variant of most sans serif families now. Early one by M. F. Benton, 1908, ATF, shown below, still called Lightline Gothic.
ABCDEFGHIJKLMNOPQRSTUVWXYZ&
abcdefghijklmnopqrstuvwxyz 1234567890

SANS SERIF OUTLINE SHADOW. First shown as Sans Surryphs Shaded, by William Thorowgood in 1839, the face at left is now Sans Serif Shaded, SB. At right is a modern ized version, Orplid, by Hans Bohn, 1929, K, now S. ¶ Graphique, H, S, is a condensed; Gill Shadow, M(E), is wider; Orbis, S, is more styled.
ABCDEFGHIJKLM ABCDEFGHIJKLMNOP 123

SAPHIR or SAPPHIRE. Hermann Zapf, 1953, S. Festival Numerals, S, are matching. Shown: 20D pt.

ABCDEFGHIJKLMNOPQRSTU 1234

SCHADOW. Georg Trump, 1938–52, W.

ABCDEFGHIJKLMabcdefghijklmnopqrst123

ABCDEFGHIJKLMabcdefghijklmnopqr123

SCOTCH ROMAN. Probably based on Richard Austin face, c. 1810; may have been U.S. design ordered by Samuel Nelson Dickinson from Miller and Richard, Edinburgh, and cast by Dickinson, 1839. Now I, L, M. Shown: M(E) 137.

ABCDEFGHIJKLMNOPQRSTUVWXYZ1234567

abcdefghijklmnopqrstuvwxyz*ABCDEG1234567890 89*

abcdefghijklmnopqrstuvwxyzHJKLMQRSTWXYZ

SIGNAL. Walter Wege, 1931, Be. ¶ Britannic, Ba; Mandate, Lu; Monoline Script, M(E); Romany, ATF; Scriba, E; Veltro, N. Shown: Light and Medium.

ABCDEFGHIJKLMNOPQRSTUVWXYZ123abcdefghijklmnopqrstuvwxyz123

ABCDEFGHIJKLMNOPQRSTUVWXYZ abcdefghijklmno123

SIMPLEX. Based on classical uncial alphabet. S. H. De Roos, 1939, A. Shown: Bold.

abcdefghijklmnopqrstuvwxyz&12345

SLAB SERIFS. The first was Memphis or Girder, by Rudolf Wolf, 1929, S; also L. Other families are: Beton, BG, I; Cairo, I; Cheops, E; Karnak, Lu; Rockwell, M; Scarab, SB; Stymie, ATF, M; Tempo, S; Welt, L&M. Shown: (1) Memphis Medium, L; (2) Beton Extra Bold: (3) Karnak Light, Black Condensed; (4) Rockwell; (5) Stymie Medium.

(1) ABCDEFGHIJKLMNOPQRSTUVWXYZ123456789

abcdefghijklmnopqrstuvwxyz*abcdefghijklmnopq*

rstuvwxyzABCDEFGHIJKLMNOPQRSTUVWXYZ

(2) **ABCDEFGHIJKLabcdefghijklmnopqrstuvwxyz**

(3) ABCDEFGHIJKLMNOPQRSTUVWXYZabcdefgh

ijklmnopqrstuvwxyz**ABCDEFghijklmnopqr*STUVwxyz12***

(4) ABCDEFGHIJKLMNOPQRSTUVWXYZabcdefg

hijklmnopqrstuvwxyz*ABCDEFGhijklmnopqrst*

(5) ABCDEFGHIJKLMNOPQRSTUVWXYZ1234567

abcdefghijklmnopqrstuvwxyz*abcdefghijklmnopqr*

SLAB SERIF OUTLINE SHADOW. A slab serif family variant, as with Rockwell Shadow, M(E) at right below. At left are Forum I and II, by Georg Trump, W, in more stylized treatment; Superba, H, is similar.

ABCDEFGHIJKLMNOQRSTUVWX

SMARAGD. Gudrun Zapf-von Hesse, 1954, S.

ABCDEFGHIJKLMNPQRSTUVWXYZ123

SOUVENIR. Morris F. Benton, 1914, ATF, in 6 to 36 pt. roman only, one weight. With the consent of ATF, redesigned by Ephram Benguiat, 1973, International Typeface Corp., in range of weights and italic for cold-type use. L made mats in text sizes in 1976, based on Benguiat; ATF reissued its face. Benguiat face thus becomes the first fully successful cold-type family to be put into hot metal. Shown: (1) ATF Souvenir; (2) ITC Souvenir Light Italic; (3) L Souvenir Light and Demi Bold, 12 pt.

(1) ABCDEFGHIJKLMNOPQRSTUVWXY&Z abcdefghijklmnoprstuvwxyz 1234567890 (2) *ABCDEF GHIJKLMNOPQRSTUV abcdefghijklmnopqrstuvwxyz*

(3) ABCDEFGHIJKLM**NOPQRSTUVWXYZ** abcdefghijklmnopqrstuvwxyz **abcdefghijklmnopqrs**

SPECTRUM. Jan Van Krimpen, 1952, E; also M(E). Romulus, E, M(E). Shown: (M) with 10 pt.

ABCDEFGHIJKL*MNOPQRSTUVWXYZ* ABCDEFGHIJKLMNOPQRSTUVWXYZ abcdefghijklmnopqrstuvwxyz

abcdefghijklmnopqrstuvwxyz*abcdefghijklmnopqrstuvwxyz*

STELLAR. R. H. Middleton, 1929, Lu. Shown: Stellar and Stellar Bold.

ABCDEFGHIJKLMNOPQRSTUVWXYZ&1234567890abcdefghij klmnopqrstuvwxyz**ABCDEFGHIJKLMNOPQRabcdefghijklmnop**

STENCIL. Gerry Powell, 1936, ATF; also Lu. ¶ Chaillot, D&P; Tea Chest, SB. (See Page 122)

STOP. Walter Hohnisch, 1939, L&M. (See Page 122)

STRESSED SANS SERIFS. Radiant, by R. H. Middleton, 1939, Lu, shown here, is perhaps the best-known. Others: Chambord, O; Globe Gothic, ATF; Lyerson, L; Touraine, D&P. Britannic and Rothbury, SB, are blacker, more styled. Shown: Radiant and Radiant Heavy.

ABCDEFGHIJKLMNOPQRSTUVWXYZabcdefghijklmnop qrstuvwxyz1234567890*ABCDEFGHIJabcdefghijklmnop*

ABCDEFGHIJKLMNOP abcdefghijklmnopqrst

STRESSED SANS SERIFS, OVER-CONDENSED. Empire (ATF) or Iris (A), designed by M. F. Benton, 1938, shown below, is typical. Hastile, N; Radiant Extra-Condensed, Lu.

ABCDEFGHIJKLMNOPQRSTUVWXYZ 1234567890

STYLED SANS SERIFS. Erbar, by Jakob Erbar, 1922, L&M (later also L), was the first modern sans serif available; the first fully successful one was Kabel (or Cable) by Rudolf Koch, 1927, K, and later M(L) as Monotype Sans Serif; also I as Vogue. ¶ Other faces which relieve geometric sans with style: Art Grotesque, SB; Bernhard Gothic, ATF; Berthold Grotesque, Be; Electra, FTF; Elegant Grotesque, S; Gill Sans Serif, M(E); Granby Grotesque, SB; Metro, L; Neuzeit Grotesque, S, L; Nobel Grotesque, A, I; Recta, N; Sans Serif, SB; Sans Serif No. 2, I; Semplicita, N; Stemple Sans Serif, S, L; Tempo, Lu. Shown: (1) Kabel Light and Kabel Bold; (2) Gill Sans Serif; (3) Erbar Medium Condensed, L; (4) Metroblack; (5) Bernhard Gothic Medium; (6) Granby Extra Bold, SB; (7) Tempo Bold.

(1) ABCDEFGHIJKLMNOPQRSTUVWXYZ & abcdefghijklmnopqrst uvwxyz1234567890 **ABCDEFGHIJabcdefghijklmnopqrstuvwxyz**

(2) ABCDEFGHIJKLMNOPQRSTUVWXYZ&1234567890 abcdefghijklmnopqrstuvwxyz*abcdefghijklmnopqrstuvwx*

(3) **ABCDEFGHIJKLMNOPQRSTUVWXYZ& abcdefghijklmnopqrstuvwxyz 1234567890**

(4) **ABCDEFGHIJKLMNabcdefghijklmnopqrstuvwxyz**

(5) ABCDEGHJKMNPQRSTabcdefghijklmnopqrstuvwxyz

ABCDEFGHIJKLMNOPQRST abcdefghijklmnopqrstuvwx

(7) **ABCDEFGHIJKLMNOabcdefghijklmnopqrstuvwxyz**

THOMPSON QUILLSCRIPT. Tommy Thompson, 1953, ATF. ¶ Heritage, ATF.

AAABCDEEFFGGHHIJJKKLLMMNNOPQRSTTU UVVWWXYZ&& abcdeffghhijklmnopqrstuvwxyz 1234567890

THUNDERBIRD. A Tuscan revived in recent resurgence of Victorian faces. Shown: 18 pt.

ABCDEFGHJKLMN23

TIME SCRIPT. Georg Trump, 1956, W. ¶ London Script, SB. Shown: Light, Medium and Bold.

ABCDEFGHIJJKabcdefghijklmnopqrstuvwxyz

ABCDEabcdefghABCDEabcdefg 1234

TIMES NEW ROMAN and TIMES BOLD. Originally designed with Linotype in mind by Monotype, the design supervised by Stanley Morison, 1932; M(E), L and SB, and later I, Lu. ¶ Life, Sim. Shown: M(E) 327 and M(E) 334.

ABCDEFGHIJKLMNOPQRSTUVWXYZ123456

abcdefghijklmnopqrstuvwxyz*abcdefghijklmnop*7890

qrstuvw ABCDEFGHIJKLMNOPQRSTUVWXYZ

ABCDEFGH*JKLMNOPQ*abcdefghijklm*abcdefghij*

TOOLED FACES. Narciss or Narcissus, shown below, by Walter Tieman, 1921, K, now S, introduced the modern variant. Others: Cameo, Lu; Cloister Bold Tooled, ATF, I; Dominus, SB; Goudy Hand-Tooled, ATF, M(L); Gravure, ATF; Hermes, A; Imprint Shadow, M(E).

ABCDEFGHIJKLMklmnopqrstuvwxyz123

TORINO. 1908, N. First called Romano Moderno, by N. ¶ Mademoiselle, Ba; Victoria Condensed, M(E). Shown: 24 pt. large.

ABCDEFGHIJKLMNOPabcdefghijklmnopq 123456

ABCDEFGHIJKLMNabcdefghijklmnop123456

TOWER. M. F. Benton, 1934, ATF. Karnak Obelisk, Lu

ABCDEFGHIJKLMNOPQRSTUVWXYZ& abcdefghijklmnopqrstuvwxyz 1234567890

TRAFTON SCRIPT or QUICK. H. A. Trafton, 1933, BG; called Etoile, D&P.

ABCDEFGHIJKLMNOPQRSTU abcdefghijklmnopqrstuvwxyz

TRAJANUS. Warren Chappell, 1939, S. ¶ Athenaeum, N. Shown: Trajanus and Trajanus Bold.

ABCDEFGHIJKLMNOPQRSTUVWXYZ abcdefghijklmnopqr

stuvwxyz *ABCDEFGHIJKLMNOPQRSTUVWXYZ* 1234567890

abcdefghijklmnopqrstuvwxyz1234 **ABCDEFGHIJ abcdefghij123456789**

TRUMP GRAVUR. Georg Trump, 1960, W. Open 3-dimensional version of Trump Mediaeval. (See use as initial on Page 93)

TYPO UPRIGHT. Based on French Ronde handwriting, and first called French Script. Now ATF; called Parisian Ronde, SB. Gloria or Fulgar, A; Interscript, I; Lino Script, L.

ABCDEFGHIJKLMNOPQRSTUVWXYZabcfghijklmpqrstuvwxy123

UMBRA. R. H. Middleton, 1932, Lu. ¶ Gill Sans Shadow, M(E); Plastica, Be; Semplicità Ombra, N; Stridon, Wa. Called Rhumba by Los Angeles. ¶ Same technique with other styles: Memphis Luna, S, slab serif; Phoebus, D&P, wedge serif; Shadow, ATF, I, condensed rounded grot roman.

ABCDEFGHIJKLMNOPQRSTUVWXYZ&

UNION PEARL. James Grover, c. 1690; mats now owned by SB.

ABCDEFFGGHIJJKLMNOPQRSTTUVWXYZQu&,.

abbcddefghhijkllmnopqrsftuvwxyzſhſtj

VAN DIJCK. Based on 17th century Dutch old style faces, by Christoffel van Dijck. Jan Van Krimpen advised on design, 1935, M(E). Shown with 10 pt.

ABCDEFGHIJKLMNOPQRSTUVWXYZ&abcdefghijklmnop
qrstuvwxyz *ABCDEFGHIJKLMNOPQRSTUVWXYZ&* 12345
ABCDEFGHIJKLMNOPQRSTUVWXYZ abcdefghijklmnopqrstuvwxyz
abcdefghijklmnopqrstuvwxyz *ABCDEFGHIJKLMNOPQRSTUVWXYZ abcdefghijklmnopqrstuvwxyz* 6789

VENDÔME. François Ganeau, 1952, O; also BG. ¶ Meridién, D&P.; Trump Mediaeval, W, L(F).

ABCDEFGHIJKLMNOPQRSTUVWXYZ
abcdefghijklmnopqrstuvwxyz

VILLAGE No. 2. Frederic W. Goudy, 1932, M(L). Designed as the house face of Goudy's Village Press, supplanting the original Village type of 1903. Shown 14 pt. (only 14, 18 pt. available M; some 12 pt. and 16 pt. handcast by Goudy)

ABCDEFGHIJKLMNOPQRSTUVWXYZ abcdefghijklmnopqrstuvwxyz1234567890

VIRTUOSA I and II. Hermann Zapf, 1949-52, Stempel. Capitals in I are more flourished than II; lowercase of both identical. II is shown. ¶ Boulevard, Be; Stradivarius, BG; Symphonie, BG.

ABCDEFGHIJKLMNOPQRSTUVWXYZ&abcdefghijklmno
pqrstuvwxyz 1234567890

WALBAUM. Cut by Justin E. Walbaum, early 19th century. Reissued, 1919, Be; also L(F), I, M(E). Waverley, I. Shown: M(E) 24D.

ABCDEFGHIJKLMNOPQRSTUVWXYZ1234567
abcdefghijklmnopqrstuvwxyz*1234567890* 890
ABCDEFGHIJKLMabcdefghijklmnopqrstuv

WALLAU. Rudolf Koch, 1925–30, K, now S. The lowercase is a rotunda Spire Gothic.

ABCDEFGHIJKLMNOPQRSTUVWXYZ
abcdefghijklmnopqrſstuvwxyz 1234567890

WEISS ROMAN and INITIALS. Emir Rudolf Weiss, 1926, BG; also I (except initials). ¶ Elizabeth, BG. Shown: Weiss Roman, Weiss Bold, Weiss Swash Capitals, and Weiss Initials No. 1.

ABCDEFGHIJKLMNOPQRSTUVWXYZabcdefghijklmnopq
rstuvwxyz1234567890 *ABCDEFGHIJKLMNOPQRSTUVWXYZ*
abcdefghijklmnopqrstuvwxyz12345 **ABCDEabcde** *ABCDEFG* ABCDE

WHEDONS GOTHIC OUTLINE. Whedon Davis, 1965, ATF. The first modern recutting of the simple outline face. ¶ Gothic Outline, ATF; Outline Gothic, Lu.

ABCDEFGHIJKLMNOPQRSTUVWXYZ abcdefghijklmnopqrstuv1234

WINDSOR. Cut c. 1905, SB, in regular, Elongated and Outline. One of the "rugged" faces, with rimpled edges of the turn of the century. This was the one recently popularized. Others: Morland, SB; Pabst Old Style, ATF; Rimpled, ATF; Roycroft, ATF. Shown: Windsor and Windsor Elongated.

ABCDEFGHIJKLMNOPQRSTUVWXYZ abcdefghijklmnopqrstuvwxyz1234 st
ABCDEFGHIJKLMNabcdefghijklmnopqr

ZEPHYR. Michael Harvey, 1964, Lu. ¶ Riccardo, H.

ABCDEFGHIJKLMNOPQRSTUVWXYZ&
1234567890

THE INITIALS USED IN CHAPTER HEADINGS

The initials used in the chapter headings constitute a sampler of such faces. Here are their names, together with reasons (some obviously fanciful) for their use. Numbers in parentheses indicate the page on which the letter appears:

A(6), Cloister Initials, cut by Frederic W. Goudy for ATF, appropriate for a "beginner-designer" chapter because Goudy began designing typefaces without any special training, and went on to become one of the greatest in all history. (Most experts doubt this would be possible for a beginner without formal training today!)

B(9) a Dutch Bloemen initial, in the collection of punches, matrices and type Dr. John Fell, Bishop of Oxford, bequeathed to the University in 1676. "The Fell types" have played a substantial role in advancing the cause of typography.

C(12) Initial used in England, late 19th century.

D(16) Based on Mazarin Bible of the 12th century.

E(19) Another 12th century hand-lettered initial.

F(20) Early Anglo-Saxon manuscript letter.

G(23) The Caroline g as rendered by F. W. Goudy.

H(27) An illuminated initial from the Gutenberg Bible.

I(31) By Erhard Ratdolt, in Incunabula period.

J(33) Believed 11th century ecclesiastical letter.

K(37) A geometric construction by Geofroy Tory.

L(44) A 19th century letter that really projects itself.

M(49) Recent photo-letter, to point up fact that music, too, has been printed from type.

N(52) Caslon capital in mortised border, typical of mechanized interchangeability even of initial letters.

O(59) Bodoni Panelled, one of the Monotype Bodoni family.

P(62) Letter from Kelmscott Chaucer of William Morris.

Q(65) Calypso type, an unusual ribboned effect.

R(72) Prisma type, reflecting what the prism can do to type.

S(75) An experimental "scannal" computer letter. (See P 76)

T(77) Rondo Bold, suggesting the problems of classification.

U(84) Cristal type; the transparent goblet of readable type, or the crystal ball to help choose a face?

V(86) Sapphire type, friends being jewels.

W(90) Lilith type, anent the problems of recognition.

X(91) Gill Cameo Ruled type; also called Airport Relief, and relief (a different kind, true) is what a hobby brings.

Y(93) Trump Gravur type. Professor Trump will not mind the suggestion that knowledge is an important trump to hold.

Z(95) Molé Foliate, to suggest the great verdure of further reading about type.

APPENDIX II

THE BODY-SIZE TYPORAMA

BODY SIZE SPECIMENS

shown for comparison and to indicate the range

On the following pages, 48 different typefaces have been set with the same "copy" (wording or message) and in the same "text" or body size of type and the same number of lines of the same width, so that you may compare them with one another in respect to their "color" (appearance and general effect), legibility and readability, and use of space. (See Page 33 for an explanation of "body type.")

The type size used is 10-point, throughout, even though comparing faces such as Helvetica and Bembo may make you doubt it. The type is set "10 on 11," meaning it is cast on an 11-point body to provide one point of space between the lines—a normal "leading," although some faces in the group require none at all (i.e., could be set "solid") and some could use much more.

It is differences such as this, in fact, that you should find as you look at the specimens.

If a face has small capitals as part of the font, these are used immediately after the face's name in the specimen block. The last two lines of the specimen are set in the companion or matching italic, if there is one. Some fonts have a matching bold instead, and this is used in such instances. Certain English Monotype fonts have both italic and bold, so both are included. Some few faces, as you will notice, have neither.

Four specimens vary from this general format, to allow an extra kind of comparison:

Cheltenham is shown half in Light and half in Bold, because Cheltenham Bold is one of the most famous and most used faces in modern printing history, and thus deserves equal billing with the lighter variant.

Electra shows two italics in two lines each. The original Italic is really a slanted roman, and the true italic, called Electra Cursive, was added later to meet printer (and designer) demand for a companion face with more contrast than the Italic.

Kabel, as noted in the text, is a Styled Sans. However, again, printers and designers have demanded another version—in this case, less individualized. So Lanston Monotype's Kabel (its version is named Sans Serif) now has "alternate Futura characters," to substitute for the stylized letters. Here, the first half of the specimen block is set in the original Kabel style and the second half with the Futura-like alternates, so you may see the different effect.

Univers is set in four different variants to suggest the variety available.

The faces shown here are not to be taken as judgment of the best or most prominent body faces. There are many others fully as worthy of inclusion. But including even a few "dated" faces shown for still another kind of comparison, the specimens do represent a valid cross-section of the different kinds of type available for setting text matter—the Body-Size Typorama.

If there were any doubt that the minute differences of style and detailed design could really be meaningful in final appearance, even the briefest of glances will show you that something is at work to yield so many different colors, textures and patterns from the same basic alphabet.

It is those little changes in these particular faces that affect the bulk of what you read.

ABOUT THE REST OF THE COPY . . .

Type specimen blocks, such as those on the facing page, traditionally are set from "copy" that is longer than needed, to be sure there is enough message for even the smallest face to be set to the full length intended. This means that there is always an unprinted ending to the copy—and sometimes the message has interest enough for the user to wonder what the rest of the copy said.

This time, it is different. Because this book has tried to leave nothing unsaid which ought to be included, here is the rest of the message:

. . . the knowledgeable reader can have his own pleasure in second-guessing the designer and printer as he studies the completed printed piece. Not that the reader can be dogmatic about his preference any more than the designer, because there are many good typefaces in our Typorama for any conceivable purpose, and no one right way to do the job. This freedom for personal expression is one of the great attractions of typography.

THE TYPESETTING JOB

The 48 different type specimen blocks shown here may well be the largest number ever assembled for other than specialized professional use. To obtain them all under the same specifications and high standards took genuine interest and co-operation, which is hereby acknowledged with thanks, from the following individuals and companies (from New York except as noted):

Bert Clarke and David Way, Clarke and Way, Inc.; Terry Halpine, Terry Linotyping, Inc.; Horace Hart, Lanston Monotype Co.; Robert Johannesen, Baxter & Spencer, Inc.; Oscar E. Kantor, Atlantic Linotype Co.; Leo Kleiman, Crowell Typographers, Inc.; Karl H. Koether, The H. W. Wilson Co.; Dr. Robert L. Leslie and Irving Levine, The Composing Room, Inc.; Hy Needleman, King Typographic Service Corp.; Edwin Ogden, A. Colish, Inc. [Mount Vernon, N.Y.] and Edwin W. Shaar, Intertype Co., for the first edition, and Dave Ostrowsky, MGA Graphics, and Pat Taylor, Out of Sorts Letter Foundery [Larchmont, N.Y.], for material in this edition.

Baskerville, Italic and Bold (English Monotype)

BASKERVILLE MAY BE COMPARED with other typefaces in many ways. First is readability: some faces help the eye more than others. Second is color: letters in mass can appear light or dark, dull or sparkling. Third is tone: faces suggest authority, richness, modernity, simplicity, etc. Fourth is efficiency for a given job—fitness for the size *of type and sheet required, the kind of paper, the printing process to be used. Since no one typeface is likely to be best in every respect,* **these matters have to be balanced. Which typeface to use is thus a fascinating choice each time, and**

Bell and Italic (Monotype)

BELL MAY BE COMPARED with other typefaces in many ways. First is readability: some faces help the eye more than others. Second is color: letters in mass can appear light or dark, dull or sparkling. Third is tone: faces suggest authority, richness, modernity, simplicity, etc. Fourth is efficiency for a given job—fitness for the size of type and sheet required, the kind of paper, the printing process to be used. Since no one typeface is likely to be best in every respect, *these matters have to be balanced. Which typeface to use is thus a fascinating choice each time, and the knowledgeable reader can*

Bembo, Italic and Bold (Monotype)

BEMBO MAY BE COMPARED with other typefaces in many ways. First is readability: some faces help the eye more than others. Second is color: letters in mass can appear light or dark, dull or sparkling. Third is tone: faces suggest authority, richness, modernity, simplicity, etc. Fourth is efficiency for a given job—fitness for the size of type and sheet required, the kind of paper, the printing *process to be used. Since no one typeface is likely to be best in every respect, these matters have to be balanced. Which typeface to use is thus a fascinat-* **ing choice each time, and the knowledgeable reader can have his own pleasure in second-guessing the designer and printer**

Bodoni Book and Italic (Monotype)

BODONI BOOK MAY BE COMPARED with other typefaces in many ways. First is readability: some faces help the eye more than others. Second is color: letters in mass can appear light or dark, dull or sparkling. Third is tone: faces suggest authority, richness, modernity, simplicity, etc. Fourth is efficiency for a given job—fitness for the size of type and sheet required, the kind of paper, the printing process to be used. Since no one typeface is likely to be *best in every respect, these matters have to be balanced. Which typeface to use is thus a fascinating choice each time,*

Bookman Old Style (Lanston Monotype)

BOOKMAN OLD STYLE MAY BE COMPARED with other typefaces in many ways. First is readability: some faces help the eye more than others. Second is color: letters in mass can appear light or dark, dull or sparkling. Third is tone: faces suggest authority, richness, modernity, simplicity, etc. Fourth is efficiency for a given job—fitness for the size of type and sheet required, the kind of paper, the printing *process to be used. Since no one typeface is likely to be best in every respect, these matters*

Bulmer and Italic (Intertype)

BULMER MAY BE COMPARED with other typefaces in many ways. First is readability: some faces help the eye more than others. Second is color: letters in mass can appear light or dark, dull or sparkling. Third is tone: faces suggest authority, richness, modernity, simplicity, etc. Fourth is efficiency for a given job—fitness for the size of type and sheet required, the kind of paper, the printing process to be used. Since no one typeface is likely to be *best in every respect, these matters have to be balanced. Which typeface to use is thus a fascinating choice each*

Caledonia and Italic (Linotype)

CALEDONIA MAY BE COMPARED with other typefaces in many ways. First is readability: some faces help the eye more than others. Second is color: letters in mass can appear light or dark, dull or sparkling. Third is tone: faces suggest authority, richness, modernity, simplicity, etc. Fourth is efficiency for a given job – fitness for the size of type and sheet required, the kind of paper, the printing process to be used. Since no one *typeface is likely to be best in every respect, these matters have to be balanced. Which typeface to use is thus*

Caslon Old Style No. 337 and Italic (Monotype)

CASLON OLD STYLE MAY BE COMPARED with other typefaces in many ways. First is readability: some faces help the eye more than others. Second is color: letters in mass can appear light or dark, dull or sparkling. Third is tone: faces suggest authority, richness, modernity, simplicity, etc. Fourth is efficiency for a given job—fitness for the size of type and sheet required, the kind of paper, the printing process to be used. Since *no one typeface is likely to be best in every respect, these matters have to be balanced. Which typeface to use is thus*

Centaur and Arrighi Italic (English Monotype)

CENTAUR may be compared with other typefaces in many ways. First is readability: some faces help the eye more than others. Second is color: letters in mass can appear light or dark, dull or sparkling. Third is tone: faces suggest authority, richness, modernity, simplicity, etc. Fourth is efficiency for a given job—fitness for the size of type and sheet required, the kind of paper, the printing process to be used. Since no typeface is likely to be best in every respect, these matters have to be balanced. Which typeface to use is *thus a fascinating choice each time, and the knowledgeable reader can have his own pleasure in second-guessing the designer and printer as he studies the com-*

Century Schoolbook and Italic (Monotype)

CENTURY SCHOOLBOOK MAY BE COMPARED with other typefaces in many ways. First is readability: some faces help the eye more than others. Second is color: letters in mass can appear light or dark, dull or sparkling. Third is tone: faces suggest authority, richness, modernity, simplicity, etc. Fourth is efficiency for a given job—fitness for the size of type and sheet required, the kind of paper, ***the printing process to be used. Since no one typeface is likely to be best in every respect, these matters have***

Cheltenham Old Style and Bold (Lanston Monotype)

CHELTENHAM MAY BE COMPARED with other type faces in many ways. First is readability: some faces help the eye more than others. Second is color: letters in mass can appear light or dark, dull or sparkling. Third is tone: faces suggest authority, richness, modernity, simplicity, **CHELTENHAM BOLD may be compared with other type faces in many ways. First is readability: some faces help the eye more than others. Second is color: letters in mass can appear light or dark, dull or sparkling. Third is tone: faces**

Clearface and Italic (Lanston Monotype)

CLEARFACE may be compared with other typefaces in many ways. First is readability: some faces help the eye more than others. Second is color: letters in mass can appear light or dark, dull or sparkling. Third is tone: faces suggest authority, richness, modernity, simplicity, etc. Fourth is efficiency for a given job—fitness for the size of type and sheet required, the kind of paper, the printing process to be used. Since no one typeface is likely to be best in every respect, these matters have to be balanced. Which typeface to use is thus a fascin-

Cochin Bold (Monotype)

COCHIN BOLD may be compared with other typefaces in many ways. First is readability: some faces help the eye more than others. Second is color: letters in mass can appear light or dark, dull or sparkling. Third is tone: faces suggest authority, richness, modernity, simplicity, etc. Fourth is efficiency for a given job—fitness for the size of type and sheet required, the kind of paper, the printing process to be used. Since no one typeface is likely to be best in every

Craw Clarendon Book (Lanston Monotype)

CRAW CLARENDON BOOK may be compared with other typefaces in many ways. First is readability: some faces help the eye more than others. Second is color: letters in mass can appear light or dark, dull or sparkling. Third is tone: faces suggest authority, richness, modernity, simplicity, etc. Fourth is efficiency for a given job—fitness for the size of type and sheet required, the kind of paper,

De Vinne and Italic (Linotype)

DEVINNE MAY BE COMPARED with other typefaces in many ways. First is readability: some faces help the eye more than others. Second is color: letters in mass can appear light or dark, dull or sparkling. Third is tone: faces suggest authority, richness, modernity, simplicity, etc. Fourth is efficiency for a given job—fitness for the size of type and sheet required, the kind of paper, the printing process to be used. Since no one typeface is *likely to be best in every respect, these matters have to be balanced. Which typeface to use is thus a fascinating*

De Vinne Condensed (Monotype)

De VINNE CONDENSED may be compared with other typefaces in many ways. First is readability: some faces help the eye more than others. Second is color: letters in mass can appear light or dark, dull or sparkling. Third is tone: faces suggest authority, richness, modernity, simplicity, etc. Fourth is efficiency for a given job—fitness for the size of type and sheet required, the kind of paper, the printing process to be used. Since no one typeface is likely to be best in every respect, these matters have to be balanced. Which

Deepdene and Italic (Monotype)

DEEPDENE MAY BE COMPARED with other type faces in many ways. First is readability: some faces help the eye more than others. Second is color: letters in mass can appear light or dark, dull or sparkling. Third is tone: faces suggest authority, richness, modernity, simplicity, etc. Fourth is efficiency for a given job—fitness for the size of type and sheet required, the kind of paper, the printing process to be used. Since no one type face is likely to be best in every respect, these matters have to be balanced. Which *type face to use is thus a fascinating choice each time, and the knowledgeable reader can have his own pleasure in second-guessing the designer and printer*

Egmont Light and Italic (Intertype)

EGMONT LIGHT MAY BE COMPARED with other typefaces in many ways. First is readability: some faces help the eye more than others. Second is color: letters in mass can appear light or dark, dull or sparkling. Third is tone: faces suggest authority, richness, modernity, simplicity, etc. Fourth is efficiency for a given job—fitness for the size of type and sheet required, the kind of paper, the printing process to be used. Since no one typeface is likely to be best in every *respect, these matters have to be balanced. Which typeface to use is thus a fascinating choice each time, and the*

Electra, Cursive and Italic (Linotype)

ELECTRA MAY BE COMPARED with other typefaces in many ways. First is readability: some faces help the eye more than others. Second is color: letters in mass can appear light or dark, dull or sparkling. Third is tone: faces suggest authority, richness, modernity, simplicity, etc. Fourth is efficiency for a given job—fitness *for the size of type and sheet required, the kind of paper, the printing process to be used. Since no one typeface is likely to be best in every respect, these matters have to be balanced. Which typeface to use is*

Excelsior and Italic (Linotype)

EXCELSIOR MAY BE COMPARED with other typefaces in many ways. First is readability: some faces help the eye more than others. Second is color: letters in mass can appear light or dark, dull or sparkling. Third is tone: faces suggest authority, richness, modernity, simplicity, etc. Fourth is efficiency for a given job—fitness for the size of type and sheet required, the kind of paper, the printing process to be used. *Since no one typeface is likely to be best in every respect, these matters have to be bal-*

Fournier and Italic (English Monotype)

FOURNIER MAY BE COMPARED with other typefaces in many ways. First is readability: some faces help the eye more than others. Second is color: letters in mass can appear light or dark, dull or sparkling. Third is tone: faces suggest authority, richness, modernity, simplicity, etc. Fourth is efficiency for a given job—fitness for the size of type and sheet required, the kind of paper, the printing process to be used. Since no one typeface is likely to be best in every respect, these matters have to be balanced. *Which typeface to use is thus a fascinating choice each time, and the knowledgeable reader can have his own pleasure in second-*

Futura Medium and Italic (Intertype)

FUTURA may be compared with other typefaces in many ways. First is readability: some faces help the eye more than others. Second is color: letters in mass can appear light or dark, dull or sparkling. Third is tone: faces suggest authority, richness, modernity, simplicity, etc. Fourth is efficiency for a given job—fitness for the size of type and sheet required, the kind of paper, the printing process to be used. Since no one typeface is likely to be best in every *respect, these matters have to be balanced. Which typeface to use is thus a fascinating choice each time, and the*

Garamond No. 3 and Italic (Linotype)

GARMOND NO. 3 MAY BE COMPARED with other typefaces in many ways. First is readability: some faces help the eye more than others. Second is color: letters in mass can appear light or dark, dull or sparkling. Third is tone: faces suggest authority, richness, modernity, simplicity, etc. Fourth is efficiency for a given job—fitness for the size of type and sheet required, the kind of paper, the printing process to be used. Since no one typeface is likely to be best in every re*spect, these matters have to be balanced. Which typeface to use is thus a fascinating choice each time, and the knowledge-*

Garamont and Italic (Lanston Monotype)

GARAMONT MAY BE COMPARED with other typefaces in many ways. First is readability: some faces help the eye more than others. Second is color: letters in mass can appear light or dark, dull or sparkling. Third is tone: faces suggest authority, richness, modernity, simplicity, etc. Fourth is efficiency for a given job—fitness for the size of type and sheet required, the kind of paper, the printing process to be used. Since no one typeface is *likely to be best in every respect, these matters have to be balanced. Which typeface to use is thus a fascinating choice each*

Goudy Modern and Italic (English Monotype)

GOUDY MODERN MAY BE COMPARED with other typefaces in many ways. First is readability: some faces help the eye more than others. Second is color: letters in mass can appear light or dark, dull or sparkling. Third is tone: faces suggest authority, richness, modernity, simplicity, etc. Fourth is efficiency for a given job—fitness for the size of type and sheet required, the kind of paper, the printing process to be used. Since no one typeface is likely to be best in every respect, these matters have to be balanced. Which *typeface to use is thus a fascinating choice each time, and the knowledgeable reader can have his own pleasure in second-guessing*

Goudy Old Style and Italic (Monotype)

GOUDY OLD STYLE MAY BE COMPARED with other typefaces in many ways. First is readability: some faces help the eye more than others. Second is color: letters in mass can appear light or dark, dull or sparkling. Third is tone: faces suggest authority, richness, modernity, simplicity, etc. Fourth is efficiency for a given job—fitness for the size of type and sheet required, the kind of paper, the printing process to be used. Since *no one typeface is likely to be best in every respect, these matters have to be balanced. Which typeface to use is thus*

Granjon and Italic (Linotype)

GRANJON MAY BE COMPARED with other typefaces in many ways. First is readability: some faces help the eye more than others. Second is color: letters in mass can appear light or dark, dull or sparkling. Third is tone: faces suggest authority, richness, modernity, simplicity, etc. Fourth is efficiency for a given job—fitness for the size of type and sheet required, the kind of paper, the printing process to be used. Since no one typeface is likely to be best in every respect, *these matters have to be balanced. Which typeface to use is thus a fascinating choice each time, and the knowledgeable*

Helvetica and Italic (Linotype)

HELVETICA may be compared with other typefaces in many ways. First is readability: some faces help the eye more than others. Second is color: letters in mass can appear light or dark, dull or sparkling. Third is tone: faces suggest authority, richness, modernity, simplicity, etc. Fourth is efficiency for a given job—fitness for the size of type and sheet required, the kind of paper, the printing process to be *used. Since no one typeface is likely to be best in every respect, these matters have to be balanced.*

Imperial and Italic Bold (Intertype)

IMPERIAL MAY BE COMPARED with other faces in many ways. First in readability; some faces help the eye more than others. Second is color: letters in mass can appear light or dark, dull or sparkling. Third is tone: faces suggest authority, richness, modernity, simplicity, etc. Fourth is efficiency for a given job—fitness for the size of type and sheet required, the kind of paper, the printing process *to be used. Since no one typeface is likely to be best in every respect, these matters have to be*

Janson and Italic (Lanston Monotype)

JANSON MAY BE COMPARED with other type faces in many ways. First is readability: some faces help the eye more than others. Second is color: letters in mass can appear light or dark, dull or sparkling. Third is tone: faces suggest authority, richness, modernity, simplicity, etc. Fourth is efficiency for a given job—fitness for the size of type and sheet required, the kind of paper, the printing process to be used. Since no one type face is likely to be *best in every respect, these matters have to be balanced. Which type face to use is thus a fascinating choice each time, and the*

Kabel Light [Sans Serif No. 329] with last five lines using Futura alternates (Lanston Monotype)

KABEL may be compared with other type faces in many ways. First is readability: some faces help the eye more than others. Second is color: letters in mass can appear light or dark, dull or sparkling. Third is tone: faces suggest authority, richness, modernity, simplicity, etc. Fourth is efficiency KABEL may be compared with other type faces in many ways. First is readability: some faces help the eye more than others. Second is color: letters in mass can appear light or dark, dull or sparkling. Third is tone: faces suggest authority, richness, modernity, simplicity, etc. Fourth is

Kennerley and Italic (Lanston Monotype)

KENNERLEY MAY BE COMPARED with other typefaces in many ways. First is readability: some faces help the eye more than others. Second is color: letters in mass can appear light or dark, dull or sparkling. Third is tone: faces suggest authority, richness, modernity, simplicity, etc. Fourth is efficiency for a given job—fitness for the size of type and sheet required, the kind of paper, the printing process to be used. Since no one typeface is likely to be best in every re-*spect, these matters have to be balanced. Which typeface to use is thus a fascinating choice each time, and the knowledgeable*

Melior and Italic (Linotype)

MELIOR may be compared with other typefaces in many ways. First is readability: some faces help the eye more than others. Second is color: letters in mass can appear light or dark, dull or sparkling. Third is tone: faces suggest authority, richness, modernity, simplicity, etc. Fourth is efficiency for a given job—fitness for the size of type and sheet required, the kind of paper, the printing process to be *used. Since no one typeface is likely to be best in every respect, these matters have to be balanced.*

Memphis Light and Bold (Linotype)

MEMPHIS LIGHT may be compared with other typefaces in many ways. First is readability: some faces help the eye more than others. Second is color: letters in mass can appear light or dark, dull or sparkling. Third is tone: faces suggest authority, richness, modernity, simplicity, etc. Fourth is efficiency for a given job—fitness for the size of type and sheet required, the kind of paper, the printing process to be used. **Since no one typeface is likely to be best in every respect, these matters have to be balanced. Which**

Modern No. 8 and Italic (Monotype)

MODERN NO. 8 MAY BE COMPARED with other typefaces in many ways. First is readability: some faces help the eye more than others. Second is color: letters in mass can appear light or dark, dull or sparkling. Third is tone: faces suggest authority, richness, modernity, simplicity, etc. Fourth is efficiency for a given job—fitness for the size of type and sheet required, the kind of paper, the printing process to be used. Since no one *typeface is likely to be best in every respect, these matters have to be balanced. Which typeface to use is thus a*

Modern Antique No. 26 (Monotype)

MODERN ANTIQUE may be compared with other typefaces in many ways. First is readability: some faces help the eye more than others. Second is color: letters in mass can appear light or dark, dull or sparkling. Third is tone: faces suggest authority, richness, modernity, simplicity, etc. Fourth is efficiency for a given job—fitness for the size of type and sheet required, the kind of paper, the printing process to be used. Since no one typeface is likely to be best in every respect,

News Gothic and Bold (Intertype)

NEWS GOTHIC MAY BE COMPARED with other typefaces in many ways. First is readability: some faces help the eye more than others. Second is color: letters in mass can appear light or dark, dull or sparkling. Third is tone: faces suggest authority, richness, modernity, simplicity, etc. Fourth is efficiency for a given job—fitness for the size of type and sheet required, the kind of paper, the printing process to be used. **Since no one typeface is likely to be best in every respect, these matters have to be balanced. Which**

Optima and Italic (Linotype)

OPTIMA may be compared with other typefaces in many ways. First is readability: some faces help the eye more than others. Second is color: letters in mass can appear light or dark, dull or sparkling. Third is tone: faces suggest authority, richness, modernity, simplicity, etc. Fourth is efficiency for a given job—fitness for the size of type and sheet required, the kind of paper, the printing process to be used. Since no *one typeface is likely to be best in every respect, these matters have to be balanced. Which typeface to use*

Palatino and Italic (Linotype)

PALATINO MAY BE COMPARED with other typefaces in many ways. First is readability: some faces help the eye more than others. Second is color: letters in mass can appear light or dark, dull or sparkling. Third is tone: faces suggest authority, richness, modernity, simplicity, etc. Fourth is efficiency for a given job—fitness for the size of type and sheet required, the kind of paper, the printing process to be used. Since no one type-*face is likely to be best in every respect, these matters have to be balanced. Which typeface to use is thus a*

Perpetua and Italic (English Monotype)

PERPETUA MAY BE COMPARED with other typefaces in many ways. First is readability: some faces help the eye more than others. Second is color: letters in mass can appear light or dark, dull or sparkling. Third is tone: faces suggest authority, richness, modernity, simplicity, etc. Fourth is efficiency for a given job—fitness for the size of type and sheet required, the kind of paper, the printing process to be used. Since no one typeface is likely to be best in every respect, these matters have to be balanced. Which typeface *to use is thus a fascinating choice each time, and the knowledgeable reader can have his own pleasure in second-guessing the designer and printer as*

Plantin and Italic (English Monotype)

PLANTIN MAY BE COMPARED with other typefaces in many ways. First is readability: some faces help the eye more than others. Second is color: letters in mass can appear light or dark, dull or sparkling. Third is tone: faces suggest authority, richness, modernity, simplicity, etc. Fourth is efficiency for a given job—fitness for the size of type and sheet required, the kind of paper, the printing process to be used. Since no one typeface is likely to be best in every respect, these *matters have to be balanced. Which typeface to use is thus a fascinating choice each time, and the knowledgeable reader*

Primer and Italic (Linotype)

PRIMER MAY BE COMPARED with other typefaces in many ways. First is readability: some faces help the eye more than others. Second is color: letters in mass can appear light or dark, dull or sparkling. Third is tone: faces suggest authority, richness, modernity, simplicity, etc. Fourth is efficiency for a given job—fitness for the size of type and sheet required, the kind of paper, the printing process to be used. *Since no one typeface is likely to be best in every respect, these matters have to be balanced.*

Scotch Roman and Italic (Monotype)

SCOTCH ROMAN MAY BE COMPARED with other typefaces in many ways. First is readability: some faces help the eye more than others. Second is color: letters in mass can appear light or dark, dull or sparkling. Third is tone: faces suggest authority, richness, modernity, simplicity, etc. Fourth is efficiency for a given job—fitness for the size of type and sheet required, the kind of paper, the printing process to be used. Since no one *typeface is likely to be best in every respect, these matters have to be balanced. Which typeface to use is thus a fasci-*

Souvenir and Souvenir Bold (Linotype)

SOUVENIR MAY BE COMPARED with other typefaces in many ways. First is readability; some faces help the eye more than others. Second is color: letters in mass can appear light or dark, dull or sparkling. Third is tone: faces suggest authority, richness, modernity, simplicity, etc. Fourth is efficiency for a given job—fitness for the size of type and sheet required, the kind of paper, the printing process to be used. Since **no one typeface is likely to be best in every respect, these matters have to be balanced. Which typeface to**

Times New Roman and Italic (English Monotype)

TIMES ROMAN MAY BE COMPARED with other typefaces in many ways. First is readability: some faces help the eye more than others. Second is color: letters in mass can appear light or dark, dull or sparkling. Third is tone: faces suggest authority, richness, modernity, simplicity, etc. Fourth is efficiency for a given job—fitness of the size of type and sheet required, the kind of paper, the printing process to be used. Since no one typeface is likely to be *best in every respect, these matters have to be balanced. Which typeface to use is thus a fascinating choice each*

Univers 685, 689, 693 and 696 (English Monotype)

UNIVERS, 685, 689, 693, 696, may be compared with other typefaces in many ways. First is readability: some faces help the eye more than others. Second is color: letters in mass can appear light or dark, dull or sparkling. *Third is tone: faces suggest authority, richness, modernity, simplicity, etc. Fourth is efficiency for a given* **job—fitness for the size of type and sheet required, the kind of paper, the printing process to be used. Since no one typeface is likely to be best in every respect, these matters have to be bal-**

Walbaum, Italic and Bold (English Monotype)

WALBAUM MAY BE COMPARED with other typefaces in many ways. First is readability: some faces help the eye more than others. Second is color: letters in mass can appear light or dark, dull or sparkling. Third is tone: faces suggest authority, richness, modernity, simplicity, etc. Fourth is efficiency for a given job—fitness for the size of type and *sheet required, the kind of paper, the printing process to be used. Since no one typeface is likely to be best in every respect,* **these matters have to be balanced. Which typeface to use is thus a fascinating choice each time, and the**

Weiss and Italic (Intertype)

WEISS MAY BE COMPARED with other typefaces in many ways. First is readability: some faces help the eye more than others. Second is color: letters in mass can appear light or dark, dull or sparkling. Third is tone: faces suggest authority, richness, modernity, simplicity, etc. Fourth is efficiency for a given job—fitness for the size of type and sheet required, the kind of paper, the printing process to be used. Since no one typeface is likely to be best in every respect, these matters have to be balanced. Which *typeface to use is thus a fascinating choice each time, and the knowledgeable reader can have his own pleasure in second-guessing*

INDEX

A WORD TO THE READER ABOUT THIS

This index is a conscientious effort to help a beginner (and the professional!) find what he is looking for, not simply by the technical term but also by a common word which leads to the general subject.*

It is comprehensive, also, out of the belief that a subject worth putting into a book is worth including in the index.

NOTE, IMPORTANTLY, that the alphabetization follows the "nothing-before-something" or "word-by-word" mode, because it tends to keep like terms together. By this system, which is now becoming enshrined by computer logic, a blank space precedes punctuation, and punctuation precedes additional letters. Thus *Book title* precedes *Book, invention of*, which in turn precedes *Bookface*—the exact opposite of the order in old style alphabetization.

COMMERCIAL TYPEFACE NAMES (only) ARE SHOWN IN ITALIC

A

*And a GLOSSARY-IN-CONTEXT
This book provides--in helpful context--hundreds of simple definitions and illustrations, shown by dots (•) in this index.

• indicates page with glossary material

• indicates page with glossary material

• indicates page with glossary material

F

• indicates page with glossary material

G

H

• indicates page with glossary material

I

• indicates page with glossary material

J

K

L

• indicates page with glossary material

M

• indicates page with glossary material

P

• indicates page with glossary material

Q

R

S

• indicates page with glossary material

• indicates page with glossary material

• indicates page with glossary material

The text of this book is set in Monotype Times New Roman, 9 on 10 pt., with captions in 9 on 10 pt. Monotype Times New Roman Italic, both enlarged photographically in the main body of the book. The headings on the Typorama specimens are 6 pt. Times New Roman, and the specimens thenselves are the sizes indicated. The index is Linotype Times Roman, 9 pt. solid, slightly reduced. Cover and related headings are in Palatino Semi-Bold, with other display in various sans serifs.

Corrections and additions for this second edition were set by Pat Taylor at his Out of Sorts Letter Foundery, Larchmont, New York. The very extensive revisions in this edition simply would not have been possible without his patient, devoted and careful cooperation. The revised and expanded index was set similarly by Norman and Mark Cordes at the Under the Cellar Steps Press, Ridgewood, New Jersey.

THE LAST WORD IS YOURS:

The intent of The Myriade Press is to produce books which are helpful, accurate and comprehensive within the scope of the subject. Therefore, corrections, comments and suggestions for improvement are invited and always welcome. Please address the publisher.